SKEPTICAL MUSIC

SKEPTICAL MUSIC

Essays on Modern Poetry

DAVID BROMWICH

THE UNIVERSITY OF CHICAGO PRESS
CHICAGO AND LONDON

DAVID BROMWICH is the Housum Professor of English
at Yale University. He is the author of numerous essays on poetry
and of several books, including *Disowned by Memory*,
published by The University of Chicago Press.

The University of Chicago Press, Chicago 60637
The University of Chicago Press, Ltd., London
© 2001 by David Bromwich.
All rights reserved. Published 2001
Printed in the United States of America
10 09 08 07 06 05 04 03 02 01   1 2 3 4 5

ISBN: 0-226-07560-5 (cloth)
ISBN: 0-226-07561-3 (paper)

Library of Congress Cataloging-in-Publication Data

Bromwich, David, 1951–
Skeptical music : essays on modern poetry / David Bromwich.
p.   cm.
Includes index.
ISBN 0-226-07560-5 (alk. paper) —
ISBN 0-226-07561-3 (pbk. : alk. paper)
1. American poetry—20th century—History and criticism.
2. English poetry—20th century—History and criticism.   I. Title.

PS323.5 .B76   2001
811'.509—dc21   00-046714

To Maria DiBattista

Too many waltzes have ended. Yet the shapes
For which the voices cry, these, too, may be
Modes of desire, modes of revealing desire.

Too many waltzes—The epic of disbelief
Blares oftener and soon, will soon be constant.
Some harmonious skeptic soon in a skeptical music

Will unite these figures of men and their shapes
Will glisten again with motion, the music
Will be motion and full of shadows.

— Wallace Stevens,
"Sad Strains of a Gay Waltz"

CONTENTS

This book collects some of my essays and reviews on modern poetry. No program more exalted than individual taste was ever offered to support the judgments, and it is too late to suppress the evidence of a critic educating himself in public. I regret this very much. It has been said that the love of a young writer for the old writer he will some day be is ambition in its most laudable form. However craftily the judgment must be qualified to be true of artists generally, I have no doubt that it applies to critics. But the whole truth is even more peculiar. Critics have "nor youth nor age, / But as it were an after-dinner's sleep / Dreaming on both." Actually to renounce an opinion would mean for us to disclaim the unearned confidence that led to the opinion. But this we cannot do. So a view once set down becomes a positive token, as if for all time, of a perception that was most firmly planted at one time. The more vivid the response, the better it carries the feeling of the moment. And yet, the more vivid the response, the greater the temptation to suppose it universally true and hence to falsify. We differ even from ourselves—a fact of experience that dawns on anyone who has ever reread a poem, a play, a story, or a novel.

Critics of poetry may be divided into two types. There are those who expound a poet's probable meanings and allow them to become more widely known and shared. That job is visibly done in order to help readers. Invisibly, it serves the writer's amour propre by displaying a credible empathy for the poet, aiming also, under cover, to excite some recognition in return ("You have understood me"—a form of approval critics desire more than we dare to confess). There is another walk of criticism, less hygienic but more fascinating, at least for the critic. It tries to say what was in the poet's mind, or what was in the poem's mind, on the theory that certain thoughts and feelings are worth the trouble to characterize because of their strangeness or their originality. Poems are thus treated as part of the natural history of intellect, in one of its more recent manifestations, the work of consciousness. The first sort of criticism is close to reviewing; the second, closer to psychology and fiction writing. My criticism has always been an impure blend of these ideal types—shaded, as time goes on, by a growing preference for the second kind of work.

In writing the longer essays on Ashbery, Stevens, Moore, and Bishop, or on literary relationships like those between Bishop and Moore, or between Crane and Eliot, my method was to revive my sense of the poets in question by rereading their work, until in each case the work started to seem a conversation with itself, and getting to know it came to be an experience like getting to know a person. I take the analogy only part way. But reading can indeed offer the consistency of interest, the mutual attraction of temperaments, the "give" at surprising places which psychologists in speaking of persons call responsiveness and critics in speaking of poems call subtlety or depth. The two kinds of acknowledgment have the same endlessness. Yet it makes a difference just when, in the history of acquaintance with a poet, one elects to cast one's continuing interest into argumentative shape. When I wrote about Ashbery, I was most gripped by the volumes from *The Double Dream of Spring* to *A Wave*. With Stevens, it was the poems of the thirties and forties collected in *Parts of a World*. With Eliot and Crane, and again with Bishop and Moore, I found myself drawn by the early writings most of all. It does seem a truth about modernist poetry that the poet is apt to be most in earnest where the work feels least transparent. This often happens early, with a poet's first discovery of a new way of saying and seeing things.

It is no accident that so many of these essays turned out to be about Americans. A great deal of the most original poetry in the twentieth century was written by Americans. This was a coherent addition to a new way of feeling in the arts, and it was great in the same way the jazz was great that migrated from the Ellington and Basie bands to the smaller groups with shifting leaders (Gillespie, Monk, Parker, Davis, Rollins, Gordon, Evans, Coltrane) that dominated the fifties and early sixties, and in the same way that the Hollywood stars were great (Stanwyck, Lupino, Grant, Cagney, Bogart, Davis, Stewart, Mitchum) who in the period now called classic gave an enchanted meaning to the accents of a style equal to daily experience. The actor builds up effects by the detail of gesture and reaction; the jazz artist, by minute articulations of phrase; and the poet? The poet works from the line and again the line.

Modern poetry is where you go to look for lines that have captivated the mind's ear before you had any idea of what they could mean; lines like

The troubled midnight and the noon's repose,

and

> lords of unquiet or of quiet sojourn,

lines that stand out with an immediate relish of statement:

> A thousand golden sheaves were lying there,
> Shining and still, but not for long to stay,

or with a declarative rightness:

> Hugely, spring exists again. The weigela does its dusty thing
> In fire-hammered air,

lines that calmly establish a poem's ending, like these:

> Remember me when I am dead
> and simplify me when I'm dead,

or like these:

> The pensive man . . . He sees that eagle float
> For which the intricate Alps are a single nest,

—all finally for the sake of working around to another beginning:

> Earliest morning, switching all the tracks
> that cross the sky from cinder star to star,
>   coupling the ends of streets
>   to trains of light.

As a reader of poetry, I live for such effects. I do not know what to say to the reader who lives for anything else.

But what does one read criticism for? Mainly, I think, quotations. A critic exists to reveal the evidence of taste and touch, of sound and sight, of feeling and of thought, by which infallibly one knows the presence of a poet. So any critic who quotes vividly has done half of the job one wants to see done. Randall Jarrell, a wonderful and immensely readable critic, was so good a quoter he could sometimes make poets of middling distinction, in whom he took a temporary interest, sound far better than they were close-up, and he could make poets of real distinction who partly annoyed him seem for the length of a review entirely absurd. Yet he was a critic more graced by fairness than most. It is simply the rule that one seeks out the most telling impression and never a happy or impartial medium. I have worked hardest at getting the right quotations, if I could: words of a language that is not overexplicit or overcooked; trite, talky, rigged, slack, or inert; not puffed-up and impressed with itself, or spiffy and pleased with itself. There are so many ways of being bad. To recognize the skill with which the artist averts them all is to realize as Coleridge once said that in depth of judgment every true artist is already a critic. The miracle of great art is to look as if the right way through the labyrinth of error was inevitable.

The aesthetic that governs the appreciations is mostly implicit, but I have defined it as far as possible in an introductory essay, and it should be plain that in calling poetry an art without importance I mean among other things an art unencumbered by the expectations of a countable public, a commercial sponsor, a thick network of enabling mediators. For better and worse—but not only for worse—poetry operates without much visible proximity to money. The experience it offers, in order to be genuine, still must largely be known in solitude. It does not follow that personal taste is an aesthetic matter exclusively, and in two further essays, "Poetic Invention and the Self-Unseeing" and "How Moral Is Taste?" I notice some points at which, in poetry as in the other arts, aesthetic and moral considerations uneasily converge. Perhaps only the essay on Hemingway calls for a word of justification. Among serious readers he is now the least mentionable of the great moderns, yet his practice continues to be exemplary for poetry as well as prose. Hemingway's discipline of the sentence lies close to the modern discipline of the line, and I include this homage by way of confirming a poet's description of him as "a poet of extraordinary actuality."

A word about the title. Skeptical music is a phrase that recalls a pitch or tonality that certain poets share—a poise and not an aloofness. In its original context, in Stevens's lovely but polemical poem "Sad Strains of a Gay Waltz," the words leave a doubt whether the music comes from an effort to make a worldly order prevail or to find and keep an order of the spirit. In the end a spiritual good matters most to Stevens, and the music takes on a resonance beyond its occasion. This is a feature of all great poetry, of course, but of the moderns emphatically. The delicacy of the effect is captured by the twentieth-century use of the word *style* in an extended sense, to denote an accent or inflection of character, a presence of mind on the surface from which a depth can be inferred. "If a dismal political season is in store for us," wrote Kenneth Burke in the thirties, "shall we not greatly need a campaign base for personal integrity, a kind of beneath-which-not? And I wonder whether we might not find this beneath-which-not in a more strenuous cult of style." Some such rallying point seems to have been a motive, hidden from the author at the time, for writing all of the pieces that are gathered here.

I started reading poetry—and the moderns came first, for me—about the age of fourteen. My favorites were Cummings, Jeffers, Eliot, Auden, Spender, Crane, Tate, Lowell, Empson, Karl Shapiro, and Dylan Thomas, in anthologies edited by Oscar Williams and Louis Untermeyer. Later, I had the rare good luck to study poetry with Harold Bloom, and our conversations were a starting point for several trains of thought I have since pursued. Sam Hynes and Walt Litz, during the many years when we taught British and American poetry together, enlarged my sense of the field by steady collegial resourcefulness. Jonathan Etra and Ross Borden were generous early with shared enthusiasms, as were Vernon Shetley and Ellen Levy; and I have a debt beyond friendship to John Hollander, for the incitement offered by the range of his memory and intuition. Chance discoveries and the talk they lead to are the best part of criticism because they are the most intense. Compared to the sensation of discussing a new or unfamiliar poem, anything one can say in print comes after the fact. But a certain abstraction seems in the nature of critical writing. One tries to compensate by a certain precision, and I am grateful to three editors for their encouragement. Ben Sonnenberg and Leon Wieseltier were a pleasure to write for, both on topics they found and on those they welcomed. Richard Poirier suggested that I work toward a book of essays. This is not quite the book we imagined in 1983, when he asked me to write a series on the modern poets for *Raritan,* but I hope in some way it represents the spirit of that journal.

In going over these pieces, I have made local revisions and cuts for the sake of clarity, and added a short postscript on Geoffrey Hill's *Triumph of Love.* The first essay was written last, and expressly for the book, though it does not pretend to tie things together. The book owes its existence to Alan Thomas at the University of Chicago Press; the selection has also been shaped by the comments of two anonymous readers for the press. The original places of publication are as follows: "Poetic Invention and the Self-Unseeing," *Grand Street,* autumn 1987; "T. S. Eliot and Hart Crane," *High and Low Moderns,* ed. Maria DiBattista and Lucy McDiarmid (Oxford University Press, 1996); "Crane in His Letters," *New Republic,* January 5 and 12, 1998; "Stevens and the Idea of the Hero," *Raritan,* summer 1987; "Marianne Moore as Discoverer," *Poetry,* March 1982; "'That Weapon, Self-Protectiveness': Notes on a Friendship," in *Marianne Moore: The Art of a Modernist,* ed. Joseph Parisi (UMI Research Press, 1990); "Elizabeth Bishop's Dream-Houses," *Raritan,* summer 1984; "The Making of the Auden Canon," *TLS,* September 17, 1976; "Answer, Heavenly Muse, Yes or No," *Hudson Review,* autumn 1979; "Geoffrey Hill and the Conscience of Words," *New Republic,* September 16 and 23, 1985; "Ted Hughes's *River,*" *Grand Street,* autumn 1985; "A Poet and Her Burden," *New Republic,* November 8, 1993; "John Ashbery: The Self against Its Images," *Raritan,* spring 1986; "Hemingway's Valor," *Grand Street,* winter 1988; "How Moral Is Taste?" *Yale Review,* winter 1994.

David Rosen read the proofs attentively and the book has profited from his corrections as well as his advice.

Grateful acknowledgment is due for permission to reprint the following poems:

"Summer" and "Definition of Blue" by John Ashbery, from *The Double Dream of Spring,* by John Ashbery, copyright © 1970 by John Ashbery, reprinted by permission of Georges Borchardt, Inc., for the author. "Wet Casements" by John Ashbery, from *Houseboat Days* by John Ashbery, copyright © by John Ashbery, reprinted by permission of Georges Borchardt, Inc., for the author. "City Afternoon" by John Ashbery, from *Self-Portrait in a Convex Mirror,* by John Ashbery, copyright © 1974 by John Ashbery. Used by permission of Viking Penguin, a division of Penguin Putnam Inc. All four John Ashbery poems are used also by permission of Carcenet Press Limited.

"Voyages V" and "Possessions" by Hart Crane, from *The Complete Poems of Hart Crane,* edited by Marc Simon, copyright © 1933, 1958, 1966 by Liveright Publishing Corporation, copyright © 1986 by Marc Simon, reprinted by permission of Liveright Publishing Corporation.

"The Death of a Soldier" by Wallace Stevens, from *Collected Poems* by Wallace Stevens, copyright 1923 and renewed 1951 by Wallace Stevens, reprinted by permission of Alfred A. Knopf, a Division of Random House, Inc., and Faber and Faber Ltd. "Parochial Theme" by Wallace Stevens, from *Collected Poems* by Wallace Stevens, copyright 1942 by Wallace Stevens, reprinted by permission of Alfred A. Knopf, a Division of Random House, Inc., and Faber and Faber Ltd.

"Ovid in the Third Reich" by Geoffrey Hill, from *New and Collected Poems, 1952–1992* by Geoffrey Hill, copyright © 1994 by Geoffrey Hill.

ONE

An Art without Importance

Modernist poetry was a method of giving order to history and nature that favored the aesthetic experience of the poet. If this sounds romantic, a distinction of practice remains: in modernist work, the poet holds a place of privilege without any help from the ideology of a nation, an ideal of the enlightened self, or the sort of humanitarian feeling the nineteenth century called the religion of the heart. Poetic modernism gives up these sources of consolation and makes a dry conclusive gesture, though one that need not be mistaken for a sign of defeat. It buries the creator in the medium, the poet in the words of writing.

So runs a familiar story which I still in part believe. But there are other stories: for example, that modernism was a direct consequence of the First World War. This explanation looks historical, and it will cover all the arts, but it does not cover the facts. Planned ugliness, miming a revulsion from the horrors of war, can be traced in the dissonance and clotted alliterations of war poems such as Wilfred Owen's "Anthem for Doomed Youth": "Only the stuttering rifles' rapid rattle / Can patter out their hasty orisons." Yet effects like these belong to a mode of derangement that had penetrated the arts before 1914. The splayed, slung-around cloven hoof that completes the mask of the voyeur in Picasso's *Demoiselles d'Avignon* is within the same range of effects, a rip in the aesthete's daydream of sensualism, as Owen's lines are a shock to the reverie of the hero's farewell. Picasso tearing the curtain aside and shoving toward the spectator that grotesque mirror image—"You! hypocrite lecteur!"—was drawing on an arsenal of tactics with sources far back in the previous century.

A metaphysical summary has emerged in the last few years to supplement the older aesthetic and historical markers. Modernism on this view was an ideology that borrowed a kindred and antithetical energy from the political movements of the age. With their ultimate defeat, modernism reached an inevitable terminus. In *Farewell to an Idea,* T. J. Clark observes of this common enterprise: "So cold and optimistic, modernism. So sure that it will get there eventually." The comment seems to hold true for poetry as well as painting when one looks into Stevens's *Comedian as the Letter C:*

> How many poems he denied himself
> In his observant progress, lesser things
> Than the relentless contact he desired.

But why should a modern artist choose to associate his art with an ascetic self-denial? Stevens replies with another question:

> What was the purpose of his pilgrimage,
> Whatever shape it took in Crispin's mind,
> If not, when all is said, to drive away
> The shadow of his fellows from the skies,
> And, from their stale intelligence released,
> To make a new intelligence prevail?

As admirers, we may grant the radical value of the modernist formalization of experience; grant an origin of the movement close to the unprecedented catastrophe of the First World War; grant that it was the aesthetic counterpart of political idealisms not less single-minded. There remains a problem with all the historical accounts, and the problem is that they are historical. They look on modernism as a completed project now entirely submerged in a distant past.

And yet the movement continues to hold us. It does so because the passion in certain works (born of a distrust of utility and effect) seems a rarer thing than the glamour of the acceptance world that now defines every alternative view (where the fine arts obey with docility the law of commerce and consumption). Modernism involved a kind of detachment, a drawing away, a refusal that is bound to look strange or ascetic when placed alongside the contemporary cultures of improvement and practice on the self. The necessity of the refusal—the need to say to an audience familiar with programmed sensations, "It is human nature to stand in the middle of a thing, but you cannot stand in the middle of this"—helps to explain why modernist poetry like painting tended toward abstraction. The same gesture of refusal goes some way to explain the revival of satire as a major mode, in the work of an intellectual cartoonist like Wyndham Lewis, a nihilist of the monologue like Céline, a comedian like Beckett whose mockery does not bend to the reader's wish for a drama, a moral, a bit of pathos one might finally trust. Yet satire is only part of the story. From the prevalence of a strident tone in the new writing of the 1910s and 1920s, and the prestige of works like *Sweeney Agonistes* and *Antic Hay,* one could hardly derive a clue to the verbal procedures of the Ithaca episode of *Ulysses.*

The criterion of the modern that I have in mind comes closer to a trait of idiom and rhetoric. It has long been said by commentators that modernism was the art-historical movement that escaped from rhetoric at last. But that cannot be. Rhetoric is the skin of language as persuasion is the clothing of belief. Maybe some who thought themselves modern believed that they were creating a beliefless language—as much is suggested in certain utterances of Mallarmé, and of Robbe-Grillet and the early Barthes—but these vanguard artists and publicists were wrong about their own work, to the extent that the work was communicative. It is hard to take all the communication out of language. What one can take out are the cues, the frames, the signals, the gesticulations. The aesthetic that seems to me compelling in modernism was mostly improvised from a rhetoric of understatement. This language is of ancient provenance; it is in Aeschylus, it is in Dante, it is in Shakespeare at the end of *King Lear*— "We that are young / Shall never see so much, nor live so long." What is modern is the insistence that such a language, expressive of doubt and reticence, has become uniquely adequate to the reality that poetry must express. Words written in this discipline convey, by the adjustment of accent or by repetition, a disturbance under the surface of the events of narrated action. That the trust between author and reader should have been rendered so frail, yet have remained so sure, is something new in the history of literature.

It cannot sound modern to us now, though it is beautiful and unhackneyed, for Shelley to say of Keats in *Adonais:* "He is a portion of that loveliness / Which once he made more lovely." It is distinctly modern for Stevens to say in an elegy for the most resonant of his moods: "One feels the life of that which gives life as it is." There is not even a little heightening to distract the ear from the plain sense of things, and one must have read Stevens a long time to be sure of the emotion that is beating in the line. We are given only the impartial word *life*—the name of the motive of feeling, and the cause of feelings that cannot be named. We are left to reflect on it unassisted. It is as if the poet had resolved by the slightest inflection of speech to exhibit what it is to bear witness to experience (not the same thing as "an experience"). More than this little, he seems to say, language should not undertake to deliver. Or is it so little?

There is a poem by William Empson whose first words are "Not wrongly moved." The poet is hoping not to be wrongly moved by a change in the world—a puzzling wish out of context, in any earlier time—but these very words say as much as a modern poem could wish to say for itself. They ask for the courage not to feel according to a digest of concocted attitudes, and among the attitudes in question are those that enjoy the sanction of culture. This negative aim suggests a justification for poetry close to that of thinking. What a modern poem somehow says is always Watch! listen! suppose!—and this in response to a scene or situation that does not have a story to fit into, and that may never have one. Poetry, on this understanding of its function, is always involved in a resistance to cliché. Empson's criticism was part of the same resistance when it connected the imaginative interest of poetry with ambiguity; so that an artist's statement-in-words could never be reduced to a merely emotive or persuasive meaning. The words of a poem are not to be supposed less intricate than experience itself. And concerning our own experience, we know that it cannot be reduced to a final understanding, whether as evidence, message, behavior, or example.

There remain effective modern poems that move us and do not scruple how they do it: Sylvia Plath's "Daddy," for example. This kind of work is the cultural stuff, the tabloid or pasteboard backing, against which the artist separates out a distinct purpose. The great British director Michael Powell said of his propaganda film *The 49th Parallel:* "I made it to drag the Americans into the war." The craft worker of aesthetic sensations, like the artist on holiday, can always assign an adequate motive for a piece of work. It is done to drag the spectator into something. In the examples that follow, I sketch a characteristic tendency of modern poetry by discussing some poems that do not drag the reader anywhere. An argument like this, touching on one of the things modern poetry is not, can hardly begin to answer the question of what modern poetry is. I aim to typify not to define, and I do so across a narrow range. These poems would not go together on any normal index of comparison. As a matter of scholarly presumption, it is usual for one or more of them to be excluded from canonical histories of modernism. But the history looks different, I mean to suggest, when one ceases to think of it as an affair mainly of techniques and schools.

START WITH Edward Thomas's "Cock-Crow," a poem that is formally compact and deals with an experience ordinary enough to have been shared by most readers.

Out of the wood of thoughts that grows by night
To be cut down by the sharp axe of light,—
Out of the night, two cocks together crow,
Cleaving the darkness with a silver blow:
And bright before my eyes twin trumpeters stand,
Heralds of splendour, one at either hand,
Each facing each as in a coat of arms:
The milkers lace their boots up at the farms.

Nothing is more startling here than the allegory of the opening line, the plain statement of the closing line, and the light and shade they bring out when placed together. The work of the poem is simply a bridge between these points. But at its heart, one finds a separate world of dream thoughts, whose rule over the mind at night is broken by the cock-crow. There are two cocks, and to mark the symmetry the poem is cast, unusually for so short a lyric, in the form of couplets. However one interprets this formal choice, the cocks of the opening lines are dutiful laborers. Somehow, soon after, they turn into heralds to convey the sleeping men into the morning: heralds, we are meant to see, in the sense of heraldry too, for one might find the images of such creatures on either side of a farmyard gate.

The subject of the psychological progression from the third to the seventh line is an imperceptible return to mundane life; and, through all this vivid stretch of interpretative writing, the tone of the poem holds steady. Then we are given the last line, homely and masculine, familiar and assured. The change seems true to an experience of waking: that, at a certain moment, by the impression of some quite arbitrary image or sound, you are conducted from sleeping thoughts into the everyday world. And the poem exists just for the sake of this contrast between sleep and waking: it is noted, and calmly captured, and the poem ends. We might say that it stops rather than ends, except that the recognition every reader can supply from experience does end it.

Well, but is it a *modern* poem? If so, the reason has to do with an undersong, a pitch that suggests it will hold for a moment only, that needs attending to and so commands attention. Every imaginable climax is refused. Not even Wordsworth, in poems about fortuitous encounters with lowly persons, or poems about the naming of places, stood so far back from claiming any prior dignity for his subject matter. The preface to *Lyrical Ballads* promised to show how the feeling in poetry might give importance to the situation, and not the situation to the feeling. Thomas, with a minimum of dramatic emphasis, has taken the implications of this aesthetic beyond Wordsworth, as if he saw that the feeling might be nothing more than a record of a perception, an intimation of thought, without any inferred motive to support it. No change of heart, no recollection of who one essentially is. This omission of importance is remarkable. One finds it again and again in the great and small achievements of modernism.

I turn now to a poem about the war, "Break of Day in the Trenches," written by a soldier, Isaac Rosenberg.

> The darkness crumbles away.
> It is the same old druid Time as ever,
> Only a live thing leaps in my hand,
> A queer sardonic rat,
> As I pull the parapet's poppy
> To stick behind my ear.
> Droll rat, they would shoot you if they knew
> Your cosmopolitan sympathies.
> Now you have touched this English hand
> You will do the same to a German
> Soon, no doubt, if it be your pleasure
> To cross the sleeping green between.
> It seems you inwardly grin as you pass
> Strong eyes, fine limbs, haughty athletes,
> Less chanced than you for life,
> Bonds to the whims of murder,
> Sprawled in the bowels of the earth,
> The torn fields of France.
> What do you see in our eyes
> At the shrieking iron and flame
> Hurled through still heavens?
> What quaver—what heart aghast?
> Poppies whose roots are in man's veins
> Drop, and are ever dropping;
> But mine in my ear is safe—
> Just a little white with the dust.

Here again the action is simple, though it holds an irony in reserve: the man who speaks the poem in a language of affectionate mockery has been startled when the rat jumped over his hand. A soldier, exposed to the limits of bodily suffering, he is afraid briefly from a trivial cause. A sharper reversal of expectation is held for the end of the poem: the rat looks in the soldier's eyes and is imagined to see the truth of an expression known to soldiers. "What do you see in our eyes . . . What quaver—what heart aghast?" The difficult and suggestive phrase "druid Time" must mean that the war makes earth a scene of human sacrifice. From this continuous disaster, the poet extracts the humblest of tokens, a poppy—related by myth to the blood of men, but also, in these fields of France, growing out of a soil that is watered by men's blood. The two final couplets mark a contrast: "Poppies whose roots are in man's veins / Drop, and are ever dropping" (hieratic, declamatory)—and then the comfort (oddly domestic) of "But mine in my ear is safe— / Just a little white with the dust." The soldier is satisfied to know that the poppy is safe behind his ear, as if it were lucky and he made it so. At the same time, the words "Just a little white with the dust" are also a reminder of death. One comes to feel that the writer has faced his predicament with a courage entirely informed by terror of his probable end. He has then turned away from that impression, back to the scene where he lives with the war and his companions in it. As much as Edward Thomas's poem, this one avoids a dramatic climax, or any moral to capitalize the significance of the incident.

THE ABSENCE OF overt justification, the absence even of a discursive clue to the argument of a poem, becomes a normal procedure of modernism, where it existed as an anomaly before. We might call it a desire for exposure. The feeling, if it is to give importance to the situation, must be made to stand alone. In this regard, the difference between modernist and non-modernist work can sometimes be glimpsed within a single *oeuvre*. Yeats was striking a familiar romantic posture when he spoke of "A lonely impulse of delight" that drove an airman to his death in the war. The poem that has that line at its center, "An Irish Airman Foresees His Death," rounds off its image of sacrifice with a calculated stoicism:

> I balanced all, brought all to mind,
> The years to come seemed waste of breath,
> A waste of breath the years behind
> In balance with this life, this death.

The speaker and subject is Major Robert Gregory, the son of the poet's patron, whom Yeats in a full-length elegy would describe as "Our Sidney and our perfect man." But this shorter poem, with its pretense of restraint, still glorifies the same martial virtue as the elegy. A death so clearly foreseen must have been selfless, but it was also, Yeats implies, an act of admirable indulgence. The poem celebrates the aristocratic blood of a man who was a lover of heights, of risk in all its seductive kinds, and he remains at his end a conscious and properly dramatic hero. Instinct drove him to choose this way of death: in a cool hour, he approved of his own gesture, which he knew to be sufficiently arbitrary. We are asked only to share his approval. For Yeats, the airman's death makes above all a satisfying aesthetic image. Life and death are joined as a painter may measure a stroke of a brush, by the work of the discriminating eye. "I balanced all, brought all to mind."

By contrast, "Easter 1916" seems a direct public poem of commemoration—a performance very different in kind, and not even potentially a place for ambivalence. And yet the poet's stance here—far more than in his poem about the airman's death—is subdued in the modern way. He is dealing with a subject even more apt to invite an aestheticizing embellishment. Indeed, the subject lay open to bitter satire as well as commemoration. Perhaps a faint undertow, from the satirical treatment Yeats never pursued, does get into the poem as we have it. But, if so, the hint is kept to a hint: there is no suggestion that he could conceivably "balance all, bring all to mind." The poem recognizes that the heroes of the Easter uprising have appeared, by a sudden deed, to embody all the stirrings for a national culture with which Yeats himself was strongly associated at an earlier time. On the other hand, their nationalist cause was never the same as his, and he looked on them in the light of prose as dangerous and reckless men. The reservations he felt about "MacDonagh and MacBride / And Connolly and Pearse"—felt and half concealed, with a cunning that Roy Foster's biography has begun to trace in detail—are gathered into the poem with an effect of dry declaration. Neither of Yeats's divided motives, not his wish to exalt and not his wish to deplore, will be allowed to control the work of public memory, and so the words have their peculiar poise:

> I have met them at close of day
> Coming with vivid faces
> From counter or desk among grey
> Eighteenth-century houses.
> I have passed with a nod of the head,
> Or polite meaningless words,
> Or have lingered awhile and said
> Polite meaningless words,
> And thought before I had done
> Of a mocking tale or a gibe
> To please a companion
> Around the fire at the club,
> Being certain that they and I
> But lived where motley is worn:

> All changed, changed utterly:
> A terrible beauty is born.

Yeats's thought does not stop at the aesthetic sublimity of the uprising, though "a terrible beauty" says as much as can be said for it. Rather, this stanza and the poem that follows are intent on what it may be to witness the birth of an order of experience. It comes into the world violently: any comment beyond this, Yeats fears, will cross into palpable untruth. His politeness once fell short of meaning, he says. The hope of this poem is not to repeat that failure of sympathy and not to warm an approving public with the balm of available sentiments. So his detachment comes alike from an intimation of the valor of the heroes and a scruple about criticizing them. One hesitates to say that the rhetoric of the poem is uniquely modern: there is something like it in Marvell's "Horatian Ode upon Cromwell's Return from Ireland"—the work of a poet who needed, like Yeats, to appear much farther above the battle than he actually was. But new conditions had rendered such a stance intuitively appropriate in Yeats's generation, confronted by an appetite, ambition, and ferocity in the ideologies of fascism and communism which brooked no compromise with art. To find a way to station oneself against or alongside the forces making for a revolution outside art is only a problem to the modernist. It is not a problem to the artist who aims at politicizing art or aestheticizing politics.

"NO IDEAS but in things" was the motto of William Carlos Williams—a prescription carried over from imagism into work of a much later phase. Considered as practical advice, it offers a memorable caution against all sentimentalism, but to take it literally is not compatible with the use of imagination. In poems like "The pure products of America go crazy," "Perpetuum Mobile: The City," and "These," Williams was a poet of vivid and disturbing energy, and the truth in his ban on ideas is a modern poet's scorn for the exquisite diction of 1905. By contrast, Stevens always had a generous way with both ideas and things: the two are hard to separate in his poetry, which depends on the complex work of the mind. Yet Stevens wrote some poems severe enough to comply with Williams's exclusion of "any humanity that suffuses" an object "in its own light" (I quote from "Nuances of a Theme by Williams"). The poems by Stevens I have in mind were written early and late, but all in their different ways are about not being wrongly moved. One of the best, "The Death of a Soldier," is another of elegy of the First World War.

Life contracts and death is expected,
As in a season of autumn.
The soldier falls.

He does not become a three-days personage,
Imposing his separation,
Calling for pomp.

Death is absolute and without memorial,
As in a season of autumn,
When the wind stops,

When the wind stops and, over the heavens,
The clouds go, nevertheless,
In their direction.

One says the soldier falls as one says the wind stops. He is not rendered important by a hero's ceremony: the funeral train, the wake, the official burial. Rather, the event in the life of a man is joined to the event in the life a season—"As in a season of autumn, / When the wind stops." Of course there *is* metaphor here, autumn for the season of death, the stopping of wind for the cessation of life, but the poem stands back and returns to a moment when such metaphors had the literal force of accident. Nature does not mourn, "The clouds go, nevertheless, / In their direction" (a line break with a chastening power)—Stevens says this as one might say of a person that he goes his own way. But the effect is even odder than that. The perspective that here joins the living to the lifeless does not suggest despair any more than gratitude. The cold sense in which this poem affirms that life goes on is consistent with its assertion that life does so indifferent to human concerns. "Nevertheless" is a logical expression, but without the trace of will one is apt to read into it, and "in their direction" means no more than "whatever direction they are seen to go in."

What happens if we generalize the aesthetic that "The Death of a Soldier" implies? Once again I think the innovation depends on an effect of omitted importance. This goes with the repetitions of the poem, which leave an impression of something found rather than made, and the sense of withdrawal that displaces a predictable climax at the end. Averted endings are a familiar feature of Eliot's early poetry, too—"'Put your shoes at the door, sleep, prepare for life.' / The last twist of the knife"—though the frequency of the abrupt irony in Eliot suggests an inhibition. Such movements of withdrawal anyway limit the kind of truth that art may claim. But within the limitation, a modern poet may come upon a new intensity of psychological power. Here is Stevens's "Domination of Black."

> At night, by the fire,
> The colors of the bushes
> And of the fallen leaves,
> Repeating themselves,
> Turned in the room,
> Like the leaves themselves
> Turning in the wind.
> Yes: but the color of the heavy hemlocks
> Came striding.
> And I remembered the cry of the peacocks.
>
> The colors of their tails
> Were like the leaves themselves
> Turning in the wind,
> In the twilight wind.
> They swept over the room,
> Just as they flew from the boughs of the hemlocks
> Down to the ground.
> I heard them cry—the peacocks.
> Was it a cry against the twilight
> Or against the leaves themselves
> Turning in the wind,
> Turning as the flames
> Turned in the fire,
> Turning as the tails of the peacocks
> Turned in the loud fire,
> Loud as the hemlocks
> Full of the cry of the peacocks?
> Or was it a cry against the hemlocks?
>
> Out of the window,
> I saw how the planets gathered
> Like the leaves themselves
> Turning in the wind.
> I saw how the night came,
> Came striding like the color of the heavy hemlocks.
> I felt afraid.
> And I remembered the cry of the peacocks.

Formally this is close again to the mainstream of imagist practice. Stevens has resolved to obey all the rules that Williams's motto "No ideas but in things" had aimed to enforce. Yet the poem transgresses every affective boundary for the sake of which those rules were devised. The objects of choice for imagism were commonly frozen at a single moment, or in arrested motion like "The apparition of these faces in the crowd; / Petals on a wet, black bough." Yet nothing in the nature of an image, as it strikes the eye and the mind, ever required a poetry with this degree of simplification. Stevens for his part has chosen images in motion, indeed images of things that can hardly be imagined except in motion: fire, wind, tail feathers of peacocks and branches of hemlocks. Even the planets, which might be imagined stationary to the eye, are pictured only as they "gather."

The poem is the work of a master of refrain. In the twelve lines of "The Death of a Soldier" were two repeated lines, a shift of implication being asserted by both repetitions, but it would be impractical to try to count the repetitions and refrains of "Domination of Black." You would end by counting the entire poem. The effect of sheer redundancy goes with another feature hard to track to a cause. Every trace of action has been suppressed. Except for the reiterations, and the pauses for questions that check their effect, dramatically nothing seems to happen. Yet something has changed in the speaker at the end, from a cumulative impression of the mood: "I felt afraid." A battle has been fought, to find meaning in the counted details, with a disturbing result to the mind.

A single word, *against,* has peculiar force here, a force hard to account for except through the influence of an archaic meaning. It used to be said that one made provision against a possible occurrence, where "against" could mean at once "until" and "in order to prevent." The word acknowledged an inevitability, even as it stood in the way. "Against that time, if ever that time come, / When I shall see thee frown on my defects"—as far back as Shakespeare the older sense could flow into some casual reaches of modern usage. Yet this urgency runs counter to the mood of a deliberate blending of sensations, prized by an aesthete who plays texture against texture and color against color. The jostle of these meanings has an effect in the poem first of distraction, then of ominous uncertainty. What is worked out gradually but unmistakably is a portrait of a mind adrift.

Under the hallucinatory assault of images, the poet does not find a token of his will. The search to make some meaning from the shuffle of the leaves, which seem to be autumn leaves as they reflect the light and colors of the fire—this effort leads to nothing but a mimic display of further leaves, the feathers of the peacocks; and then the terrible cry of the peacocks, so eerily like a human cry of pain that the poet has to remind himself "I heard them cry—the peacocks." There is a pressure of pathos in the scene which his mind can do nothing with. The things he would have wished to turn to a purpose continue opaque, while other things transform themselves as if they had the will he lacks. Orpheus with his lyre made the wilderness bend to his song, but the "heavy hemlocks" of this poem "come striding" unbidden. The final emotion I think is terror—a terror that comes from an attempt of imaginative assertion that is resisted by the mind's own impediment. The last two lines suggest that the speaker has been shaken beyond comprehension. Yet all we know is that something has happened, and that it has not been good.

I make these comments as if such an underplot could be rendered finally lucid. Yet I know that such reconstruction is slow and difficult, the work of many readings; and it is made so by the resolute enforcement of a pitch of description close to apathy. This Stevens accomplishes through the use of simple conjunctions like *and*, where the significance cannot but be complex; through the use of anaphora; and through the apparent innocuousness of reflexive metaphors: "The colors of the bushes . . . Turned in the room / Like the leaves themselves." It is also done by words that give priority to the appearances of direct sensation—"I say," "I felt," "I remembered"—though, as the title partly concedes, for all the impartial manner what is described is a moment of dark self-absorption. "Domination of Black" in all these ways is a work of original power, yet what it represents cannot be pictured, and can hardly be restated in words. "A jump of the mind from meditation and feeling to an awareness of an absence of feeling"—perhaps that is the best a paraphrase can do.

There is a curious resonance of Beckett's prose in these lines by Stevens. "But I confess I attended but absently to these poor figures, in which I suppose my sense of disaster sought to contain itself." "After the fiasco, the solace, the repose, I began again, to try and live, cause to live, be another, in myself, in another. How false all this is. No time now to explain. I began again." The aesthetic I have been describing, with its rhythm of unemphatic closure, was not limited to poetry and it was not, I think, necessarily limited to words. A style of indirection and ellipsis, which the realist cinema discovered around 1945 as if it were a given grace of film, had been quietly inherited from modernist poetry and prose. As a reminder of the range of this practice, whose strength is to imply only the shadow of a narrative, I close with two passages from a famous short story by Hemingway, "A Clean, Well-Lighted Place." Such stories were written by others too—by Turgenev and Chekhov, by Joyce and D. H. Lawrence and Elizabeth

Bowen—to suggest a possibility of self-possession that they do not dramatize. This motive the story writers share with poets like Thomas, Rosenberg, and Stevens.

"A Clean, Well-Lighted Place" begins with an indifferent exchange of words about suicide, a fragment of a conversation in the small hours between two persons in relation to whom we are not permitted to satisfy a personal interest. It touches a depth of solitude that can only be known in society.

> It was late and every one had left the café except an old man who sat in the shadow the leaves of the tree made against the electric light. In the day time the street was dusty, but at night the dew settled the dust and the old man liked to sit late because he was deaf and now at night it was quiet and he felt the difference. The two waiters inside the café knew that the old man was a little drunk, and while he was a good client they knew that if he became too drunk he would leave without paying, so they kept watch on him.
> "Last week he tried to commit suicide," one waiter said.
> "Why?"
> "He was in despair."
> "What about"
> "Nothing."

The last line might be heard as a dismissal of the anecdote, but I cannot see that we are meant to take it so. The ending is really no different, except that the solitude has become still more ordinary. We are in the life occupied by one of the voices, fully exposed to disaster, yet holding disaster at bay.

> "You want another copita?" the barman asked.
> "No, thank you," said the waiter and went out. He disliked bars and bodegas. A clean, well-lighted café was a very different thing. Now, without thinking further, he would go home to his room. He would lie in the bed and finally, with daylight, he would go to sleep. After all, he said to himself, it is probably only insomnia. Many must have it.

A COMMON AIM of modernist art, part aesthetic, part ethical, sometimes went by the name "impersonality." It came to be known best in T. S. Eliot's formulation in "Tradition and the Individual Talent," where he refers to the "continual extinction of personality" as an accompaniment of the artist's surrender to something more valuable than himself. Even when Eliot proposed it, in the context of a polemical essay, this was a far-fetched conceit, not entirely free of metaphysical dandyism. But Eliot added a qualification later in the essay: "Poetry is not a turning loose of emotion, but an escape from emotion; it is not the expression of personality, but an escape from personality. But, of course, only those who have personality and emotions know what it means to want to escape from these things." Here the argument becomes more interesting. It sounds as if the "continual extinction" had been a therapy known to Eliot himself, a practice devised for certain occasions and associated with a kind of poetry he admired and wanted to produce. He was right about its connection with his own best work. A reason for the superiority of *The Waste Land* to *Four Quartets* is that the latter has come to care about plausibility. The "mature" poet plots himself into every recess of the poem. He plots in even the reader's response to his own response to himself. The writing of poetry at this remove from all but the finer tactical emotions becomes a practice closely akin to diplomacy.

But impersonality need not be thought so recondite a matter as Eliot made it seem. It is known prosaically to any writer who has revised. The more you take out, the more telling the hints of a purpose. And that is the true argument against confessional poetry: that it will not take that step; and so it drives out the poet's ability to edit. A different kind of failure to imagine or write outside oneself can be felt in the personalism of a cannily mobile professional style in letters today. On this subject it is better to say nothing than to say too little, for the style is not visible in poetry only. It is the kiss of gentle knowingness that attends the mannerly fiction of the day, and it portions out the higher journalism in symmetrical slices of prudence, glitz, and a cost-free self-mockery. Its master trait is a suavity that makes the poet or story writer or reviewer signal everywhere "But, hey. You don't need to take this *very* seriously. I'm doing it because it's the way we do it now." The *I* is always on the scene, and it always stands for a collection of other people's attitudes. In this situation an idea of impersonality may still have salutary power, even as a distant ideal. It may be a necessary part of the resistance to cliché.

One learns more nearly what was at stake in the modernist wish for impersonality if one looks at Eliot's precursors in his polemic. They were, in fact, the romantic poets and critics—a continuity remarked by Frank Kermode in *Romantic Image* and by Iris Murdoch in "Against Dryness." The aesthetic demand for a purging of the self goes back to Keats's wish for "negative capability," or that state of suspense "when a man is capable of being in uncertainties, Mysteries, doubts, without any irritable reaching after fact & reason." This, for Keats, was a mood of susceptible imaginings, because it did not subject itself to any wish for enlightenment or edi-fiction; a mood of nervous (not irritable) unease, whose peculiarity is that it looks toward neither satisfaction nor any concrete result. Keats does not specify the sort of fact and reason to which the poet should be indifferent, but in his case a particular provocation was the moralism of Wordsworth: "we hate poetry that has a palpable design upon us." A poem should not impose itself on a realm of action or intention outside the poem; that is getting credit on the cheap, and is to be deplored like any vulgar mixing of virtues—as when a politician tells you what a good husband he is. "A poet is the most unpoetical of any thing in existence; because he has no identity."

Keats went furthest to clarify his counter-ideal in writing to a generous fellow poet whom he admired, but whom he took to be another moralist tempted by the rewards of fact and reason, Percy Shelley. "A modern work it is said must have a purpose, which may be the God—an artist must serve Mammon—he must have 'self concentration' selfishness perhaps. You I am sure will forgive me for sincerely remarking that you might curb your magnanimity and be more of an artist, and 'load every rift' of your subject with ore. . . . My Imagination is a Monastery and I am its Monk." An artist of the sort Keats aims to exemplify must stand apart from our usual understanding of power and identity. To adapt a pertinent remark from Henry James's essay on Turgenev, the artist hopes to gain, in return for his secluded labor, "something which it is idle to pause to call much or little so long as it contributes to swell the volume of consciousness." Poetry that has a palpable design moves in the opposite direction: it returns to its origin and lets us see the author's hand on the materials, always guiding our response; it makes sure of our sympathies by leaving no doubt what the author's are and how pleasing our conversion will be.

Let me conclude with some theses on the Keatsian and Eliotic, the romantic and modern idea of a selfless capability, beyond which the art of poetry has not yet advanced.

1. The work seeks out objectification—of a subject matter that lay undigested in experience; of the author's anger or envy or enthusiasm; of data about the world that have found no other calculus. Objectification, in this sense, implies neither "dryness" as to form nor "anti-humanism" as to ideology. It has nothing to do with what the work of art describes, or with what it asserts. It is merely a way of establishing how it wants to be taken.

2. We are made to feel a deep and at the same time unfathomable relation between the work and its author. Flaubert saying that *he* was Madame Bovary was executing a stroke of wit or paradox within the impersonal

aesthetic and at its expense. Yet, in any other regime of the arts, such a comment would hardly seem witty or poignant. It would amount to what any reader might be pardoned for assuming. "The opinions expressed by the characters in this book are necessarily the opinions of the author."

3. Belief is of no consequence. Kierkegaard said that the motto of the Christian is "As thou believest, so it comes to pass; or As thou believest, so art thou; to believe is to be." The modern artist envisioned by Keats and Eliot has escaped the force of this imperative, being, by choice and calling, nothing himself. He consoles the regret this may cause by reflecting that very good doctrine can make very bad poems.

4. The work attempts to give no account of itself. As Stevens said in a letter (June 3, 1941): "What I intended is nothing."

T. W. Adorno in *Aesthetic Theory*—the one great book of its kind that belongs to modernism—distinguished between the good of objectification in a work of art and two aims that are sometimes confused with it: the cult of immediacy (associated with photographic realism and the values of exhaustive information and rapid access), and the fetish of perfection (associated with the nineteenth-century idea of the masterpiece, the single work that becomes the focus of an entire career). "Art will live on only as long as it has the power to resist society. If it refuses to objectify itself, it becomes a commodity." To speak favorably of objectification, as Adorno does here, may be only another way of saying that "in every work of art something appears that does not exist." In a formula that Adorno often repeats, art vindicates itself as a *promesse du bonheur*, an implied image of a culture less mingled with barbarism than any the artist can have known. This means that the work of art is a token of a happiness that can never become a promise kept to the artist.

The promise does matter nonetheless. There is a relation, difficult to specify but known to every reader, between the idea of a distant and maybe unattainable happiness in society and the pointless ideal of objectification in art. It has something to do with the non-utilitarian good of perfection as an end in itself. It may have more to do with the hope of bringing into the world of appearance a thing that does not exist in the world. The connection anyway suggests a reason why a poet might still suppose today that one cannot write well if one writes for the present moment. To evoke posterity is mawkish if it means to weep on your own grave with the help of an unfalsifiable chorus. But the interest of posterity may have a very different source. There are times when the fact and reason of the present appear so tidal an onrush that they threaten to carry off any possible imagining of a future. All that throng of worthy or energetic purposes, of fashions that exert an unchallengeable command, are a provocation that the poet may turn away from simply for the sake of imaginative freedom. Posterity then becomes the name of a power of resistance—one of the necessary motives of abstraction, or impersonality, or "'self concentration' selfishness perhaps."

TWO

Poetic Invention and
the Self-Unseeing

Thomas Hardy wrote the poem called "The Self-Unseeing" from which I have taken part of my title. It is a poem of memory, in three stanzas: first, a return to a cherished place, which is haunted now by the memory of a past moment; second, a tableau of that moment—a gathering of a family or intimate friends, with a woman staring into a fire and a man playing a fiddle; finally, a comment from the perspective of memories closer to the present.

> Childlike, I danced in a dream;
> Blessings emblazoned that day;
> Everything glowed with a gleam;
> Yet we were looking away!

The poem feels like a small romantic piece with no anomaly of motive. The most commanding of its details—the way the last three lines give a chiming emphasis to the commonplace materials—is partly a result of foreshortening. But the title is difficult. One can suppose it belongs to one of the jargons that Hardy liked to make up from poem to poem and then to forget. He found late in life that he was having trouble with the meanings of certain words, but he got no help from a dictionary, which, when he turned to it, cited his early books for its only recent examples of the usage in question. Another of Hardy's poems, however, has a similar title, "The Self-Unconscious." So the kind of meaning he wanted to enforce by calling his subject the self-unseeing was important enough to have been unforgettable to him.

Some clear senses for the phrase come from the story that the poem recounts. "All this happened a long time ago; I couldn't know then how much it mattered. I was just *there,* and it was happening. The self that was going to become me was already part of the scene; but that is something I see only now." The poem allows one to moralize this in a Proustian way: "I see it vividly now because I wasn't seeing it then. But this disparity and this recognition are just what the self is. Things prepare for us, as if in our absence, a text which we read later on, and when we read it we say, 'These things were mine; together, all these are myself.'" They can be mine, Hardy wanted the readers of his title to see, only on the condition of my having once been unaware of their significance. They do inescapably look personal now, since I did not live with the desire of making them so. It would be plausible to think of the poem as showing that an intense retrospect is the reward of an earlier unseeing.

But maybe it is fairer to exclude the very idea of a reward. It would be more like Hardy to suppose that one's uses of experience are unreflective, even to the point of a stupefied endurance; and that this is a cost of secreting something peculiar to oneself, something that can be recognized but never realized. Some readers think they can hear a sentimental grace note in the very last line, and they find it an annoyance: as if Hardy were wishing to live twice, the second time as a knowing contemporary of the objects of his nostalgia. I think they have heard it wrong. The poem is an analysis of a condition. It is in the nature of the self Hardy describes to have been unseeing. Or, rather, merely to have been. Around this constant limit, which the occasions of memory leave unfixed, a self is crystallized in writing. It is a powerful abstraction which one comes to know apart from experience. The sense in which this is so, I want to argue, is a subject of modern poetry, almost its defining subject. I am construing poetry narrowly here to mean the work of a single person that may preserve (unexpectedly) or change (unexpectedly) the habitual understandings of a common life. Poetry in this sense, like other writing but more acutely, shows the possibility and the difficulty of the creation of individuals. I started with Hardy's word "self" and have now switched to "person" and "individual." I will be using the three indifferently from now on. The latter two are longer but also less metaphysical-sounding, and they run less risk of getting distracted by side issues.

A discussion of "the function of poetry" meets a big enough problem anyway in the shape of that phrase. When Matthew Arnold lectured on the function of criticism, he conceded a lot in advance to an ordinary ideal of social responsiveness. Literature, including poetry, was, on the view Arnold proposed, itself a kind of response, a "criticism of life." In framing his discussion like this, Arnold was joining an argument with utilitarianism: not perhaps with its own weapons, but certainly on its own ground. His way of thinking is still a point of departure for those who grant the propriety of speaking at all about poetry's relation to a more general life. Eliot, for example, who was reluctant to talk about poetry in terms of function, often said that the value of poetry related somehow to conscious beliefs: just the beliefs that, when they gave credence to religious institutions, could be the cement of a social order. It is impossible now to share Arnold's motive of constructing a defense of poetry with an equal rebuke to utilitarian planners and romantic sages. And few people would have agreed with Eliot even in 1930 when he urged poets to submit their art to the liberating order of institutions. I do not think in fact that one can assert a function for poetry without some reference to beliefs. But they may be beliefs that are closer to our usual idea of instinct. They cooperate with the processes of social development and decay, and they are as accidental as every other element of those processes. When they are given form by poetry, we read them as if they were part of a design that included ourselves.

This was Shelley's argument in the "Defence of Poetry," and in the remarks to come I will be adding nothing to it. Shelley regarded the poet as a figure of partial autonomy: the kind of figure without whom any claim of solidarity with others is apt to become repressive. The poet stands for autonomy because his work bears a relation to its circumstances which looks strange and therefore inventive. We can look back at it much later and see that this relation was determinate after all. Yet it appears to define the lives of readers as well as poets, and it does so in advance of their usual practices. Thus the range of values that Shelley associates with poetry cuts across the modern division between the language of aesthetics and the language of morals. Moral philosophers, Iris Murdoch observed in her essay "On 'God' and 'Good,'" work now with pieces of an older tradition that has become unreal to them. They are left therefore

> with a denuded self whose only virtues are freedom, or at best sincerity, or, in the case of the British philosophers, an everyday reasonableness. Philosophy, on its other fronts, has been busy dismantling the old substantial picture of the "self," and ethics has not proved able to rethink this concept for moral purposes. The moral agent then is pictured as an isolated principle of will, or burrowing pinpoint of consciousness, inside, or beside, a lump of being which has been handed over to the other disciplines, such as psychology or sociology. On the one hand a Luciferian philosophy of adventures of the will, and on the other natural science. Moral philosophy, and indeed morals, are thus undefended against an irresponsible and undirected

self-assertion which goes easily hand in hand with some brand of pseudo-scientific determinism. An unexamined sense of the strength of the machine is combined with an illusion of leaping out of it.

The situation that Murdoch described seems to me to hold true for literature, with the difference perhaps that literary people are more trustful of that "isolated principle of will, or burrowing pinpoint of consciousness." At least we talk as if we were.

Toward a richer conception of both morals and aesthetics, Murdoch proposed an idea of freedom. She called it tragic freedom because it was unconnected with any universal order or harmony satisfying to the reason. Art, as she saw it, was uniquely fitted to exemplify such an idea: by its very existence, it taught the reality of something apart from either self-assertion or a thoroughgoing determinism. This was an attitude of attention to the being of others and therefore to a good outside oneself. In another, more programmatic, essay, "The Sublime and the Good," Murdoch admitted that even in works of art there was no "social totality within which we can come to comprehend differences as placed and reconciled. We have only a segment of the circle. Freedom is exercised in the confrontation by each other, in the context of an infinitely extensible work of imaginative understanding, of two irreducibly dissimilar individuals. Love is the imaginative recognition of, that is respect for, this otherness." To make these words apply to poetry, and not, as they were chiefly meant, to works of fiction and drama, one has to qualify and slightly contract the description of what literature does. The love Murdoch spoke of was, of course, severe in character rather than sentimental, but even so lyric poetry is not the place to look for it. To the extent that we do find it there, we are looking at borrowings from somewhere else: from the moralizing interjections of a novelist, for example, or the implicit gratitudes and cordial regards that may be at home in friendship. By poets, when poetry is not what they are up to, the reader is sometimes treated as a credible surrogate for a docile or dependable friend. This is another way of saying that the lyric poetry which has dominated the last two centuries cannot dramatize the confrontation of two irreducibly dissimilar individuals. What it can dramatize is something more elementary: the sense of relationship that emerges from the coalescence of separate moments of an individual life. But this may lead us in turn to think of the moments of more than one individual.

What Murdoch called an attention to the being of others is not a matter of indifference to the poet. It is what makes him write rather than sing, or pray, or merely observe the concatenation of his thoughts and dreams.

And it is what makes him interested in being read. But poetry has a sufficient function now in showing the possibility and the difficulty of the creation of individuals. I mean the sort of showing that Hardy gives in the third stanza of "The Self-Unseeing," and also the sort that Elizabeth Bishop wrote about, in a passage that ought to be better known than it is.

> Dreams [she wrote in a letter to Anne Stevenson], works of art (some), glimpses of the always-more-successful surrealism of everyday life, unexpected moments of empathy (is it?), catch a peripheral vision of whatever it is one can never really see full face but that seems enormously important. I can't believe we are wholly irrational—and I do admire Darwin!—But reading Darwin, one admires the beautiful solid case being built up out of his endless heroic *observations*, almost unconscious or automatic—and then comes a sudden relaxation, a forgetful phrase, and one *feels* the strangeness of his undertaking, sees the lonely young man, his eyes fixed on facts and minute details, sinking or sliding giddily off into the unknown. What one seems to want in art, in experiencing it, is the same thing that is necessary for its creation, a self-forgetful, perfectly useless concentration.

Apart, then, from this act of useless concentration, poetry is without an ambition to edify. Its end is to produce a text from life that counts as an exemplary case of the emergence of an individual.

THE TWO ILLUSTRATIONS I now want to give are by John Ashbery and Geoffrey Hill, poets who are close to being identified with the antipodes of contemporary practice. So I need to begin by saying what the common background is for the individuals we first come to know in their work. It is, above all, a background of anonymity, against which the poet emerges as a named being. That anonymity may appear as an effect of regarding human life in the context of the behavioral sciences, as Murdoch's analysis asserted, or in the context of natural history, as Bishop's seemed to suggest. In the two poems I will quote, the force of anonymity is connected, first, with the techniques of mass culture and, second, with the techniques of modern war. Both technologies, of course, were developed in a conscious effort to destroy the idea of persons who can feel and think alone rather than in the mass. Little as these poems share of temperament or idiom, it is striking that they both begin by mimicking a style of anonymity that they mean to resist. The process by which a named being does emerge is gradual in both cases, and indeed imperceptible unless one compares their ends with their beginnings. Somewhere between these points, the poems succeed in making a strange resolution vivid to us. They look on their inhuman objects as dead things which one may outlast if one is able to make them one's own. Since I find that very few people who admire one of these poets have any time for the other, I may as well add that it was the sort of tenacity and resistance I have just described, the feeling of refusing to deliver themselves easily, which, through these poems in particular, first attracted me to the work of Ashbery and Hill. They do seem to me to share a certain asceticism. One may think of it as the other side of an assurance that they are whatever they will be found to have been while they were looking away.

Here is Ashbery's "Definition of Blue."

The rise of capitalism parallels the advance of romanticism
And the individual is dominant until the close of the nineteenth century.
In our own time, mass practices have sought to submerge the personality
By ignoring it, which has caused it instead to branch out in all directions
Far from the permanent tug that used to be its notion of "home."
These different impetuses are received from everywhere
And are as instantly snapped back, hitting through the cold atmosphere
In one steady, intense line.

There is no remedy for this "packaging" which has supplanted the old
    sensations.
Formerly there would have been architectural screens at the point where the
    action became most difficult
As a path trails off into shrubbery—confusing, forgotten, yet continuing to exist.
But today there is no point in looking to imaginative new methods
Since all of them are in constant use. The most that can be said for them further
Is that erosion produces a kind of dust or exaggerated pumice
Which fills space and transforms it, becoming a medium
In which it is possible to recognize oneself.

Each new diversion adds its accurate touch to the ensemble, and so
A portrait, smooth as glass, is built up out of multiple corrections
And it has no relation to the space or time in which it was lived.
Only its existence is a part of all being, and is therefore, I suppose, to be prized
Beyond chasms of night that fight us
By being hidden and present.

And yet it results in a downward motion, or rather a floating one
In which the blue surroundings drift slowly up and past you
To realize themselves some day, while you, in this nether world that could not be
    better
Waken each morning to the exact value of what you did and said, which
    remains.

The opening three-and-a-half lines are spoken, evidently, by a lecturer on the History of the Great Ideas, who wields his broad commonplaces with an ease that is both definitive and bland. In describing the phenomena of mass culture, he affects to judge them from a position outside their control. But this is in fact a tone of voice that can register no difference at all from the standard idioms of that culture.

The metaphors that complete the stanza look like members of a single family: the branching out in all directions, the tug of home, the impetuses from everywhere, and the instant snapping back. One can accordingly construe them as elements of a single figure even if their discontinuities do not give much hope for a satisfying result. But what is remarkable about the passage is this. It feels so categorical and propositional, in so anomalous a way, that one is compelled to read it personally after all, against what had seemed to be its aim. In the same way, the mass practices that the speaker has set out to portray appear to yield something characteristic in spite of themselves, with the "one steady, intense line" that marks the rebound of the personality. What Ashbery calls the personality and what I have been calling the individual asserts its claim by an apparently hermetic but actually mundane turn of speech. It reads its own features in the hidden places of a language it could not remedy. This does not imply acceptance. It is only that "today," as Ashbery puts it, "there is no point in looking to imaginative new methods / Since all of them are in constant use." Methods, I suppose, would be formal properties, like those architectural screens that once concealed or disclosed the movements of the characters on whom our attention was meant to fall. Now the poet leaves the perfection of such methods to the adepts of packaging. But he notices the rate at which each invention succeeds the last. To seize the thing, at a moment of its decomposition, and make it serve as a decoy for one's purposes, is to have a personal signature. A conviction of impersonality may come therefore from the very tonalities that the poet learns from mass culture. But in his writing it gives weight to a self-revelation that is the more affecting for having been subdued to a colorless medium. This seems to me incidentally a clue to a deep affinity between much of Ashbery's work and the vein Eliot was exploring in "Preludes," "The Fire Sermon," and a few other poems.

In the most surprising of the metaphors here, Ashbery speaks of "erosion." He seems to have in mind the wearing out of new methods and of the habits of recognition they bring. This erosion, he says, "produces a kind of dust or exaggerated pumice / Which fills space and transforms it, becoming a medium / In which it is possible to recognize oneself. / Each new diversion adds its accurate touch to the ensemble, and so / A portrait, smooth as glass, is built up out of multiple corrections / And it has no relation to the space or time in which it was lived." It is these multiple corrections, then, which yield a self-portrait distinct from every stereotype. Such a portrait "has no relation to the space or time in which it was lived," in the sense that an exhaustive account of its conditions would still fall short of projecting its qualities. But in another sense the portrait is wholly formed by circumstance, its multiple corrections built up out of ready materials that are known to all. The difference between the poet and others is that they did not wish for the diversions. The last stanza is, it seems to me, a kind of envoi to those others, who inhabit the blue surroundings to which a definition will be given "some day." For now, the portrait alone represents, as its maker cannot, the exact value of what he did and said, which remains.

I have been reading "Definition of Blue," as I would read some other poems by Ashbery, as if it were part of the wisdom literature of our culture. But one must add that it is wisdom literature of a peculiar sort. For the audience it cares for and the instruction it gives are confined to an aesthetic idea of the self. In Geoffrey Hill's "Ovid in the Third Reich," there is perhaps a limitation of an opposite sort. The audience it cares for and the instruction it gives are confined to an ethical idea of the self. What I believe we have to know about Ovid—with whom Hill's title and epigraph go some way to identify the speaker of his poem—are moral and not artistic facts. He kept his distance, out of necessity more than choice, from an imperial government in an evil time. Thus he was a prime instance of the moral luck which may be another name for moral good. The citizen who cannot escape into exile, and who fails to obstruct the crimes of a state, is an instance of his antithesis. This poem, concerned with the necessity of judging, is chastened by an awareness of how entirely, and uncreditably, our own fortunes are mingled with our duty to praise and blame.

> *non peccat, quaecumque potest peccasse negare,*
> *solaque famosam culpa professa facit.*
> (Amores, III, xiv)

I love my work and my children. God
Is distant, difficult. Things happen.
Too near the ancient troughs of blood
Innocence is no earthly weapon.

I have learned one thing: not to look down
So much upon the damned. They, in their sphere,
Harmonize strangely with the divine
Love. I, in mine, celebrate the love-choir.

I said that this poem had a first-person speaker. But at some point in one's thinking about it, the moods of the two stanzas begin to sound so disparate that one thinks of them as belonging to separate speakers.

The first stanza makes a remark about innocence which may or may not be trying to appease a suspicion of guilt. Anyway it knows well the place where such suspicions arise. By contrast, the second stanza gives its verdict judicially, from a position of detachment. The first is cast in the present, the second in the perfect tense: "I love . . . ," "I have learned. . . ." Some way into this effort of comparison, one may notice an unpleasant thing. The banal locutions of the first speaker—"I love my work and my children," "Things happen"—belong to the timeless chatter of extenuating circumstances. They were employed in a wholesale fashion in the years after the fall of the Third Reich, and they embody the standard apology of the "little man." This is the citizen who was close enough to criminal acts to be looked on as their accomplice. However powerful he may have been once, he feels small now beside the circumstances that seem to condemn him. In this light the sentence, "God is distant, difficult," is perhaps not the admission of doubt one took it for, or not only that. It, too, may be merely exculpatory. The "ancient troughs of blood" are the camps. That is a phrase that appears to hold nothing in reserve either for sympathy or palliation. But, as I hear it, the word "ancient" implies the figuratively true, but literally consoling and corrupt fiction that, human nature being what it is, the same troughs were always there. The whole last sentence of this stanza is precarious—it wants to be both found out and let off. "Too near the ancient troughs of blood / Innocence is no earthly weapon." Thus perhaps: "We all live too near them. Our innocence as victims, or as guiltless accomplices, cannot prevent us from being killed, or from being judged." Or, if one imagines it said by someone who actually lived near the camps: "One might have lived farther off, and so have been ignorant, as well as plausible in one's ignorance. Luck alone decides the question about oneself that others will see as striking at one's essence. This fact leaves every person equally weaponless." About the speaker of this stanza, if one imagined his utterance stopping here, one would know very little humanly, except that he could argue most tribunals into an acquittal.

The second stanza offers a judgment that is exceptional because it is unappeasable. And yet, its most striking trait is the austerity with which the moralizing tenor of such a judgment is withheld. "Not to look down / So much upon the damned": it is a different thing from not looking down, not admitting that they are damned. One may be helped in interpreting this by a parallel suggestion in another of Hill's poems, "Annunciations." We are enjoined there to "strive / To recognize the damned among your friends." But to do so is repellent to self-love, as, for example, striving to recognize your friends among the damned would not be repellent. Here, in a recognition of the guiltless or guilty accomplices of the Third Reich, Hill observes that "They . . . harmonize strangely with the divine / Love." Between a line ending and a full stop, Love is almost as hard to say in this poem as God, between a full stop and a line ending. And "they" harmonize strangely; not harmonize: they are in their sphere and he is in his. He celebrates for the moment, in writing, what they were not, rather than condemn what they were. But now, having reached this point, I have to ask again how far a distinction can be sustained between the two voices that one may hear in these stanzas. Hill could have separated them by giving quotation marks to just one. He chose not to do so. I am grateful anyway for this doubt since it makes me sure the poem succeeds in something unexampled. It gives a single tonality to habits of speech that might belong to persons of wholly distinct fortunes and conduct.

I hope I have interpreted both of these poems accurately; I have tried as well to interpret them tendentiously. The purpose has been to show how, in both, the poet claims a kinship with an anonymous texture of life, which had seemed to rule out the possibility of his utterance. The portrait that we read is built up out of multiple corrections of something—it does not matter greatly whether we call it a "sphere" or "surroundings"—with which the poet could not have been supposed to acknowledge an affinity. This plot, of the emergence of a person against a background of impersonal forces, is enough to account for certain similarities of gesture between the two poems, notwithstanding their total incommensurability of feeling. The closing recognitions that one finds in them also suggest an answer to the question, What is poetry for?—a question it is still right to ask if one cannot accept the answers that center on magic, or craft, or free play. Both Ashbery and Hill portray the judging or defining person as a site of resistance that can only be known as the subject of recognitions like these. But recognition after all may be too special and literary a word. I prefer Iris Murdoch's word, "attention."

ON THE VIEW I am proposing, the modernity of certain poems is at once anomalous and paradigmatic for modern culture. It is marked by a discovery of attention that characterizes a self in writing. Poetry, on this side of its work, performs an altogether different task from the descriptive writing, whether in prose or verse, whose mode is artful portraiture and whose end is self-presentation. The work that I have quoted is recessive. Work of the other kind is dominant, and it comes with a caption: "I am a person of such and such a type, and you will find me charming." The confidence is not always misplaced. But, from the point of view I have sketched, its appeal lies outside poetry. To stress, for a last time, how little this difference has to do with the formal division between verse and prose, I want to end by quoting a passage from Hardy's novel *A Pair of Blue Eyes*. Even more than his poem "The Self-Unseeing," it seems to me an epitome of poetic invention, but like the poem it has some details of context that need explaining. Henry Knight has slipped at the edge of a cliff and hangs suspended over the ocean, his face against the rock face and his fingers clutching "a knot of starved herbage." Hanging thus, as Hardy describes him, "from the inner face of the segment of a hollow cylinder, having the sky for a top and the sea for a bottom, which enclosed the bay to the extent of nearly a semicircle," he looks at what is directly in front of him.

> By one of those familiar conjunctions of things wherewith the inanimate world baits the mind of man when he pauses in moments of suspense, opposite Knight's eyes was an imbedded fossil, standing forth in low relief from the rock. It was a creature with eyes. The eyes, dead and turned to stone, were even now regarding him. It was one of the early crustaceans called Trilobites. Separated by millions of years in their lives, Knight and this underling seemed to have met in their place of death. It was the single instance within reach of his vision of anything that had ever been alive and had had a body to save, as he himself had now.
>
> The creature represented but a low type of animal existence, for never in their vernal years had the plains indicated by those numberless slaty layers been traversed by an intelligence worthy of the name. Zoophytes, mollusca, shell-fish, were the highest developments of those ancient dates. The immense lapses of time each formation represented had known nothing of the dignity of man. They were grand times, but they were mean times too, and mean were their relics. He was to be with the small in his death.
>
> Knight was a fair geologist; and such is the supremacy of habit over occasion, as a pioneer of the thoughts of men, that at this dreadful juncture his mind found time to take in, by a momentary sweep, the varied scenes

that had had their day between this creature's epoch and his own. There is no place like a cleft landscape for bringing home such imaginings as these.

In this passage of the sublime-grotesque, Knight reaches the point at which one says "I" only of something that will have been.

Yet Knight comes to his moment of attention just where one would have expected the self to have become as insubstantial, and the will as intensified, as possible. It occurs, that is, when an irrefutable sense of the strength of the machine has seemed to combine with a desperate hope of leaping out of it. Instead, he chooses this interval to cover the lapse of time between the trilobite and himself, so that he catches in its dead eyes an image of himself looking away: "It was the single instance within reach of his vision of anything that had ever been alive and had had a body to save, as he himself had now." Here if anywhere is an instance of perfectly useless concentration. It is the furthest thing imaginable from an idea of recovery, which would allow one to know, and in anticipation to cherish, the thing that is to be recovered. But curiously, as Hardy narrates the close of this scene, it does not end in resignation, or for that matter in a renewed vitality. "The previous sensation, that it was improbable he would die, was fainter now. However, Knight still clung to the cliff." Hardy's is a peculiarly dry treatment of a melodramatic occasion. It exhibits indeed the reverse of a poet's "reckless courage in entering the abyss of himself." And in this again it resembles the other inventions I have been discussing. Faced by the annihilation of an individual life, the writers of these words regard the idea of themselves as an almost material deposit. To write poems is, for them, to be a fair geologist. Accordingly, the catastrophe that interests them is never extinction as such, but rather a fate of namelessness which others have suffered before.

Hardy was not a meliorist of the imagination. Wallace Stevens, who was, said that poetry began with "A seeing and unseeing in the eye," and he added that the effect of making its objects "Visible or invisible or both" would be "An abstraction blooded, as a man by thought." His words accurately describe the work of poetry now, if we construe abstraction literally, as a drawing apart of two things that leads to a redescribing of both. Abstraction is emphatic reduction. It is the movement by which poetry joins with another life, or what readers once could bear to call the stream of life. We may prefer to think of it as the inner face of the segment of a hollow cylinder. If the life there returns the poet's gaze, it does so with the fixed eyes of a dead thing. But the encounter leads out from the present moment as something suffered and back to the same moment as something defined. Aesthetic and moral thought, I said near the start, are not well equipped to discuss, or even perhaps to notice such encounters. But whether or not we speak of them in a language we already know, they matter to the larger self-image of a community like ours, with which both aesthetic and moral thought are concerned. They have as much consequence as the record of a survival has for one who may or may not survive. None of this ought to imply an enhanced sense of vocation for the poet. Poetry itself must always be indifferent to the pathos of its own implication in the life it sometimes touches. It goes on being written from an impulse no more admirable than the painter's, the judge's, the geologist's, or the trilobite's. Like them it clings to the cliff.

1987

THREE

T. S. Eliot and Hart Crane

The poems were not epicurean; still, they were innocent of public-spiritedness: they sang of private disgust and diffidence, and of people who seemed genuine because they were unattractive or weak. The author was irritated by tea parties, and not afraid to say so, with the result that his occasional "might-have-beens" rang out with the precision of a gong. . . . Here was a protest, and a feeble one, and the more congenial for being feeble. For what, in that world of gigantic horror, was tolerable except the slighter gestures of dissent?

— E. M. Forster on reading T. S. Eliot in 1917

By 1940 T. S. Eliot had emerged as the representative English poet of modernism. This was one of those transitions that feel natural after they have happened—that can seem to settle a reputation once and for all with a finality mysterious to readers who witnessed the struggle for fame. Of such a moment it is always fair to ask how far the climax it affords is a trick of retrospect, a shadow we mistake for a necessary part of the landscape. What if Eliot's assimilation had occurred much faster? What if it had occurred more slowly, or on a more idiosyncratic basis? Eliot's letters and occasional criticism are sown with doubt and wonder at the definitive quality of his triumph. The way a few of his poems joined with a few of his polemical essays to secure a unique place for his poetic achievement is one of those inspired accidents that history casts up from time to time to challenge our determinisms. Of course, this was the outcome Eliot desired all along. But the readers who first cared for his poetry must have seen the possibility of a different development.

Suppose that his poetry had been spurned in every quarter of the literary establishment for a decade or two after *The Waste Land*. What then?

Eventually he might have found a place among the unassimilables, the recessive geniuses of English poetry—the company of Collins and Beddoes rather than Donne and Dryden. There would have been much justice in this. The author of *Prufrock and Other Observations* was felt by his contemporaries to be an elusive and not an imposing presence. His charm lay most of all in the relief he offered from importance. Nor did *The Waste Land* seem at first a drastic departure from the earlier sources of his appeal. It commanded respect as an experiment with voices, like "Prufrock" and the Sweeney poems. To think of it in that light may still be more pertinent than to honor it teleologically for the qualities it shares with *Ash Wednesday* and *Four Quartets*. The passing characters of the poem—Mrs. Porter, Mr. Eugenides, the Young Man Carbuncular—these figures were hardly notable for their continuous gravity. They were phantoms of a mind delicately questing after sensations, and their aim was "a new art emotion," to adapt a phrase from Eliot's criticism. Their creator appeared to be a poet averse to no stimulus, however morbid—a cautious welcomer of any experience, however drab—whose peculiarities of temperament had much to do with the dignity of his art.

Some of Eliot's essays of the period lend themselves to a similar description. "Hamlet and His Problems," now commonly read as a manifesto for dramatic objectivity, was a paradox in the vein of *The Authoress of the Odyssey*, a fit of character criticism against the character critics. Eliot's bogus primerlike title (which could be added to the books on the shelf in Beerbohm's caricature of Yeats: *Short Cuts to Mysticism, Half Hours with the Symbols, Reality: Its Cause and Cure, Hamlet and His Problems*) mocked the orderliness of his clinical tone. Even "Tradition and the Individual Talent," to a reader who weighed the chemical analogy in the second part as carefully as the axioms of culture in the first, could seem a late flower of the dandyism of Poe. These essays were, among other things, deliberate curiosities, out-of-the-way solutions to problems the reader was meant to see as in no way impersonal. The solemn reception of Eliot's criticism in the next generation, as if it had been written by a more judicious Matthew Arnold, enhanced his stature in the short run only, and on dubious terms.

I have been trying to convey the susceptible mood in which the young Hart Crane would have approached the poetry of Eliot. But the obstacles to an adequate view of the subject have been planted by Crane as much as by Eliot. Open and impulsive as Crane's letters generally are, they give a misleading impression of this particular debt. His quotable statements of general aims and theories, which align his poetry with Eliot's, tend to take an adversarial stance when Eliot himself is in the picture. This happened,

I think, in part because Crane had resolved early to write *The Bridge* as an answer to *The Waste Land*. Another motive may have been that his frequent correspondent in matters concerning Eliot was Allen Tate, a contemporary who shared Crane's advocacy of Eliot's poems but who was already, in their exchanges of letters in the 1920s, on the way to admiring Eliot as a prophet of civilization. The influence of "Gerontion" on the "Ode to the Confederate Dead" differs in character from the influence of *The Waste Land* on *The Bridge*. In the first case the relation is that of principle and illustration, in the second that of statement and counter-statement. Affinity seems a truer word than influence to describe the latter sort of kinship—a point I can bring out by comparing the early poems "La Figlia che Piange" and "My Grandmother's Love Letters."

BOTH POEMS address a feminine presence that is not quite maternal, and that is touched by erotic warmth; a presence whose memory must be appeased before the poet can venture into his own acts of love and imagination. Yet the poems exhibit, and exemplify for the sake of each poet's future, distinct uses of sympathy. Eliot's is a tenderness that will at last be detached from erotic passion, whereas Crane is seeking a temporary freedom from familial piety, earned by an intense avowal of such piety. Notwithstanding this divergence of motives, the poems share a single story and a music. The wish of the poets to serve as guardians at a scene of their former lives, protectors of something that was suffered there, is curiously blended with a self-command that makes them stand back from the scene. The result is a tone at the brink of an irony that neither poet entirely wants to formulate. The revealing point for comparison, it seems to me, is the "turn" of the poems—the place in each where the poet speaks of his seclusion from the image with which he began. In "La Figlia che Piange" that image is the glimpsed attitude of a woman at the top of a stair, holding a bunch of flowers; in "My Grandmother's Love Letters," it is a view of a nook by the corner of the roof where the letters have long been stored. Self-conscious in their bearing toward the women they write about, both poets are also safely hidden in their watching; and a sense of memory as a sheltering medium, protective for the rememberer and the image, touches with regret their knowledge of the person whose life cannot be recovered.

From this fortunate position—a voyeur but one not in search of a voyeur's pleasure—Eliot imagines a meeting with a possible consummation between the woman and a man. (The man, we are free to imagine, is the speaker himself in a different life.)

So I would have had him leave,
So I would have had her stand and grieve,
So he would have left
As the soul leaves the body torn and bruised,
As the mind deserts the body it has used.
I should find
Some way incomparably light and deft,
Some way we both should understand,
Simple and faithless as a smile and shake of the hand.

She turned away, but with the autumn weather
Compelled my imagination many days,
Many days and many hours:
Her hair over her arms and her arms full of flowers.
And I wonder how they should have been together!
I should have lost a gesture and a pose.
Sometimes these cogitations still amaze
The troubled midnight and the noon's repose.

The compromised interest of the observer has much in common with the attitude of a Jamesian narrator, though even by the terms of that analogy the speaker of "La Figlia che Piange" is evasive—calling his anxiety and bewilderment "cogitations" and his shadowy desire a concern with "a gesture and a pose." He is troubled most by an intimation that the woman is morally innocent, as he somehow is not. And yet her life will be filled to a depth of experience he does not hope to share.

A larger impulse of ordinary sympathy is at work in Crane's poem. He tries—one can feel the pressure of the effort—to associate his fancies with the actual life of the woman he writes about. Yet as his ingenuity stretches to cover the distance between them, the questions his poem asks take on a careful obliqueness like Eliot's. The love that his grandmother felt seems now so far off that, if he should cross the house to retrieve her letters, each step would feel like a passage of countless years:

Over the greatness of such space
Steps must be gentle.
It is all hung by an invisible white hair.
It trembles as birch limbs webbing the air.

And I ask myself:

"Are your fingers long enough to play
Old keys that are but echoes:
Is the silence strong enough

To carry back the music to its source
And back to you again
As though to her?"

Yet I would lead my grandmother by the hand
Through much of what she would not understand;
And so I stumble. And the rain continues on the roof
With such a sound of gently pitying laughter.

I would, the phrase that governs the last several stanzas of Eliot's poem, is displaced by Crane to the last four lines; the entire closing montage of "La Figlia che Piange," with its surprising sudden exterior (a scene of both pathos and indifference), has been miraculously condensed. Crane has the same need to find "Some way incomparably light and deft, / Some way we both should understand" to connect person with person and present with past. Hence the difficult question he asks himself: whether he is strong enough "To carry back the music to its source / And back to you again / As though to her?" The phenomenal life of the world, which continues untroubled as before, at the ends of both of these poems may be a sign that the connection has not been achieved.

"La Figlia che Piange" and "My Grandmother's Love Letters" are linked more subtly by a seasonal counterpoint, Eliot's poem starting in spring and passing into autumn, Crane's set in an autumn that looks back on someone else's spring. There are resonances too between the sunlit and moonlit spaces in which the poems create their distinctive moods of stillness. And (the detail that feels most like conscious allusion) the separate line of "My Grandmother's Love Letters,"

It is all hung by an invisible white hair

recalls a line repeated in Eliot's opening stanza,

Weave, weave the sunlight in your hair

and never returned to in the later stanzas, the weight of which nevertheless carries implicitly through the rest of Eliot's poem. The closing notes of the poems differ perhaps by a nuance of decisiveness. Eliot ends with the amazement or bemusement that was for him at this period a familiar and almost a reassuring motif: one hears it in nearly the same key at the end of the monologue "Portrait of a Lady." By contrast, the sympathy Crane had begun with deepens, as he turns from this memory to other memories.

The sense that is rich in "My Grandmother's Love Letters," of a pity that touches the poet unaccountably from a slight but charged detail of the setting, has its own precedent elsewhere in Eliot. The penultimate stanza of "Preludes" confesses:

> I am moved by fancies that are curled
> Around these images, and cling:
> The notion of some infinitely gentle
> Infinitely suffering thing.

Three further lines close "Preludes" in a vein of average irony—"Wipe your hand across your mouth, and laugh"—but "My Grandmother's Love Letters" includes the fancies as if they would do without a retraction.

"Preludes" is the poem by Eliot that seems most steadily resonant in Crane's early work. Comprising discrete impressions of a city—several perspectives, offered by a "consciousness" or "conscience" not easily distinguishable into a single person—this poem's montage tries out the shifts of tense and mood that will be more gravely performed in *The Waste Land*. It covers a matter-of-fact range, not the intensities of Tiresias, without a claim of supervening authority and without the cues of false or true guidance which would come later, with the demand of Eliot's poetry that it be read as prophetic speech.

For Crane I think the appeal of "Preludes" lay in its intuition of the city's unemphatic routine as an incitement to the poet.

> The morning comes to consciousness
> Of faint stale smells of beer
> From the sawdust-trampled street
> With all its muddy feet that press
> To early coffee-stands.
> With the other masquerades
> That time resumes,
> One thinks of all the hands
> That are raising dingy shades
> In a thousand furnished rooms.

This landscape was often in Hart Crane's mind when he wrote his shorter poems of the 1920s; hints of it appear as late as the subway entry sequence of "The Tunnel." He remembered the same passage in a sort of private joke in a letter: arrested drunk one night in 1927, "the next I knew the door crashed shut and I found myself behind the bars. I imitated Chaliapin fairly well until dawn leaked in, or rather such limited evidences of same as six o'clock whistles and the postulated press of dirty feet to early coffee stands." The casual echoes have a wider meaning. The most difficult task of Crane's poetry, as he comes close to saying elsewhere in his letters, is to connect the thought of an "infinitely gentle, infinitely suffering thing" with some surmise about the emotions proper toward the hands in those "thousand furnished rooms."

His first full response was "Chaplinesque":

> We make our meek adjustments,
> Contented with such random consolations
> As the wind deposits
> In slithered and too ample pockets.
>
> For we can still love the world, who find
> A famished kitten on the step, and know
> Recesses for it from the fury of the street,
> Or warm torn elbow coverts.
>
> We will sidestep, and to the final smirk
> Dally the doom of that inevitable thumb
> That slowly chafes its puckered index toward us,
> Facing the dull squint with what innocence
> And what surprise!
>
> And yet these fine collapses are not lies
> More than the pirouettes of any pliant cane;
> Our obsequies are, in a way, no enterprise.
> We can evade you, and all else but the heart:
> What blame to us if the heart live on.
>
> The game enforces smirks; but we have seen
> The moon in lonely alleys make
> A grail of laughter of an empty ash can,
> And through all sound of gaiety and quest
> Have heard a kitten in the wilderness.

The poem answers directly with the poet's voice an experience "Preludes" reported as occurring once to someone, the experience that brought "Such a vision of the street / As the street hardly understands."

The "smirk" can seem a mystifying detail even to a reader who feels its rightness. It suggests the improbability of human contact in the city's crowds, where the "squint" looking for the main chance blots out every other concern. The tone is a good deal like "Wipe your hand across your mouth, and laugh"; and maybe for a moment this poem is testing a similar note of scorn. Then the gesture is looked at differently: "The game enforces smirks; but we have seen / The moon in lonely alleys make / A grail of laughter." The game may be the one Walt Whitman spoke of in *Song of Myself;* "Looking with side-curved head curious what will come next, / Both in and out of the game, and watching and wondering at it." Crane's mood suggests something of this poise and inquisitiveness. The kitten, a child of the city, has wandered in from outside the game, a chance embodiment of the "suffering thing." To keep it safe from the fury of the street is a charity worthy of Chaplin's tramp.

The modern artist exists to invent a shelter for the most vagrant sympathies. Crane said so in the letter to William Wright in which he also declared his interest in Chaplin:

> I am moved to put Chaplin with the poets (of today); hence the "we." In other words, he, especially in "The Kid," made me feel myself, as a poet, as being "in the same boat" with him. Poetry, the human feelings, "the kitten," is so crowded out of the humdrum, rushing, mechanical scramble of today that the man who would preserve them must duck and camouflage for dear life to keep them or keep himself from annihilation. . . . I have tried to express these "social sympathies" in words corresponding somewhat to the antics of the actor.

This summary brings to light the active impulse Crane speaks of missing in Eliot. But one must resist the temptation to suppose that either poet was aiming for effects the other accomplished. I doubt that Eliot, given the diffusive emotions that matter to him, would have thought of offering a setting to such lines as

> Recesses for it from the fury of the street

or

> And through all sound of gaiety and quest,

lines that are touchstones of the confidence and isolation of the man who wrote them. A certain striding eloquence seems natural to Crane, and fits with the truth he speaks to the antagonist of "Chaplinesque" (the boss or agent of the state, the character in Chaplin's films who sizes up the tramp with a lowering grimace): "We can evade you, and all else but the heart: / What blame to us if the heart live on." It is the reverse of Eliot's sentiment at the end of "Preludes": "The worlds revolve like ancient women / Gathering fuel in vacant lots." The steps of the women may look random as they cast about for bits of fuel, but a capricious determinism governs their smallest movement. At times the steps of the tramp will look no different. But "Chaplinesque" takes its buoyancy from a resolve—the mood of someone going somewhere—which the tramp asserts at irregular intervals. The forward motion is an illusion, but one that Crane brings to enchanted reality by siding with this hero.

MY COMMENTS on Eliot and Crane are shaped by an aesthetic judgment as personal as any other. *Prufrock and Other Observations* and *White Buildings* seem to me among the greatest achievements of modernity, quite as original in what they accomplish as *The Waste Land* and *The Bridge*. One of the cheats of high modernist theory, abetted by Eliot in "*Ulysses,* Order, and Myth" and embraced by Crane in the conception of his longer poems, was the supposition that the virtual order of human knowledge must stand in some interesting relation to literary form. It followed that one could make the modern world systematically intelligible for art by respecting and executing the proper form of a knowledge special to art—by viewing the novel, for example, as the genre of the "transcendent homelessness of the idea" (the phrase is Lukács's, from *The Theory of the Novel*). With modernism, genre itself briefly and misleadingly became, as it had been in the eighteenth century, a master clue to the earnestness of the author's claim to represent reality. To writers like Eliot and Crane, this suggested the tactical propriety of expanding the lyric to claim again the scope of the epic. Of the pretensions of modernist poetry, none has dated so badly as this.

The *Waste Land* and *The Bridge* were not assisted imaginatively by the encyclopedic ambition to which they owe their conspicuous effects of structure. The miscellaneous texture of the poems is truer to their motives. A little more consistently than Eliot's early poems, *The Waste Land* divides into two separate registers for the portrayal of the city, the first reductive and satirical, the second ecstatic and agonistic—the latter, in order to be released, often seeming to require the pressure of a quotation. At any moment a detail such as "The sound of horns and motors, which shall bring / Sweeney to Mrs. Porter in the spring" may modulate to a style less easily placed:

> O City city, I can sometimes hear
> Beside a public bar in Lower Thames Street,
> The pleasant whining of a mandoline
> And a clatter and a chatter from within
> Where fishmen lounge at noon: where the walls
> Of Magnus Martyr hold
> Inexplicable splendour of Ionian white and gold.

Though the transitions of *The Bridge* are less clear-cut, part of Crane's method lies in a pattern of allusions to *The Waste Land*. This plan had emerged as early as his letter of September 11, 1927, to Otto H. Kahn, and later, piece by piece, in the echoes he found of Phlebas the Phoenician, who "Forgot the cry of gulls, and the deep sea swell / And the profit and loss"— lines that haunted him already in "For the Marriage of Faustus and Helen."

Let us turn to a kind of allusion more precisely dependent on context. Eliot in *The Waste Land*, himself looking back to Shakespeare's *Tempest*, overhears a character in "The Fire Sermon" in an unexplained trance of thought.

> While I was fishing in the dull canal
> On a winter evening round behind the gashouse
> Musing upon the king my brother's wreck
> And on the king my father's death before him. . . .

Pondering those lines in "The River," Crane added to the Old World image of destiny the local accretions of a childhood in the American Midwest. The effect is a startling recovery and transformation:

> Behind
> My father's cannery works I used to see
> Rail-squatters ranged in nomad raillery,
> The ancient men—wifeless or runaway
> Hobo-trekkers that forever search
> An empire wilderness of freight and rails.
> Each seemed a child, like me, on a loose perch,
> Holding to childhood like some termless play.
> John, Jake or Charley, hopping the slow freight
> —Memphis to Tallahassee—riding the rods,
> Blind fists of nothing, humpty-dumpty clods.

The allegory of both poets tells of a child set loose from his moorings; but discrete elements of erotic feeling are at work in the two passages. The poet's distance from the allegory is widened by Eliot as far as possible. It is narrowed by Crane to an unembarrassed intimacy with the humble materials from which any cultural myth can be made.

The Bridge, like *The Waste Land*, is spoken by a man reluctant to conquer a landscape he imagines in the form of a woman, a landscape which itself has suffered the assault of earlier generations of men. The king of *The Waste Land* owns an inheritance that has shrunk to nothing. At its outer reach he is dimly conscious of the Thames maidens who "can connect / Nothing with nothing." The same intimation of despair is in the familiar landscape of the child Hart Crane as he watches the hobo-trekkers, but in *The Bridge* the possibility of connection is not despised:

> They lurk across her, knowing her yonder breast
> Snow-silvered, sumac-stained or smoky blue—
> Is past the valley-sleepers, south or west.
> —As I have trod the rumorous midnights, too.

The narrator of the last line is noticeably mortal, and idiosyncratic in what he confides, unlike the Tiresias of *The Waste Land*.

Tiresias was fated to endure sexual experience as a man and a woman, then punished with blindness by Hera for his report that woman's pleasure was greater, and, in compensation, rewarded with the gift of prophecy by Zeus. His self-knowledge, as the poem presents it, is a version of all knowledge. "As I have trod the rumorous midnights, too" implies a more local and personal claim. It is possible that this narrator, too, has known experience in both sexes. If so he has evidently derived feelings of potency from both. And if the word *rumorous* is a further memory of Eliot— "aetherial rumours / Revive for a moment a broken Coriolanus"—the roughs of the "empire wilderness of freight and rails" connect the memory with a different nostalgia.

The paths a single echo may suggest are a consequence of disparate conceptions of poetic authority. When the speaker of "The Fire Sermon" sits down and weeps "by the waters of Leman," he imagines a fraternity shared with the lamenter of Psalms, a kind of fellowship that is possible only across time. The rail-squatters "ranged in nomad raillery" speak of a casual traffic among the traditions of the living; and American folk songs, some of them named in "The River," are a reminder of the energy of such traditions. You make a world in art, Crane seems to have believed, out of fragments knowable as parts of the world. With his submission to the sundry data of life—a gesture unmixed with contempt—the speaker of "The River" admits a fact of his personal life, namely, that he has had a childhood: something (odd as it feels to say so) that cannot be said of the narrator of *The Waste Land*. Crane is able here to discover a pathos foreign to Eliot, even in a line, *"Blind fists of nothing, humpty-dumpty clods,"* which itself has a strong foreshadowing in Eliot's "I will show you fear in a handful of dust" (as also in "other withered stumps of time"). "Blind fists of nothing" implies an energy in purposeless action that Eliot withholds from all his characters. The defeats or casualties in *The Bridge* are accepted as defeats without being accounted final. Sex is the motive of this contrast, with Eliot's plot steadily allying sexual completion and disgust—an event and a feeling that Crane may link incidentally, as he does in "National Winter Garden" and "The Tunnel," without implying that these show the working out of an invariable law.

Crane wrote several letters about *The Bridge* and *The Waste Land.* Only one of them says his purpose is the antithesis of Eliot's, and he offers the comparison in a mood of conjecture rather than assertion: "The poem, as a whole, is, I think, an affirmation of experience, and to that extent is 'positive' rather than 'negative' in the sense that *The Waste Land* is negative." Because of its use by the pragmatists James and Dewey, "experience," in the 1920s, was a word charged with specifically American associations. It was apt to serve a common argument that the individual—most of all the individual in a democracy—possessed among his inward resources a field of experiment sufficient to define an idea of freedom. Thus the potency Crane would ascribe to the Mississippi River belonged also to personal consciousness and imagination: "The River, spreading, flows—and spends your dream." Eliot's preoccupations were closer to metaphysical realism, and likely in the 1920s, as they were later, to allude with some urgency to a claim on behalf of reality. Knowledge of reality was, by definition, almost impossible to obtain, and that made the requirement of such knowledge all the more pressing. Eliot's usual metaphors when these concerns are in view—metaphors that have a source in the philosophy of F. H. Bradley—picture a realm where knowledge is complete, intelligible, and integral, yet by its nature undisclosed to individual consciousness. The nearest one can get to a sense of solidarity in experience is by imagining a sequence of identical privations, each knowing the character of the others because its contents mirror the contents of all others:

> I have heard the key
> Turn in the door once and turn once only
> We think of the key, each in his prison
> Thinking of the key, each confirms a prison.

The comfort this thought brings may be a sort of knowledge, but it is knowledge at the cost of experience, and what it confirms is a negation of freedom.

These theoretical self-definitions would have come home to Crane implicitly enough; he understood how much was at stake when he talked of "positive" and "negative." *The Waste Land* is a progress poem of a sort: it moves continuously through its series of sure-to-be-missed connections, in which every episode must prove to have been foresuffered. The structure of the poem is that of a theme and variations. The apparently chance encounters, improvised meetings, and assignations disclose themselves as versions of a single story which goes on with all the adventitious shifts of age and custom. A truth, we are invited to see, lies in wait beneath the accumulation of masks—a truth not susceptible to the inflections of personal will. There is no aspect or coloring of life that will not be known in advance to Tiresias. The progress of *The Bridge* feels just as repetitive but is harder to follow since it aims to resemble a process of growth. The poem loses what can be lost for the sake of a gain in experience; its recognitions have ceased to be an affair of the guilty living and the unburied dead:

> "Stetson!
> "You who were with me in the ships at Mylae!
> "That corpse you planted last year in your garden,
> "Has it begun to sprout?"

Eliot's style is dramatic and satirical—a choice emphasized in his splendid recording of the poem, with its dryness and air of continuous command. Whereas, in *The Waste Land,* nothing can come of any memory that is reengaged, *The Bridge* offers another kind of memory: a meeting of eyes in which "the stubborn years gleam and atone," as the ranger's mother says in "Indiana."

IT IS AN American hope to seek atonement through experience alone. For that reason I think Yvor Winters was right to associate *The Bridge* with *Song of Myself,* though he was wrong to suppose that this description entailed a self-evident rebuke. *The Bridge* and *Song of Myself* have the same kind of unity—of mood, texture, urgency and enterprise. Crane was conscious early of this link to Whitman, one token of which appears in "For the Marriage of Faustus and Helen." The poet presents himself in the midst of a crowd, anonymous and loitering until his name is called; the passage mingles the thought of Whitman with an echo of Eliot forgetting "the profit and loss":

> And yet, suppose some evening I forgot
> The fare and transfer, yet got by that way
> Without recall,—lost yet poised in traffic.
> Then I might find your eyes across an aisle,
> Still flickering. . . .

The traffic makes it possible to lose oneself "without recall," shorn of a past, and yet to get by, to be on the move and somehow poised. The flickering carries a range of suggestions: of a face in back of a blind; a face suggestive by its lines, though hard to see in the glancing lights of the traffic; a face in which the eyes themselves may be blinking. The aisle seems a metaphor for the canyons dividing the façades of New York's skyscrapers, or the passage between the rows of a cinema, which in turn gives a further sense to the flickering.

In "Faustus and Helen," as in *The Bridge,* eyes know more than they are conscious of; and Crane's thought once again comes from Whitman: "Who knows, for all the distance, but I am as good as looking at you now, for all you cannot see me?" From "Prufrock" on, the eyes in Eliot's poetry are uncertain that knowledge is to be desired. His eyes alight gently but do not fix; they are cast down or averted—part of a face they help you to prepare "to meet the faces that you meet." It is fitting that Crane's most tormenting poem of love should have been a countersong to "Prufrock." There are other antithetical features of "Possessions," the title of which (with its overtones of demonic possession) works against the sense of material property or furnishings. It might have been called "Dispossessions":

> Witness now this trust! the rain
> That steals softly direction
> And the key, ready to hand—sifting
> One moment in sacrifice (the direst)
> Through a thousand nights the flesh
> Assaults outright for bolts that linger
> Hidden,   O undirected as the sky
> That through its black foam has no eyes
> For this fixed stone of lust . . .
>
> Accumulate such moments to an hour:
> Account the total of this trembling tabulation.
> I know the screen, the distant flying taps
> And stabbing medley that sways—
> And the mercy, feminine, that stays
> As though prepared.
>
> And I, entering, take up the stone
> As quiet as you can make a man . . .
> In Bleecker Street, still trenchant in a void,
> Wounded by apprehensions out of speech,
> I hold it up against a disk of light—
> I, turning, turning on smoked forking spires,
> The city's stubborn lives, desires.

Tossed on these horns, who bleeding dies,
Lacks all but piteous admissions to be spilt
Upon the page whose blind sum finally burns
Record of rage and partial appetites.
The pure possession, the inclusive cloud
Whose heart is fire shall come,—the white wind rase
All but bright stones wherein our smiling plays.

The first line ends with a pun on "tryst," and the entreaty here of a witness or accomplice is ventured with much of Prufrock's urgency: "Oh do not ask what is it." But this scene of turmoil has obstructions that not only impede but chafe and penetrate; compare the lines of "Prufrock,"

It is impossible to say just what I mean!
But as if a magic lantern threw the nerves in patterns on a screen:
Would it have been worth while

with the unreluctant answer of "Possessions":

I know the screen, the distant flying taps
And stabbing medley that sways—
And the mercy, feminine, that stays.

The contrast follows from Crane's determination to write of a desire on the other side of satisfaction, to make a "Record of rage and partial appetites." So the wariness of

The eyes that fix you in a formulated phrase,
And when I am formulated, sprawling on a pin,
When I am pinned and wriggling on the wall,
Then how should I begin
To spit out all the butt-ends of my days and ways?

gives way to an agonized embrace:

I, turning, turning on smoked forking spires,
The city's stubborn lives, desires.

Crane's speaker has grown old with the spent vehemence of youth, but it is Eliot's who has the lighter step: "Prufrock" was a young man's poem about age.

And yet in "Possessions" the language of "Prufrock" has been so assimilated that its ending can seem to occur the moment after "human voices wake us and we drown." The spray of the sea, in which Prufrock's mermaids were glimpsed, is taken up in "The pure possession, the inclusive cloud" that marks the conquests and surrenders of the later poet, now burnt forever into the city's memory. "Possessions" is a homosexual poem, defiantly so. But the remarkable uncollected lyric "Legende," written when Crane was nineteen, gives a feminine motive to the same image of erotic possession and erasure. The woman there "has become a pathos,— / Waif of the tides"; the poet closes by saying, "even my vision will be erased / As a cameo the waves claim again." This sense of the good of rendering a life permanent, even as its detail is burned away, would be constant in Crane's work: that is a reason for the *we* of "Possessions" to imitate the Dantesque *we* of "Prufrock," though with a shift of emphasis. Prufrock's companion had to be knowledgeable in the ways of erotic hunger, regret, and repetition, but was largely a pretext for dramatic confidences. Crane's use of the word includes himself and his lover.

A last comparison will bring out the delicacy with which Crane could portray erotic contact as a hint of some larger acknowledgment that was never to be spoken. For his provocation he turned again to *The Waste Land* and particularly to the lines that follow the imperative "Datta":

> The awful daring of a moment's surrender
> Which an age or prudence can never retract
> By this, and this only, we have existed.

Crane's echo, at once violently explicit and curiously tacit, speaks of

> sifting
> One moment in sacrifice (the direst)
> Through a thousand nights the flesh
> Assaults outright for bolts that linger
> Hidden.

There had always been in Eliot a need to cherish the personal relation as an enigma, which by its nature belonged to a realm of untouchable grace and self-sacrifice. The anxiety of physical surrender is lest you be given something that was not yours to take: "That is not what I meant at all, / That is not it, at all." But Crane's interest is always to take everything. What survives his experience will be preserved elsewhere—it is not for him to say where— as elusive as "bright stones wherein our smiling plays." The ironic phrase at the point where memory hopes to recover something more palpable—"Accumulate such moments to an hour: / Account the total of this trembling tabulation"—suggests his view of a dry impartiality that will dispense with the work of recovery. For the idea of counting such moments is bound to be false; they are really one moment "that stays / As though prepared."

I HAVE BEEN discussing Crane's poetry and his temperament and personal traits as if these things were plainly related. Yet he is one of those poets who can persuade many readers much of the time that his poetry has shed any empirical relation to a life. One might tell a convincing story about his writing in which the ordinary elements, including the feelings he had for other writers, almost vanished. He would appear then as a romantic hero, uneasily committed in his early years to the "tremorous" moments he invoked in "Legend"—the first poem and in many ways the signature of *White Buildings*—but gravitating at last to a poetry unconfined by chance encounters with the actual world. No poet has written many poems outside those limits. Coleridge did it in "Kubla Khan," and Swinburne in "At a Month's End." Crane may have felt he was crossing a similar threshold when he wrote "Voyages VI." It is something to be the kind of writer for whom such a thought is possible.

On this view of his career, its fable of initiation is "Passage." For, like no other poem by Crane, "Passage" signals a break from experience. But what is impressive is how far even there the landscapes of Eliot, his cadences, and his imaginative predicament become for Crane a prophecy of what he himself must and must not become. In the allegory of the poem, the author is challenged to account for his life by an unnamed figure of admonition. The presence of such a figure is an artistic given—his life from the start has been a scene of risk. "Dangerously the summer burned / (I had joined the entrainments of the wind)," he declares, translating *entraînement,* a rapture or enthusiasm. The inquest continues as the weight of the landscape intensifies:

> The shadows of boulders lengthened my back:
> In the bronze gongs of my cheeks
> The rain dried without odour.
>
> "It is not long, it is not long;
> See where the red and black
> Vine-stanchioned valleys—": but the wind
> Died speaking through the ages that you know
> And hug, chimney-sooted heart of man!
> So was I turned about and back, much as your smoke
> Compiles a too well-known biography.

As in "Emblems of Conduct"—where we are told, of any present moment in art, "By that time summer and smoke were past"—smoke is a figure for a life whose pathos can be captured in a story. The Crane of "Passage" was turning away from such stories, as Eliot, at the end of *The Waste Land,* had done in the hope of subduing his inheritance. But there is no such hope and no acceptance in "Passage": its pledge is to master a fate that will elude any witness or historian of conduct. The poem bequeaths the poet to desires without a possessor, desires harbored and acted upon, to which writing will be a weak secondary clue. *Your* smoke—the possessive pronoun is impersonal, its grammar that of Hamlet's "There are more things in heaven and earth, Horatio, / Than are dreamt of in your philosophy." More is at stake in a life than the smoke that tells the story will ever compile.

Here is his source in Eliot:

> What are the roots that clutch, what branches grow
> Out of this stony rubbish? Son of man,
> You cannot say, or guess, for you know only
> A heap of broken images, where the sun beats,
> And the dead tree gives no shelter, the cricket no relief,
> And the dry stone no sound of water. Only
> There is shadow under this red rock,
> (Come in under the shadow of this red rock),
> And I will show you something different from either
> Your shadow at morning striding behind you
> Or your shadow at evening rising to meet you;
> I will show you fear in a handful of dust.

The passage, from "The Burial of the Dead," offers the first sign that the dread of *The Waste Land* has a metaphysical dimension. That poem ends with a gesture of reserve that commits the poet to an ordering of life, however provisional; a gesture honorable in its humility, when considered beside the fear and apathy the poem as a whole has described. At the end of "Passages" Crane, too, breaking one spell to cast another, faces a barren sea from the land's end where memory has set him down. It is here that he asks:

> What fountains did I hear? what icy speeches?
> Memory, committed to the page, had broke.

He may yet be released into a life more intoxicating than anything memory could yield.

What that life will be the man who prays for it "cannot say, or guess," not because he has ceased to exist, but because the thing he will be is unwritten. Crane lived to make few examples of the poetry that here beckons to him. After "Voyages VI" one can count "The Dance" and perhaps "O Carib Isle!" as efforts of an unexampled pressure of purpose. These are poems of agony—"I could not pluck the arrows from my side"—a record of suffering that testifies against the healing of the sufferer:

> Let not the pilgrim see himself again
> For slow evisceration bound like those huge terrapin

Each daybreak on the wharf, their brine-caked eyes;
—Spiked, overturned; such thunder in their strain!

But from the first there was another order of poetry that mattered to Crane, and that represents him as faithfully. An agnostic naturalism persisted from "Repose of Rivers" to "The Broken Tower." As one looks back on that span of work, its dominant note comes, one cannot fail to see, not just from the city but from the city of Eliot. What is true of "Chaplinesque" and "Possessions" is also true of "Recitative" and "To Brooklyn Bridge" and "The Tunnel." To say these poems were achieved in dialogue would be to assert too little for the poems and too little for both poets. Crane wrote poetry of a kind unimaginable without Eliot; and the accomplishment of Eliot feels somehow larger in this light.

1996

FOUR

Crane in His Letters

These are the letters of a great poet, and they do not disappoint.* But Crane had another quality, besides his distinction as an artist, which people will look to confirm in any record of his life. Because of the determination with which, as a teen-aged boy from Ohio, he planted himself in New York City and, in the 1920s, helped to make a myth of that city, he has inherited much of the glamour that attaches itself to the romantic experimenter and *poète maudit*. There was, as his friends could see, something of Melville in the quest of imaginative ecstasy that drove him on; just as, in retrospect, there is something akin to Scott Fitzgerald in the chaos of squandered energies that gradually engulfed him. "The voice of a generation"—it is a stock phrase, of course, but in Crane it answered to a deep and ingenuous ambition:

> Then, drop by caustic drop, a perfect cry
> Shall string some constant harmony,—
> Relentless caper for all those who step
> The legend of their youth into the noon.

The dramatic interest of his letters comes from our knowing how swiftly the author of those lines—from "Legend," a poem in his first book, *White Buildings*—would pass into the author of "Purgatorio," a lament of exile written from Mexico by a man with the sere countenance that his portraits show at the age of thirty:

> My country, O my land, my friends—
> Am I apart—here from you in a land

*O My Land, My Friends: The Selected Letters of Hart Crane, ed. Langdon Hammer and Brom Weber.

> Where all your gas lights—faces—sputum gleam
> Like something left, forsaken—here am I—

As they come to be better known, the letters will only enhance the legend, and in human terms one may feel ambivalent about this. We accept an aesthetic half-truth when we crave a "story" to interpret an artist's career. And yet one feels that there ought to be exorbitant lives like his; and the letters themselves are alive to that feeling. In Crane, a life and a body of work are so fused that they seem to return our gaze together.

He was born in 1899, the son of Clarence and Grace Crane, well-meaning progenitors who never let go, who stayed and sat on his life. Far on in his twenties, Hart felt obliged to respond to Clarence's offers of jobs that he could not take, and to Grace's soliciting of advice that she would not follow. Clarence had been a restaurant owner, then a candy manufacturer (he invented the LifeSaver), and from the first it was clear that Hart would have his father's support to the exact extent of his concern with the family business. He had shown bohemian inclinations, publishing, by the age of fourteen, "advanced" poems with an exquisite Pre-Raphaelite tone. Yet he appears never to have adopted the role—conventional in the generation after Ibsen—of the artist alienated from his family. He kept close to his mother, uncomfortably close as adviser, consoler, giver of practical wisdom and reassurance, more like an older brother than a son. At the same time, even after her divorce, he would never repudiate his father. But the things he could care for, and the things Clarence could even theoretically encourage, were as far apart as were his native confidence and his mother's wavering anxieties. Right to the end, in this tangle of allegiances, he was called on to tack from New York to Ohio, or from Mexico to Ohio, to unravel affairs that were still going wrong.

As a young man in New York, Crane went half way to satisfy his father's demand for a business life: he worked for several months in advertising, at the J. Walter Thompson agency. But soon after announcing to a close friend, William Wright, that a business career "is not to be scorned," that "the commercial aspect is the most promising characteristic of America," he feels compelled to assure Wright that "bowing to it" need not involve "our complete surrender of everything else." In the same letter of 1919, he goes on to speak of the world as "a devastation in my eyes," and one may suppose the reversal a sign of callowness; but the truth is that these swings were characteristic all his life, and very little in the early letters sounds unformed or mawkish.

There is a captivating frankness in the exuberance with which Crane addresses himself to the experience of people and books. Writing to Gorham

Munson—an editor and critic to whom he sent some of his best letters—he plots his name facetiously on a literary map extending from Munson and his collaborator Matthew Josephson to the leading spirits of the age. Sherwood Anderson, he says, "and Josephson are opposite poles. J., classic, hard and glossy,—Anderson, crowd-bound, with a smell of the sod about him, uncouth. Somewhere between them is Hart Crane with a kind of indetermination, still much puzzled." Amid the literary and personal vicissitudes of his early twenties, the note of adventure stays vivid, and as fresh as when he wrote to his father on his first move from Cleveland to New York in 1916: "It is a great shock, but a good tonic, to come down here as I have and view the countless multitudes. It seems sometimes almost as though you had lost yourself, and were trying to find somewhere in this sea of humanity, your lost identity." The thought of self-recognition in a crowd, recurrent in the letters, would find a deliberate echo in Crane's sequence "For the Marriage of Faustus and Helen":

> And yet, suppose some evening I forgot
> The fare and transfer, yet got by that way
> Without recall,—lost yet poised in traffic.
> Then I might find your eyes across an aisle . . .

This kind of loss and discovery he supposed was a blessing, and he searched to attain it again and again—by the mobility of his life, by his passage from one artistic idiom to another, and, always, by his erotic experience. With the letters in view, one enters into certain of his choices, and comes to realize that they were choices.

AN EDITION BY Brom Weber misleadingly called *The Letters of Hart Crane* was published in 1952, and it gave an impressive first glimpse of Crane as a letter writer. Energetic—spontaneous and considered, not careless-careful in the manner of the confider with a public eye on posterity—the letters in that edition already told much about the life of one poet, and about what it meant to be an artist in America early in this century. Because he liked to drink and was often seen drunk, and because his sexual relations were with men, some of them sailors he picked up after a night's carousing, Crane in the decades following the appearance of the letters went on being talked of and written about as a wild man—a potent warning against the artist-as-artist turned loose upon modern life. *O My Land, My Friends* ought to complete the change of perspective. It is a generous reader's edition, done with a care for accurate scholarship—there are separate introductions to successive periods of Crane's life, and a good analytical index—and though called a "selected" letters it has a better claim to representativeness than its precursor. Some early letters have been cut, but more than a third of those printed are new and they are given, as the 1952 edition did not give them, uncensored. There are now several mentions of Crane's homosexual loves. There are also far more copious draft materials, and more intense and sustained discussion of his poetry— much of it from Crane's correspondence with Yvor Winters, both sides of which were published in 1978 by Thomas Parkinson. Crane's observations on the writing of friends—the comments, for instance, on a draft of Tate's "Ode to the Confederate Dead"—will be a revelation to many readers. But the new letters are only a large reminder of qualities that might have been guessed from his public statement to Harriet Monroe, the editor of *Poetry,* in defense of his poem "At Melville's Tomb."

This touchstone of modernist poetics had been extorted from Crane in a curious manner—really by an editorial whim. Monroe agreed to publish the poem if the author would agree to explain it. Looking at its third stanza,

> Then in the circuit calm of one vast coil,
> Its lashings charmed and malice reconciled,
> Frosted eyes there were that lifted altars;
> And silent answers crept across the stars,

Monroe wrote: "I find your image of *frosted eyes lifting altars* difficult to visualize." The phrase, Crane wrote back, "refers simply to a conviction that a man, not knowing perhaps a definite god yet being endowed with a reverence for deity—such a man naturally postulates a deity somehow, and the altar of that deity by the very *action* of the eyes *lifted* in searching." And the rest of the explanation, reprinted here, proceeds in the same style, studious and deliberate, without pomp or manifesto. Crane's early reviews and letters to journals, many of them written in his teens, in defense of Joyce and Sherwood Anderson and other personal heroes, showed the same kind of forthrightness, almost simplicity of heart, on behalf of aesthetic intensity as an ultimate good.

He was among the most intelligent of artists—in the discursive sense, which entails an ability to communicate a purpose of the work of art outside the work itself. He was self-taught without the dogmatism of the self-taught, critically resourceful and (a capacity harder to hold on to) inquisitive; and he had a confidence he was able to put into words, while doing justice to the attendant doubts. The restorations in the present volume include a great many comments on his own work in progress—especially "For the Marriage of Faustus and Helen," the most learned of his poems, and in its idiom perhaps the most original. He liked to test his work on friends, and once you get used to the miscellaneous context, the letters start to seem a natural habitat for his verse.

All his revisions seem to me improvements. "The game enforces jerks," in "Chaplinesque," a line meant to catch the speed and comical stiffness of Chaplin's tramp, eventually yields for the last word "smirks"—picking up with considerable effect a word used earlier in the poem. The wonderful opening of "Van Winkle,"

> Macadam, gun grey as the tunny's pelt,
> Leaps from Far Rockaway to Golden Gate,
> For first it was the road, the road only
> We heeded in joint piracy and pushed,

is still better in the final version, where "pelt" gives way to "belt" and the last two lines become

> Listen! the miles a hurdy-gurdy grinds—
> Down gold arpeggios mile on mile unwinds.

He would save the piracy of the open road for later sections of *The Bridge;* a touch of street music was better suited to this lightly framing overture.

Crane's poetry had a reputation for difficulty, though he would have preferred otherwise, as he conceded in a vigorous letter to Yvor Winters that begins: "Dear Winters, You need a good drubbing for all your recent easy talk about 'the complete man,' the poet and his ethical place in society, etc." Difficulty had never been his aim: "It happens that the first poem I ever wrote was too dense to be understood, and I now find that I can trust most critics to tell me that all my subsequent efforts have been equally futile. . . . I write damned little because I am interested in recording certain sensations, very rigidly chosen, with an eye for what according to my taste and sum of prejudices seems suitable—or intense enough." His poems—the fact is well attested—do not yield their secret on a first or second reading, but what do we mean by difficulty? Shakespeare's sonnets are as hard as Crane's *Voyages,* and they were always hard. Great poetry is usually difficult in some way, and only the veneer of perpetual acquaintance, added by dozens of anthologies over hundreds of years, can make us believe otherwise. Anyway the illusion of familiarity has a cost. We start to be in love with the cliché that our ear has substituted for the words on the page. Crane permits that assimilation as little as any poet; and this comes to seem a mark of his integrity. He never "makes obscure" but adheres, as firmly as he can, to the motto he chose from John Donne: "Make my dark heavy poem light—and light."

These letters have been compared to those of Keats and Dickinson. The highest praise is intended, and Crane can endure the comparison, but let me confess, after many hours of many days with this volume, that I have never spent such voluntary hours at a time with the letters of Keats or Dickinson. Their letters are brilliant and fraught, always special, often on the stretch, and they pass the full test of character with a vengeance: they would burn a hole in any other prose you set beside them. But with all their attractions, they seldom make quite human company. Crane has a passion for friendship; that is his continuous and absorbing interest. His responses and daily reports have a ballast of ordinary humor, pique or distaste, mundane affection for mundane things. He has a rarer consistency, too, for though he covers various topics in various companies, he never confides in one correspondent in a manner that proves him false to another; and after fifty pages or so, anywhere except for his last years, one actually feels that one has seen friendship in practice. Some letters we read to find out something about the author; others we steal a pleasure and read as if their writers meant them for us. Crane's letters are wasted, and all the better for that.

Here is a passage from one to his mother, describing the sensations of the city, saying what it is that draws him to stay there in 1924. He would like, he says, to acquire a room with a view of the harbor:

> Mr. Opffer, who has such a back room in this house, has invited me to use his room whenever he is out, and the other evening the view from his window was one never to be forgotten. Everytime one looks at the harbor and the NY skyline across the river it is quite different, and the range of atmospheric effects is endless. But at twilight on a foggy evening, such as it was at this time, it is beyond description. Gradually the lights in the enormously tall buildings begin to flicker through the mist. There was a great cloud enveloping the top of the Woolworth tower, while below, in the river, were streaming reflections of myriad lights, continually being crossed by the twinkling mast and deck lights of little tugs scudding along, freight rafts, and occasional liners starting outward. Look far to your left toward Staten Island and there is the statue of Liberty, with that remarkable lamp of hers that makes her seen for miles. And up at the right Brooklyn Bridge, the most superb piece of construction in the modern world, I'm sure, with strings of light crossing it like glowing worms as the Ls and surface cars pass each other going and coming. It is particularly fine to feel the greatest city in the world from enough distance, as I do here, to see its larger proportions.

It is a generous sight, generously recorded, the more so when one sets it beside a stanza of "To Brooklyn Bridge" that seems to have followed the same mood of awe and forgetful gazing:

> Again the traffic lights that skim thy swift
> Unfractioned idiom, immaculate sigh of stars,
> Beading thy path—condense eternity:
> And we have seen night lifted in thine arms.

To judge by the letters, the poems Crane held in surest esteem were "For the Marriage of Faustus and Helen" and *Voyages.* "F & H," as he called it, celebrates a peculiarly modern form of beauty—an abstract experience of the city, with a pleasure in the distance at which objects now acquire their glamour—while treating the romantic theme of the "barter" of beauty for pain. The poem is also, rather disturbingly, a celebration of the clearance for new emotions made by the Great War: the settings are a city street, a nightclub dance floor, and a squadron of fighter planes. *Voyages* is a series of six poems, of tremendous erotic intensity, written for a young man, Emil Opffer, in whom Crane believed he had found "the Word made Flesh." The sequence runs a course from contemplation to ecstasy to a rededication of powers; from childhood to an imagined return by the poet after death; and as one makes out its lights and shadows, from a mid-morning prelude looking out toward the sea, to a conclusion at the edge of dawn looking in toward the shore.

Crane was right to hold a unique affection for these poems even after he went to work in a different vein; and if I had to persuade a reader of the eloquence that is his, and that belongs to no other modern, the poem I would choose is "Voyages V." It moves straight forward in a glide of farewell so that one feels, at once, Crane's aptness of image and his power to condense a phrase and a metaphor. A less conspicuous strength is evident here, namely his sense of dramatic speech—speech heightened beyond any naturalism, and yet not overwrought; speech as it would come to be known in lines not written yet by Eugene O'Neill and Tennessee Williams. The poem is centered on a dramatic situation, too—the speaker looking out at the horizon off shore, at an after-midnight hour, the decidedness of its horizon light suggesting to him an end of his love. He turns to the lover asleep beside him and recalls the betrayals that have already begun to draw them apart, and the fractures of temperament or history that will finally cause them to break off. But the poem stops short of pathos, with a look at the sleeping form beside him, and a consolation that is not a regret.

Meticulous, past midnight in clear rime,
Infrangible and lonely, smooth as though cast
Together in one merciless white blade—
The bay estuaries fleck the hard sky limits.

—As if too brittle or too clear to touch!
The cables of our sleep so swiftly filed,
Already hang, shred ends from remembered stars.
One frozen trackless smile . . . What words
Can strangle this deaf moonlight? For we

Are overtaken. Now no cry, no sword
Can fasten or deflect this tidal wedge,
Slow tyranny of moonlight, moonlight loved
And changed . . . "There's

Nothing like this in the world," you say,
Knowing I cannot touch your hand and look
Too, into that godless cleft of sky
Where nothing turns but dead sands flashing.

"—And never to quite understand!" No,
In all the argosy of your bright hair I dreamed
Nothing so flagless as this piracy.

                              But now
Draw in your head, alone and too tall here.
Your eyes already in the slant of drifting foam;
Your breath sealed by the ghosts I do not know:
Draw in your head and sleep the long way home.

All of the threat of loss in love is compressed in the ambiguous use of
filed, to mean stored up in memory, and also to mean frayed. The variations from the blank-verse meter are cunning, yet altogether natural here,
where a line like "And changed . . . There's" is deliberately fragmentary,
while "Your eyes already in the slant of drifting foam" is almost a hexame-
ter. Since I first read the poem, I have marveled at the sound and cadence
of "The bay estuaries fleck the hard sky limits": a neutral notation of landscape which has the force of an admonition. The magnificent final
stanza—almost all of it carried in words of a single syllable—gains an
added poignancy from a far-off echo of Milton: "Look homeward, Angel,
now, and melt with ruth. . . . Sunk though he be beneath the wat'ry
floor"—an echo that elaborates and explains the poet's feeling that this pre-
dawn hour is ghostly. Yet one may have read and admired the poem for a

long time without being conscious of its learning. Crane's modernism was in this sense never academic, and he has survived for three generations by the surprising communicability with which his words continue to seem, as he said in "Praise for an Urn," "Delicate riders of the storm."

WHY DID SO personal a writer take on the larger "symbolic" cultural work of self-definition that would become *The Bridge?* Part of the motive was intimate—with Opffer, he had walked "hand in hand across the most beautiful bridge of the world, the cables enclosing us and pulling us upward in such a dance as I have never walked and can never walk with another." There seems to have been a revelatory moment when he held in his mind the entire imaginative shape of the poem. He writes in a letter to Munson that he aims to suggest "a mystical synthesis of 'America.'" The conception, in 1923, is "already flickering through my mind . . . but the actual statement of the thing, the marshalling of the forces, will take me months, at best"; but he adds, "if I do succeed" there will be "such a waving of banners, such ascent of towers." Crane was much influenced by the American Revival of the 1910s, particularly Waldo Frank's *Our America.* It looked as if *The Bridge,* some of it written and most of it planned during the wait for the publication of *White Buildings,* might swell the common enterprise of a generation. The poem was also intended as a reply to the symbolic authority of Eliot's *Waste Land,* a work that Crane found impressive but "dead."

His comments on Eliot generally show an unintimidated appreciation and irony. He can say to Allen Tate, in a letter of 1922, "You will profit by reading him again and again. I must have read 'Prufrock' twenty-five times and things like the 'Preludes' more often"; but in a later exchange, when Tate has truly come under Eliot's thrall, he will warn against "that particular supine narcissism which charms so many in the poetry of our friend Eliot." He is proud to have "The Tunnel" accepted for the *Criterion* by an editor, T. S. Eliot, "representative of the most exacting literary standards of our time"; yet he wonders that "the man has dug the ground and buried hope as deep and direfully as it can ever be done"—adding with quiet mischief that Eliot's pessimism is "amply justified, in his own case." Crane was wary of a style of resignation shared by all the whole-length modernists, a movement in which incidentally he ranked Spengler, whose *Decline of the West* he read with a fascination that cooled into skepticism. He could not share the satisfaction of believing that "the fruits of civilization are entirely harvested."

The Bridge was an attempt at a "counter-statement"—a word coined by Kenneth Burke, a friend of Crane's and a favorite drinking partner. It would be published in 1929, a bad year for an epic of affirmation, and its formal structure of variations on a national theme of discovery, founding, expansion, dispossesssion, and hope, made it an improbable vehicle for the aesthetic task that Crane had embraced in a letter to Tate of 1922: "Let us invent an idiom for the proper transposition of jazz into words! Something clean, sparkling, elusive!" But he worked at the poem steadily and revised it systematically. In the meantime he wrote to Otto Kahn, a railroad financier and patron of the arts, and received a series of modest grants. These direct petitions for assistance are the work of an author with a justified confidence in his powers. They lay out a plan of the finished poem, and though its design would change as the writing advanced, Crane's informative sketches of his myth in 1926 and 1927 still make an excellent guide to the intricacies of *The Bridge*. He clearly hoped that the result would be a summing up of the "fervid covenant" between person and person, and between person and place, that had always preoccupied him. The solidarity he cared for, he seemed to think, could become as common as the open road, and he may at moments have thought of *The Bridge* as a popular poem.

It sustains an extraordinary eloquence in several of its major sections, and exhibits an integrity of purpose that does not falter. One has throughout a sense of wide vistas surveyed across time and space, for the sake of capturing a single detail; and the sweep of the writing passes from the "dip and pivot" of the seagull, in "To Brooklyn Bridge," to the pilgrimage of the Mississippi Valley settlers in "The River," whose journey becomes an allegory of the progress of a tradition or the recollections of an individual mind:

> Down, down—born pioneers in time's despite,
> Grimed tributaries to an ancient flow—
> They win no frontier by their wayward plight,
> But drift in stillness, as from Jordan's brow.
>
> You will not hear it as the sea; even stone
> Is not more hushed by gravity . . . But slow,
> As loth to take more tribute—sliding prone
> Like one whose eyes were buried long ago
>
> The River, spreading, flows—and spends your dream.

In a later section, "The Tunnel," the poem acquires a different gravity that it could not do without—a montage of scenes from an all-night subway ride, with a morbid particularity that Crane had mostly kept out of his poetry before, ending at sunrise with a view of the East River:

> Daemon, demurring and eventful yawn!
> Whose hideous laughter is a bellows mirth
> —Or the muffled slaughter of a day in birth—
> O cruelly to inoculate the brinking dawn
> With antennae toward worlds that glow and sink.

It was a very wrong report that held Crane to be an optimist of the Machine Age. On the other hand, the charge that he was a "primitivist"— made earliest by his friend Yvor Winters—can seem borne out by the figure of the medicine man and shaman whom the poet associates with himself in "The Dance." But one cannot help admiring the bravery of this headlong narrative, with its effort to claim the materials of Longfellow for a modern and psychological inquest; just as, in the pure rhapsody of "Atlantis," one stands back at the propulsive intensity with which the poem starts and keeps on lifting. Maybe "Ave Maria," a prayer of Columbus, suffered from too much premeditation: its antiquarian diction leaves an odd on-purpose aftershine. And "Indiana," a ballad of the frontier, a lovely sentimental song, remains hard to hold in solution with the rest of the poem. And yet the final feeling is incomparable: *The Bridge* makes a myth out of wholly individual episodes, both recalled and reimagined. Crane's letter of dedication to John A. Roebling, son of the builder—a letter both dignified and understated, a plain expression of gratitude—is one of the most moving in the book.

TWO REVIEWS OF *The Bridge,* by Allen Tate and Yvor Winters, did as much to affect Crane's thinking about himself as they did to influence the early reception of the poem. These were gifted critics, still in the process of defining their temperaments. They were also poets who recognized in Crane an ascendant genius. They had earlier stood up for him as unselfish allies—Tate in a fine introduction to *White Buildings,* Winters in a review of that book which pronounced its author "among the five or six greatest poets writing in English." Both critics now had a short time to collect their thoughts about an elusive work by Crane in a "visionary" mode that neither found congenial. Different as they were—Tate a devoted modernist, Winters a rational antimodernist—they came to nearly the same conclusion. They read *The Bridge* as an epic in the tradition of Whitman that exposed the failure of the tradition itself. The argument that followed makes a great point of interest in these letters, for the debate about Whitman becomes a debate about America and the morality of art.

Crane was defending himself and not just his poem, but his replies are notable for their self-possession and, except for one phrase in the letter to Winters, their freedom from asperity. Winters in his review had quoted, as powerful and deranged, a line from "The Dance": "Lie to us—dance us back to the tribal morn!" Crane replied:

> You still point with complacency, I see, to the infamous medicine-man passage. . . . I've tried before to tell you how innocent that passage is, but you will probably cite it again, somewhere else, I am sure, as an example of "moral surrender," "reversion of the species," or heaven knows what. . . . All I am saying amounts in substance to this: "Mimic the scene of yesterday; I want to see how it looked." Here again your notions of what is feeble in my character offered false premises.
>
> My acknowledgement of Whitman as an influence and living force: "Not greatest, thou,—not first, nor last,—but near," as I qualify it,—apparently this discolored the entire poem in your estimation.

He expands the defense of Whitman in his letter to Tate, and links it there to an insistence that poetry be personal rather than method-minding.

The anti-aesthetic turn of the thirties was well begun in the first year of that decade, and was already visible in a book like *Axel's Castle*. There are, Crane says, critics who look to poetry for an ethical or quasi-ethical result; for them,

> poetry as poetry (and I don't mean merely decorative verse) isn't worth a second reading any more. Therefore—away with Kubla Khan, out with Marlowe, and to hell with Keats! It's a pity, I think. So many true things have a way of coming out all the better without the strain to sum up the universe in one impressive little pellet. I admit that I don't answer the requirements. . . .
>
> This personal note is doubtless responsible for what you term as sentimentality in my attitude toward Whitman. It's true that my rhapsodic address to him in the *Bridge* exceeds any exact evaluation of the man. I realized that in the midst of composition. But since you and I hold such divergent prejudices regarding the value of the materials and events that W. responded to, and especially as you, like so many others, never seem to have read his *Democratic Vistas* and other of his statements sharply decrying the materialism, industrialism, etc. of which you name him the guilty and hysterical spokesman, there isn't much use in my tabulating the qualified, yet persistent reasons I have for my admiration of him, and my allegiance to the positive universal tendencies implicit in nearly all his best work.

Crane would be established, in the literary memory of the 1940s and 1950s, as a half-mad rebel whose want of a "moral check" at last destroyed him. But he had been more than half a mentor to Tate and Winters, and as the letters show, he knew what he was doing in the poem that lost their approval.

ONE NOTICES in these letters of self-defense, as earlier in letters to Gorham Munson, how anxious Crane is to extricate the personal impression, or the tincture of an available rumor, from the characterizations offered of his poetry. His poems, he insists, are deeper and different than any idea of his pathology may suggest, and his actual interests are wider than his poetry may show. He spoke of wanting to try his hand at prose, and there are signs of such a preparation early on: he read *Ulysses* with the passion of an initiate, and *Moby-Dick* three times (crediting it the last time with having revived his interest in life), and followed eagerly the successive volumes of Dos Passos's *USA*. He had as solid a claim as any writer of the twenties to have immersed himself in his society, to have become deliberately "lost yet poised in traffic"; but it was hard, even for friends, to make both allowances at once: to subtract the personal from the literary impression and the literary from the personal. His later life began to resemble the most tormented intervals of his poetry, while the poems came to appear a commentary on "wounds pledged once to hope—cleft to despair." His work had always shown an affinity with Whitman and Dickinson and (a particular enthusiasm) Marlowe; among contemporaries, he admired Stevens and Edward Thomas; he was eclectic enough to experiment, quite late, with the idiom of E. E. Cummings. Now most of all he came to resemble himself. The greatest of his last poems, "The Broken Tower," is a dialogue with the aspirations of his previous work, and it combs through a hoard of telegraphic self-portraits, relying, as it does so, on a reader's implicit knowledge of "Recitative," "Repose of Rivers," "For the Marriage of Faustus and Helen," and "The Dance."

He sent "The Broken Tower" to Morton Dauwen Zabel, the editor of *Poetry*, and was awaiting an answer when he took his fatal journey back to the States in April 1932. It is plain that his powers were still alive, and could still be directed upon the most complex of designs. And yet I agree with his editor, Langdon Hammer, that in the last five years or so leading up to his suicide, Crane's sense of himself had undergone a disastrous plunge. One thinks of the words of another poet, John Clare: "the vast shipwreck of my life's esteems." As Hammer remarks, not without charity, Crane now "sometimes settled for the fame of a drunkard, whose intoxicated misadventures mocked the inspired states of 'possession' he once knew and still craved."

It is heartbreaking to compare a letter to his mother in the mid-twenties, about a night on the town with Charlie Chaplin, which ends by evoking "the intense clarity of spirit that a man like Chaplin gives" and avows that he himself has that clarity—and the long succession of abject notes to Katherine Anne Porter and Peggy Cowley in apology for his drinking binges in Mexico. From one mayhem to the next, his wish to have "What I hold healed, original now, and pure" is dashed against the memory of an escapade the night before, until at last he writes to Peggy Cowley: "Why is it you love me so? I don't deserve it. I'm just a careening idiot with a talent for humor at times, and for insult and desecration at others."

The sadness of his final years comes not only from the fretful juggling of projects, the failure to obtain a release from the ties to his parents, the dependency that wears down his dearest friendships when for the first time it looks like sponging. There is another element now. His authorization to speak of despair is a new tonality in his character, and it is a terrible addition. This phase began—so it seems when one reads the letters in sequence—as early as his trip to California in 1927, as a paid intellectual companion of Herbert Wise. In San Pedro and in Hollywood, Crane would lose himself among the rough trade, then face the appalling prospect of holding up the level of refinement he had been hired to impersonate. He refers more than once to the atmosphere of southern California as a "pink vacuum," and his impression in a letter to Malcolm and Peggy Cowley is close to Nathanael West's a few years later:

> Writing is next to impossible—what with the purling of fountains, the drawling of mockingbirds, the roaring of surf, the blazing of movie stars, the barking of dogs, the midnight shakings of geraniums, the cruising of warships. . . . My philosophic moments are few, but when they do occur it is almost always possible to turn on the radio and immediately expose my soul to the rasping persuasions of Aimee Macpherson, eternally ranting and evangelizing to packed houses at the great palm-flanked arena of Angelus Temple. She broadcasts the news that people are frequently carried out in pieces, arms broken, heads smashed in the stampede for salvation which she almost nightly stages, thereby emphasizing the need of arriving early. . . . The peculiar mixtures of piety and utter abandon in this welter of cults, ages, occupations, etc. out here make it a good deal like Bedlam. Retired schoolmarms from Iowa, Ohio, Kansas and all the corn-and-wheat

belt along with millions of hobbling Methuselahs, alfalfa-fringed and querulous, side by side with crowds of ambitious but none-too-successful strumpets of moviedom, quite good to look at, and then hordes of rather nondescript people who seem just bound from nowhere into nothing.

He pulled out of this engagement early: something dismal had entered his soul. His fixed idea was now a wish to recover his former clarity. But recovery is a dead weight on desire, compared to real aspiration.

The opening lines of "The Broken Tower" acknowledge the difference, and appear to search for a spiritual transfiguration:

> The bell-rope that gathers God at dawn
> Dispatches me, as though I dropped down the knell
> Of a spent day—to wander the cathedral lawn
> From pit to crucifix, feet chill on steps from hell.

The poem, as Crane thought of it, was about his revival in a love affair with Peggy Cowley, the only heterosexual relationship of his life, and some of his letters to her are exhilarated and tender. But "O Carib Isle!"— a piece of damnation-eloquence, of a Marlovian energy, written many months earlier—caught more accurately the recurrent mood of his last sojourn:

> Slagged of the hurricane—I, cast within its flow,
> Congeal by afternoons here, satin and vacant.

His father had died in 1931, the Crane estate was involved with the threat of a lawsuit, and in this crisis he felt honor-bound to take an interest, having accepted loans from his stepmother. But his voyage back on the SS *Orizaba* turned into another scene of besotted confusion and humiliation—with Peggy Cowley laid up from accidental burns, and Crane, after a drunken scuffle with sailors, held in his room with the door boarded up. He escaped and jumped from the ship's railing; his last words to her had been: "I'm not going to make it, dear. I'm utterly disgraced." But of his actual correspondence the final words are "Permanent address—Box 604, Chagrin Falls, Ohio."

What survives in the letters is the wonder of a human being who had to imagine himself, and who performed as much as he ever promised in imagining. He wrote to his mother nine years before his death:

> If I can't continue to create the sort of poetry that is my intensest and deepest component in life—then it all means very little to me, and then I might as well tie myself up to some smug ambition and "success" (the common idol that every Tom Dick and Harry is bowing to everywhere). But so far, as

you know, I only grow more convinced that what I naturally have to give the world in my own terms—is worth giving.

And to his father, the entrepreneur, the nonstop man of schemes to possess and succeed:

> Try to imagine working for the pure love of simply making something beautiful,—something that maybe can't be sold or used to help sell anything else, but that is simply a communication between man and man, a bond of understanding and human enlightenment—which is what a real work of art is. If you do that, then maybe you will see why I am not so foolish after all to have followed what seems sometimes only a faint star.

It is hard to think of an American who knew more intimately what it must mean to live for art. He wrote his epitaph in an elegy for an Ohio friend, Ernest Nelson—"Scatter these well-meant idioms"—as if to say that an artist's life can be guessed at but never recovered.

1998

FIVE

Stevens and the Idea of the Hero

This is an essay about the work philosophy and poetry may share in imagining and justifying a way of life. My focus is a debate in Stevens's poetry between two versions of pragmatism, which I associate with William James and Nietzsche. Valuable studies of influence like Margaret Peterson's article "*Harmonium* and William James," and the chapter on Nietzsche in Milton J. Bates's recent book *Wallace Stevens: A Mythology of Self,* have aided or confirmed my thinking, and I have little to add to their findings. For my purposes, "James" and "Nietzsche" stand for two aspects of Stevens's poetry in *Parts of a World.* Both were there from the start of his career, but in this volume one can feel a gradual shift from Nietzsche to James, until they come to represent nearly antithetical habits of feeling. A great deal was at stake in this transfer of allegiance: Stevens's idea of the hero, his belief in poetry itself, and his interest in America as a place where the poet and hero might join in a natural solidarity.

Reading these poems as a scene of argument has made certain things about them clear to me for the first time. Maybe it is simply that two people arguing are easier to follow than someone arguing with himself. But I have been aware throughout of a danger of making the contest appear too amiable. The preoccupation of Stevens's work, in the late 1930s and early 1940s, was the choice of a language to persuade the mind "that war is part of itself." Those words come from "Man and Bottle," and the fierceness of the challenge, from either of the rival points of view Stevens is exploring, shows in the bitterness of many other poems as well. Yet it seems to me that the James and Nietzsche of *Parts of a World* do have a common point of departure. Both are developments from Emerson, and, more particularly, from the step Emerson took in identifying imagination with action when he said, "Every spirit builds itself a house, and beyond its house a world."

Stevens's poems of the mid-thirties (among them "Farewell to Florida," "Sad Strains of a Gay Waltz," and "Mozart, 1935") are full of an uneasy consciousness of the misery of the times. They speak of "these sudden mobs of men," of a "besieging pain" that finds no relief, of a "voice of angry fear" from the mass of the inarticulate, "an immense suppression, freed." Stevens's response for the most part is disengaged. He resembles the hero of "Sad Strains of a Gay Waltz"—the "mountain-minded" aesthete he called Hoon—"Who found all form and order in solitude. / For whom the shapes were never the figures of men." What such a character can hope for, Stevens writes, in this "epic of disbelief," is that "Some harmonious skeptic soon in a skeptical music / Will unite these figures of men and their shapes / Will glisten again." It would be a vulgar, but not a false, translation to see this as saying: the marchers will be sent home, and the whole spectacle organized on a new principle by someone who knows what order is. Of course, the protest has already been rendered a degree less unruly when the *sudden mobs* are reduced to mere *figures of men.* Some such careful establishment of distance is a motive for the characteristic deflections of *Ideas of Order.* Hearing, in "Mozart, 1935," that "the streets are full of cries," Stevens will murmur to himself: "Be seated at the piano." This is said with confidence and a sense of propriety; any other response would be unavailing, as well as insincere, if one grants the truth of the closing aphorism of "Like Decorations in a Nigger Cemetery":

> Union of the weakest develops strength
> Not wisdom. Can all men, together, avenge
> One of the leaves that have fallen in autumn?
> But the wise man avenges by building his city in snow.

This is perhaps as close as Stevens will ever come to the eloquence of Nietzsche's Zarathustra.

He would seem to have found here the wisdom of detachment. Had he found it, his poetry would have stopped. Instead, because he was not satisfied with lines like these, his poetry came to have a larger subject. The moment that interests me, which includes much of *Parts of a World,* begins with the hero as a poet and ends with the hero as a "major man"—a version of the representative man whom Stevens characterized, in a letter to Hi Simons, as "a possibly more than human human." It could be said that in making the transition he gave up a dead abstraction for a live one. But it is not quite right to leave the matter there. This change had much to do with a widening of his sense of the "noble" imagination to include many rather than few. What he gained in the process I will be recounting poem by poem. The details, I think, are necessary to explain the full force of Stevens's turn to the common soldier at the end of *Notes toward a Supreme Fiction*—his decision finally to justify himself to one of the weak whose union he had deplored, with the appeal that

> war for war, each has its gallant kind.
> How simply the fictive hero becomes the real.

But it took a long inward argument against an idea of the superhuman to bring his imaginings to that point.

An outward pressure to sustain the argument came from the reality of American soldiers going off to fight in the Second World War, for a cause which, as Stevens saw it, they could only make true by their fighting. This, in itself, is a pragmatic way of thinking about what the hero does. Yet the commonness of these soldiers has no conceivable place in the Nietzschean picture of heroism; and it is here that Jamesian pragmatism seems to have helped by suggesting an alternative picture. Now and then Stevens hoped that the two could be reconciled, as parts of a single creed; so, in "Of Bright & Blue Birds & the Gala Sun," he speaks of living in an element in which "we pronounce joy like a word of our own":

> It is there, being imperfect, and with these things
> And erudite in happiness, with nothing learned,
> That we are joyously ourselves and we think
>
> Without the labor of thought, in that element,
> And we feel, in a way apart, for a moment, as if
> There was a bright *scienza* outside of ourselves,
>
> A gaiety that is being, not merely knowing,
> The will to be and to be total in belief,
> Provoking a laughter, an agreement, by surprise.

Some of the surprise is occasioned by an agreement between the authors of *The Gay Science* and *The Will to Believe,* from the play on words by which Stevens almost blends the titles of those books. About the same time, he was speaking of the need to unite the characters whom he called in "Montrachet-le-Jardin" the superman and the root-man, in order to arrive at the grandeur he imagined in "Gigantomachia," where "in an inhuman elevation" each man "himself became the giant." All of these passages imply that Nietzschean means, in an individual life, may work toward a non-Nietzschean end in the life of a culture. The title *Parts of a World,* with its echo of James's *A Pluralistic Universe,* says something about what we may expect such a culture to be like.

ACCORDING TO THE pragmatic view of knowledge which James and Nietzsche share, the will selects certain objects to the exclusion of others. These objects of attention become meaningful as objects of use, and the work we do with them favors a certain construction of the world to the exclusion of other possible constructions. Reflection on the character of the knowledge we acquire in this way prompts James and Nietzsche to give quite distinct accounts of the sort of person who creates that knowledge. James, in *The Will to Believe,* says "*faith in a fact can help create the fact,*" and the faith he has in mind is that of a man or woman in a group. "Our faith," as he explains, "is faith in someone else's faith, and in the greatest matters this is most the case." This follows from his axiom, first announced in *The Principles of Psychology,* that the egoistic and sympathetic instincts are "co-ordinate," and that useless or antisocial instincts are weeded out by a process resembling natural selection. In an apparently similar vein, Nietzsche, in *The Will to Power,* says "it is precisely facts that do not exist, only *interpretations.*" But the conquering interpretation he has in mind will always be proposed by a solitary man. The life of such a man is defined by one continuous act of abstention from social existence; alone, he has come to know that "existence and the world seem justified only as an aesthetic phenomenon." One can say that the Nietzschean hero of knowledge is simply an artist working with a free hand; yet the description will be incomplete without some mention of the conditions that prepare for his work.

The hero's element, as Nietzsche defines it, is the "*pathos of distance*": a sublime perspective across the ranks of an immense structure of subordination, by which the hero is reminded that he owes his place to the suppression of inferior human materials. Nietzsche explores this conception at length in *The Genealogy of Morals* and *The Twilight of the Idols.* The following quotation from *Beyond Good and Evil* gives a fair idea of his usual emphasis:

> Without that *pathos of distance* which grows out of the ingrained difference between strata—when the ruling caste constantly looks afar and looks down upon subjects and instruments and just as constantly practices obedience and command, keeping down and keeping at a distance—that other, more mysterious pathos could not have grown up either—the craving for an ever new widening of distances within the soul itself, the devel-

opment of ever higher, rarer, more remote, further-stretching, more comprehensive states—in brief, simply the enhancement of the type "man."

Since Nietzsche is writing genealogy rather than history—correlating human qualities and their place of growth, without necessarily assigning the latter as a cause of the former—two distinct readings of the pathos of distance are equally plausible: either the soul redisposes in itself the differences it finds among the strata in a society, and thereby is enabled to rise above itself in order to look down on what it has overcome; or the soul writes out, in the text it makes of the world, the very differences it has found in itself, for the sake of advancing its power.

And yet, on either of these interpretations, the pathos of distance may seem a chapter in the genealogy of aesthetics which Nietzsche falsified. It is apt to seem especially so to an American poet. For once the poet has discovered "the distances within the soul," nothing obliges him to see their likeness in a pattern of social subordination, or to regard as their epitome an aristocrat or barbarian with no visible attainments comparable to the poet's. In this sense the procedure of a poem like Yeats's "In Memory of Major Robert Gregory"—the decision to represent the pathos of distance by a hero of art and action, whose early death alone assures no finite deed will mar the infinite hopes he raised—is only a dramatic way for the poet to talk about himself. Stevens understood, more subtly even than Nietzsche did, the fictive quality of all heroism; and what he aimed to do, in *Parts of a World*, was to return the pathos of distance to the individual mind alone. For him, as the native of a partly democratic life, the mind's powers were not necessarily involved with the pattern of high and low in a given social order. The next (the Whitmanian) step in forming a democratic idea of poetry would be to conceive of a fellowship of souls who share a knowledge of just such distances within themselves—to be able to say, as Whitman did to the reader of "Crossing Brooklyn Ferry," "It is not upon you alone the dark patches fall." Stevens never quite took this step. That it was always close to his imaginings goes far to explain his resistance to the hero of the Nietzschean sublime, the extra-moral agent who looks on the general life as *materia poetica* for his own creations.

An element of Nietzsche's pragmatism that Stevens found persistently attractive was the suggestion that the good of existence is change and that our most vivid acknowledgment of that good comes from the ability to imagine a life wiped clear of ourselves. The very fact that we can think like this shows, for Stevens as it did for Nietzsche, just how little we belong to the world, how unnecessary we are to its ostensible purposes, and therefore how much depends on the shape we choose to give it, once the already given schemes of God, grammar, and truth have been exposed as contingent. The first poem in *Parts of a World,* "Parochial Theme," seems to have been written with this thought in view. The title is difficult but I think it means: life is merely parochial in relation to death.

> Long-tailed ponies go nosing the pine-lands,
> Ponies of Parisians shooting on the hill.
>
> The wind blows. In the wind, the voices
> Have shapes that are not yet fully themselves,
>
> Are sounds blown by a blower into shapes,
> The blower squeezed to the thinnest *mi* of falsetto.
>
> The hunters run to and fro. The heavy trees,
> The grunting, shuffling branches, the robust,
>
> The nocturnal, the antique, the blue-green pines
> Deepen the feelings to inhuman depths.
>
> These are the forest. This health is holy,
> This halloo, halloo, halloo heard over the cries
>
> Of those for whom a square room is a fire,
> Of those whom the statues torture and keep down.
>
> This health is holy, this descant of a self,
> This barbarous chanting of what is strong, this blare.
>
> But salvation here? What about the rattle of sticks
> On tins and boxes? What about horses eaten by wind?
>
> When spring comes and the skeletons of the hunters
> Stretch themselves to rest in their first summer's sun,
>
> The spring will have a health of its own, with none
> Of autumn's halloo in its hair. So that closely, then,
>
> Health follows after health. Salvation there:
> There's no such thing as life; or if there is,
>
> It is faster than the weather, faster than
> Any character. It is more than any scene:
>
> Of the guillotine or of any glamorous hanging.
> Piece the world together, boys, but not with your hands.

In a startling passage of *The Gay Science,* Nietzsche warned: "Let us beware of saying that death is opposed to life. The living is merely a type of what is dead, and a very rare type." Stevens's poem is a meditation on that sentiment. (He observes, in an unusually revealing comment in a letter, "That poem may be summed up by saying that there is no such thing as life; what there is is a style of life from time to time.") So, for all the barbarous health of the hunters he depicts, no trace of their vigor will survive their death. "This health is holy" but without memorial. It is true "The spring will have a health of its own, with none / Of autumn's halloo in its hair." Yet the good that this change brings will belong to no one— "It is faster than the weather, faster than / Any character." All that remains is the succession of mood to mood, in which no conclusive scene, even of a public death, "Of the guillotine or of any glamorous hanging," can lend a final tenor to the landscape.

In view of his denial of every human consolation, Stevens's last line may be read as a cutting dismissal of the geniality with which James, as a "humanistic" pragmatist, sometimes announced that the whole of life belonged to no one. "Piece the world together, boys, but not with your hands" seems to say that it is dangerous work after all. Such figures of speech, with their implied metaphor of carpentry, come naturally to Stevens's own writing; and they do not always carry an admonition. A full decade later, in *An Ordinary Evening in New Haven,* he would speak of "A city slapped up like a chest of tools," and explore a psychology in which "the self, / The town, the weather, in a casual litter, / Together, said words of the world are the life of the world." What does he mean to reject in James's statement of a similar pluralism? The problem, in part, was that James had made it appear a dependable victory for the tough-minded, as if they encountered no resistance from the world itself. "There is really no inherent order," James writes in *A Pluralistic Universe,* "but it is we who project order into the world. . . . We *carve out* order by leaving the disorderly parts out." Granting this, it remains a long stretch to suppose, as he does in "Pragmatism and Humanism," that "the world stands really malleable, waiting to receive its final touches at our hands. Like the kingdom of heaven, it suffers human violence willingly." That is true to the emotions of the reformer in religion, false to the emotions of the revisionist in art. We, as well as the world, may suffer violence at such contact. As for our interest in projecting an order, the first lines of "Connoisseur of Chaos" ask us to reconsider its motives: "A. A violent order is disorder; and / B. A great disorder is an order. These / Two things are one. (Pages of illustrations.)" Looked at in this way, the inhuman metaphors of "Parochial

Theme" are a rebuke made from the perspective of a severer pragmatism like Nietzsche's.

I can clarify the last point by analyzing one instance of Jamesian "piecing-together," which takes its illustrations, very characteristically, from those habits of grammar that become our second nature in speech, just as the things we know become our second nature in action. "Everything you can think of," says James in *A Pluralistic Universe*, "however vast or inclusive, has on the pluralistic view a genuinely 'external' environment of some sort or amount. Things are 'with' one another in many ways, but nothing includes everything, or dominates over everything. The word 'and' trails after every sentence." The remark carries a vivid suggestion of the world's *readiness* for the truths we wish to engender upon it. The world's own prepositions are associative, not restrictive ("with," not "except"), and its conjunctions independent rather than subordinate ("and," rather than "but," "because," or "although"). It is this kind of pluralism that "Parochial Theme" aims to correct. Once (Stevens is telling James) this thought is really thought to the end, no sentence about the world will include an implicit and-with-me. The different shading Nietzsche gave to a parallel thought in *The Gay Science* may be instructive here:

> We laugh as soon as we encounter the juxtaposition of "man *and* world," separated by the sublime presumption of the little word "and." But look, when we laugh like that, have we not simply carried the contempt for man one step further? And thus also pessimism, the contempt for that existence which is knowable by *us?* Have we not exposed ourselves to the suspicion of an opposition—an opposition between the world in which we were at home up to now with our reverences that perhaps made it possible for us to *endure* life, and another world *that consists of us?*

To recognize this suspicion, Nietzsche argues, is directly to confront a choice: "'Either abolish your reverences or—*yourselves!* The latter would be nihilism; but would not the former also be—nihilism?" Evidently, the Nietzschean solution is to invent reverences that "consist of us" and are inseparable from the selves that made them. This does not yet entail the nihilism of abolishing either our reverences or ourselves. But it points to a difficulty James never felt in interpreting the "and" that trails after every sentence whose subject is man.

BOTH VERSIONS of nihilism described above held an absorbing interest for Stevens, and the hero of "Landscape with Boat" is an adept of the former type, with modifications: he would abolish all reverences, all sentiments, all the colors and affects of things as they have been known, to get at "a truth beyond all truths." Yet no matter how many poems he seeks to deny himself—in the manner of Crispin, the hero of *The Comedian as the Letter C*—he is still surrounded by the flowers of his eloquence. The poem opens abruptly with that irony:

> An anti-master-man, floribund ascetic.

> He brushed away the thunder, then the clouds,
> Then the colossal illusion of heaven. Yet still
> The sky was blue. He wanted imperceptible air.
> He wanted to see. He wanted the eye to see
> And not be touched by blue. He wanted to know,
> A naked man who regarded himself in the glass
> Of air, who looked for the world beneath the blue,
> Without blue, without any turquoise tint or phase,
> Any azure under-side or after-color. Nabob
> Of bones, he rejected, he denied, to arrive
> At the neutral centre, the ominous element,
> The single-colored, colorless, primitive.

As the poem goes on to suggest in the lines that follow, "the truth," which the ascetic hero aims to achieve, does not lie in the "uncreated night" that he postulates only by denying the colors of day. Rather, "it was easier to think it lay there," and to suppose it would take shape from the sum of his denials. The sole means of creation for an asceticism as thoroughgoing as his is a negation of other people's truths. When illusion has been subtracted from illusion, until he is chargeable with no imaginable bias, error, or inclination, *there,* he thinks, the truth will have shown itself.

But "Landscape with Boat" is a poem about "supposing" in a more optative sense—about what its hero might have come to had he not denied himself:

> He never supposed
> That he might be truth, himself, or part of it,
> That the things that he rejected might be part
> And the irregular turquoise, part, the perceptible blue
> Grown denser, part, the eye so touched, so played
> Upon by clouds, the ear so magnified
> By thunder, parts, and all these things together,
> Parts, and more things, parts. He never supposed divine
> Things might not look divine, nor that if nothing
> Was divine then all things were, the world itself,
> And that if nothing was the truth, then all
> Things were the truth, the world itself was the truth.

Had he been better able to suppose:
He might sit on a sofa on a balcony
Above the Mediterranean, emerald
Becoming emeralds. He might watch the palms
Flap green ears in the heat. He might observe
A yellow wine and follow a steamer's track
And say, "The thing I hum appears to be
The rhythm of this celestial pantomime."

Manifestly, to this hero's way of thinking, what was familiar in experience was also conventional, and therefore had to be removed if new discoveries of thought were to take its place. His experiment is an instance of the way asceticism, by its "mountain-minded" hostility to all existing habits and customs, may finally turn into nihilism. By contrast, Nietzsche argues that we can never stop ourselves or the things we feel from becoming part of truth. "That mountain there!" *The Gay Science* adjures its readers, "That cloud there! What is 'real' in that? Subtract the phantasm of every human *contribution* from it, my sober friends. If you *can!*" The only recovery Nietzsche can imagine, from the domination of our lives by objects themselves shaped by human moods and purposes, is the displacement of someone else's perspective by our own.

It is plain from this account that Stevens's anti-master-man is in some ways the reverse of a Nietzschean hero. Nevertheless, one can feel that he shares an important premise with the master-man, and that the poem, by discerning a connection between them, implies a single criticism of both types. Their common premise is that creation and destruction are the same thing. It is celebrated in Nietzsche's own work by his saying that "all great things bring about their own destruction through an act of self-overcoming" (in *The Genealogy of Morals*); and again, his saying that the world "becomes, it passes away, but it has never ceased from passing away—its excrements are its food" (in *The Will to Power*). This conception does not require, but in Nietzsche it does seem related to, the gnostic belief that what the self does it cannot do wrongly. In poetry, such beliefs have their touchstone in Yeats's "I am content to live it all again"; the hero is someone who consents to his fate as if for a second time. That mood, however, is foreign to the mind James portrays, from his *Psychology* on—the mind in which, as he tells us, no single moment is ever quite like any other. James distrusted the very idea of repetition and, still more, the idea of self-overcoming as a compelled repetition of suffering. To judge by *Esthétique du Mal,* Stevens agreed: "His anima liked its animal." But we are not dealing with a contrast between what Stevens himself always accepted and what he always denied. It is a question of opposite tendencies and the play of his mind between them. In the first pragmatic way of thinking, everything passes away and returns, even if as its own antithesis: the world's food for its excrement, the single-colored primitive for the many-colored exquisite. In the second way, everything stays but alters slightly, with its earlier traces somehow perceptible after the change.

With the final scene of "Landscape with Boat," there is an impressive sense of the materials of a vision remaining for all to see, even as they are transformed. The steamer is a steamer, and the sofa and balcony still have some of the palpable weight of a philosopher's desk. Something has been created. It would not be quite right to say that something has been destroyed. Let me offer now a generalization about Stevens's response to the antihuman pragmatism I have associated with Nietzsche. He believed that in thinkers of this type an attachment to mere existence was finally betrayed by a demand for perfection. "The imperfect is our paradise," Stevens attests in "The Poems of Our Climate." But he discerned in Nietzsche an opposite faith, with two distinct consequences: the cult of the superhuman and the idea of eternal recurrence. It may be odd, initially, to think of Nietzsche, the questioner of all systems and decomposer of truths, as a philosopher who sought perfection in any sense of the word. But in Nietzsche as I think Stevens read him—as, with less suspicion, Yeats seems to have read him, too—the idea that "a thing is the sum of its effects" led to a wish for effects that count irresistibly. It is this that prompts Nietzsche to say, in *The Will to Power:* "The great majority of men have no right to existence, but are a misfortune to higher men. I do not yet grant the failures the right. There are also peoples that are failures." Against both the cult of the superhuman and the idea of eternal recurrence, Stevens's poetry recoiled almost instinctively but with a conscious eloquence, during the years of the war against Hitler. I will cite some examples presently. But, from the beginnings of his poetry, nothing is more characteristic of Stevens than the number of ways he discovers of saying of a thing, feeling, or person: "No, still human, still, somehow, part of us"; and "Each time a little different from the last."

I used the closing of "Parochial Theme"—"Piece the world together, boys, but not with your hands"—to capture the general sense of a Stevensian rebuke to James. Let me now use what I believe is the crucial line of "Landscape with Boat" to imagine a Stevensian rebuke to Nietzsche. *Had he been better able to suppose,* Nietzsche would have conceived of a major man who was not masterful. He would then have moved from the idea of a great man who carves a new image of life from the acquiescent human data, to the less brutal idea of a man or woman who is made great by an enterprise in which others have a part.

IN PLACE OF Nietzsche's conquering interpretation, which leaves nothing as it was, Stevens offers his conception of what it is *to suppose.* All of his poems, in fact, have a rich sense of the specifically grammatical devices that may exhibit a "supposing" frame of mind. One is the infinitive that leans on nothing, that is changed gradually, by reiteration, from a desire to an irrevocable command:

> To be free again, to return to the violent mind
> That is their mind, these men, and that will bind
> Me round, carry me, misty deck, carry me
> To the cold. . . .

Or again:

> To discover an order as of
> A season, to discover summer and know it,
>
> To discover winter and know it well, to find,
> Not to impose, not to have reasoned at all,
> Out of nothing to have come on major weather.

A different device with similar effects is the *as if* that creates a reality out of mere subjunctive possibility: "As if the air, the midday air, was swarming / With the metaphysical changes that occur, / Merely in living as and where we live"; "As if the design of all his words takes form / And frame from thinking and is realized." A noticeable feature here is the refusal of the customary decorum for a contrary-to-fact conditional: instead of "as if it were," Stevens often says "as if it was." His are, so to speak, congruent-with-fact conditionals, expressive of the faith in a fact that may help create the fact. These devices, which Helen Vendler and others have anatomized, seem to me to typify a grammar of supposing. They belong, that is, to a pragmatism which aims to effect, instead of a transvaluation of values, a deferral of the changing value of a thing, from the interpreter who first captures it to the imaginable others who receive and use it for a while. As the person who brings about such changes, Stevens's hero is the instigator of an adaptive scheme that includes an interest in human solidarity.

How did he come to think like this? In his early poems the hero is an artist, and to become part of a common life means, for him, to be domesticated and thereby ruined for all the purposes of art. That is the fate of Crispin. As a choice of heroes we are left, then, with the solitary aesthete like Hoon, or else the upright man of action, like General Jackson in "The American Sublime," whose statue makes the curious people wonder: "What wine does one drink? / What bread does one eat?" These are the same people who, once they grow restive, will be dismissed in a contemptuous aside, as "those whom the statues torture and keep down." By the time Stevens came to write of the statue of General Du Puy, in *Notes toward a Supreme Fiction,* and to admit that "the General was rubbish in the end," a great shift of his feelings had already occurred. An explanation for this turn, as I said at the start, is that the war stirred him to an unexpected kind of sympathy. Unlike Yeats in "The Statues," he would never again count himself among those who,

> thrown upon this filthy modern tide
> And by its formless spawning fury wrecked,
> Climb to our proper dark.

Instead, he would associate himself, as in "Asides on the Oboe," with a secular hero who wears "jasmine crowns," even when "the jasmine islands were bloody martyrdoms"; the man "who in a million diamonds sums us up"; in short, the common man forced temporarily to fight in a war. The soldier has a forerunner, however, in the figure of the tramp, who appeared occasionally in Stevens's poems of the thirties.

Holly Stevens in a memoir of her father recalled that on their walks together in Hartford they used to pass by a dump. It was one of Stevens's favorite spots, and he liked to entertain her by making up stories about the tramp who lived there. A story like this, for grown-ups, is told in another poem of *Parts of a World,* which I take to be a companion to "Landscape with Boat." The tramp in "The Man on the Dump" exists as a representative of all the human qualities which—to paraphrase James on the good of drunkenness—expand, unite, and say yes, rather than diminish, discriminate, and say no. Living where he does, in a heap of flowers and junk, he cherishes no hope of ever arriving at a final truth:

> Day creeps down. The moon is creeping up.
> The sun is a corbeil of flowers the moon Blanche
> Places there, a bouquet. Ho-ho . . . The dump is full
> Of images. Days pass like papers from a press.
> The bouquets come here in the papers. So the sun,
> And so the moon, both come, and the janitor's poems
> Of every day, the wrapper on the can of pears,

> The cat in the paper-bag, the corset, the box
> From Esthonia: the tiger chest, for tea.
> The freshness of night has been fresh a long time.

The first two and a half lines present a fable, possibly in the manner of Stevens himself on one of his walks. He is speaking to someone younger than he is, or anyway someone touchable by romance; and, because it is twilight, the poem asks what to make of that time of day; what to make of it, particularly, if one is a poet for whom the sun has become almost a personal symbol, and the sense it has carried to readers is, *This world is enough.* Now that the light is fading, the world itself seems a heap of undistinguishable images: "One grows to hate these things except on the dump." But there, one has to make the most of them. The man on the dump sorts together the parts of a world that he finds, only more conspicuously than we find our own, in pieces.

In the lines that follow, the tramp, who is also the poet, will try to bend all these disposable materials to the uses of another kind of poem, in praise of the sensuous pleasure of physical things. Such a poem might begin as "The Man on the Dump" continues—"Now, in the time of spring"— and then invoke the flowers that are listed as a parenthetical afterthought: "(azaleas, trilliums, / Myrtle, viburnums, daffodils, blue phlox)." But the poet grows quickly disgusted with this pretense, and is reduced to "(azaleas and so on,)" until, feeling what he calls "the purifying change," he concludes that "One rejects / The trash." It takes a certain valor to say on the dump, "One feels the purifying change," but to reject the trash is hopeless. It is all around and may as well be used to build a world. This rejection, like that of the ascetic in "Landscape with Boat," is only an instance of the tendency James found in most abstract thinkers (philosophers, in this, resembling other fastidious dwellers in a chaotic life), "who have always aimed at cleaning up the litter with which the world is apparently filled." There remains a sense in which a pragmatist, with a degree of self-irony, could truly say that he rejects the trash. He would have to mean, "One rejects everything out of which a world answerable to one's own temperament cannot be made." But in that case, one cannot pick out in advance exactly what one will reject, from its membership in this or that category of things. Some such liberating uncertainty appears to lift Stevens to the end of his poem. "That's the time / One looks at the elephant colorings of tires." Everything else is changed by relation to that quiet redefinition of a mundane thing.

Accordingly, "The Man on the Dump" ends by embracing the particularity while rejecting the exclusiveness of what it calls "the the":

One sits and beats an old tin can, lard pail.
One beats and beats for that which one believes.
That's what one wants to get near. Could it after all
Be merely oneself, as superior as the ear
To a crow's voice? Did the nightingale torture the ear,
Pack the heart and scratch the mind? And does the ear
Solace itself in peevish birds? Is it peace,
Is it a philosopher's honeymoon, one finds
On the dump? Is it to sit among mattresses of the dead,
Bottles, pots, shoes and grass and murmur *aptest eve:*
Is it to hear the blatter of grackles and say
Invisible priest; is it to eject, to pull
The day to pieces and cry *stanza my stone?*
Where was it one first heard of the truth? The the.

Following a thought from Emerson's "Circles," James in *Pragmatism* criticized "the notion of *the* truth," conceived as "one answer, determinate and complete, to the one fixed enigma which the world is believed to propound." In a related passage of *A Pluralistic Universe,* he considered Hegel's idea of the universe as a whole composed of mutually necessary elements, and cemented by "the atmosphere of explicit negativity" of the dialectic. Given the metaphor of a "Book of Nature," James asks whether things are "improved or deteriorated by having myriads of garbled and misprinted separate leaves and chapters" printed beside "the one superb copy of a book fit for the ideal reader." Hegel, he concludes, had no choice but to propose simultaneously the superb copy and the misprints, because he was "dominated by the notion of a truth that should prove incontrovertible, binding on every one, and certain, which should be *the* truth, one indivisible, eternal, objective, and necessary, to which all our particular thinking must lead as to its consummation." However one reads the last line of "The Man on the Dump," its general drift is with the pragmatic conception of truth that is sketched in passages like these.

Stevens's was preeminently a poetry of the indefinite article, the *a;* whether one thinks of "A hand that bears a thick-leaved fruit, / A pungent bloom against your shade"; or "A curriculum, a vigor, a local abstraction . . . / Call it, once more, a river, an unnamed flowing." He says of the possible motives for the creation of poetry, "It must / Be the finding of a satisfaction, and may / Be of a man skating, a woman dancing, a woman / Combing." As for the kind of object his poetry observes and modifies, "It may be a shade that traverses / A dust, a force that traverses a shade." Stevens's own comment on his dislike of the *the* occurs, where it is likeliest to attract attention, in "On the Road Home," the next poem after "The Man on the Dump" in the arrangement of *Parts of a World*.

> It was when I said,
> "There is no such thing as the truth,"
> That the grapes seemed fatter.
> The fox ran out of his hole.

Metaphor, of course, has often been supposed to grant a version of the "philosopher's honeymoon," but the notion of *the* right comparison, which exactly fits the demands of its appropriate form, is like the notion of *the* truth. Such attempts at certainty lose track of the stride of thinking: they are, in James's terms, "saltatory" rather than "ambulatory," for they leap from point to point without any record of the space traversed. Thus, to say *invisible priest* when one hears "the blatter of grackles"—to cry *stanza my stone* on any ecstatic provocation—shows a false precision of fancy which resembles the false precision of the intellect. It is a habit of mind shared by one sort of philosopher (the rationalist) and one sort of poet (the ascetic). Of the hero who may eventually replace these, James gives a description as arresting as Stevens's. It is credible to some, he observes in "Pragmatism and Humanism," that our "strung-along unfinished world" should be formed by "an indefinitely numerous lot of eaches, coherent in all sorts of ways and degrees; and the tough-minded are perfectly willing to keep them at that valuation." Admittedly, "to rationalists this describes a tramp and vagrant world, adrift in space, with neither elephant nor tortoise to plant its foot upon." The tough-minded are those who take to the work of adapting themselves to such a place.

If the tramp in Stevens's poetry of the thirties does, as I have suggested, become the soldier in his poetry of the forties, it is an imaginative transition with moral consequences. The nature of those consequences will take some explaining. But the figures seem to be related usually in some such series as the following: misery—the many who are miserable—the tramp—tramping feet—marchers—soldiers on the way to war—soldiers fighting—death. The most striking instance of these partial equations occurs in "Dry Loaf," a poem that Stevens published in 1938:

> It was the battering of drums I heard
> It was hunger, it was the hungry that cried
> And the waves, the waves were soldiers moving,
> Marching and marching in a tragic time
> Below me, on the asphalt, under the trees.

In shifting, almost imperceptibly, his sense of the identity of the marchers, Stevens's feelings were at one with the public sentiments of the thirties and forties. The movement in his own writing can be traced vividly in the fortunes of a single word, "misery." In his early poems, it was apt to be associated with something small and mean, or stale and trite: to a confident aesthete, these come to much the same thing. There is the pathetic "misery in the sound of the wind" which one must not think of in "The Snow Man," since to do so would falsely humanize the intelligence of "a mind of winter"; or again, the

> petty misery
> At heart, a petty misery

that assails the poet in a moment of self-doubt, in *The Man with the Blue Guitar*. But the word itself is being steadily revised throughout the forties, and it is a great moment in his last poems when, in "To an Old Philosopher in Rome," Stevens turns to address Santayana as "master and commiserable man." Mastery joins here with the sense of a shared misery, of "the pity that is the memorial of this room"; and Stevens is never more himself than when he praises Santayana for a kind of consciousness he had once asked to be freed from: "Impatient for the grandeur that you need / In so much misery; and yet finding it / Only in misery." It is Stevens and not Santayana who has discovered, in that condition, "Profound poetry of the poor and of the dead."

ONE EFFECT, then, of Stevens's engagement with the pragmatic idea of world-making, was to show how a personal reading of life might include a concern with his fellow readers. Only among those others can the poet represent "a perspective, of which / Men are part both in the inch and in the mile." In this sense I think the influence of James humanized the influence of Nietzsche. But it did not for that reason efface it. When Stevens finally composed his portrait of the common soldier in the "Examination of the Hero in a Time of War," he was careful to close the distance between misery and the sort of mastery he had once supposed to exist by contrast with it. At the same time, he pointed out that such retractions could only occur when the whole life of a community was in question. This is another way of saying that the most pronounced anti-Nietzschean moment of his poetry involves a certain sacrifice of his own inventions. To make contact with the reality of war, poetry itself must cease to be aesthetic. But Stevens insists that this is the proper choice for the poet.

Modern opinion of the "Examination of the Hero" tends to be low. Harold Bloom, in *Wallace Stevens: The Poems of Our Climate*, dismisses it in a paragraph. Yet Stevens himself named it prominently as one of his favorite poems. In the light of *Parts of a World,* one can see that his estimate had to do with a moral consciousness which the "Examination" exhibits uniquely in his work. This poem makes us see how even the reticences of public speech help to establish the dignity of a public moment. Moral and aesthetic service join together, and the distinction between them is lost, in a crisis when action and speech alike are governed by necessity. The "Examination," however, presumes, without seeking to defend, the worth of such acts of service. Only by the position Stevens assigns it, at the end of *Parts of a World,* can one recognize the ways in which it completes a long progression of his writing. In this ambitious effort to speak for the fate of a community, the master-among-men is, at last, visibly displaced by a hero at once ordinary and major.

"Force is my lot" are the first words of the poem, and it is pertinent that "lot" is a submissive word for fate, common to those who must endure it and thoroughly familiar in the vulgate. James often writes of our lot; Nietzsche speaks of "my destiny." A requirement of poetry in a time of war, Stevens says, is "to grasp the hero," and he warns as early as section V that the work is difficult because "the common man is the common hero." Yet "the common hero is the hero"; and, as he notes at the start of section VI,

> Unless we believe in the hero, what is there
> To believe? Incisive what, the fellow
> Of what good. Devise. Make him of mud,
> For every day. In a civiler manner,
> Devise, devise.

By devising this hero "in a civiler manner" than ever before, Stevens hoped to make existence and the world seem justified in a time of war, and not only as an aesthetic phenomenon.

But his continuing interest in what such an aesthetic phenomenon *is* explains a good many details of the "Examination." Indeed, for several of its incidental properties, the poem is indebted to the view of art it means to question, from *The Birth of Tragedy.* There Nietzsche distinguished between the Dionysian force that is the origin of tragedy and the Apollinian image by which it is presented in art. By means of the latter alone is the subject of tragedy made endurable:

> The Apollinian tears us out of the Dionysian universality and lets us find delight in individuals; it attaches our pity to them, and by means of them it satisfies our sense of beauty which longs for great and sublime forms; it presents images of life to us, and incites us to comprehend in thought the core

of life they contain. With the immense impact of the image, the concept, the ethical teaching, and the sympathetic emotion, the Apollinian tears man from his orgiastic self-annihilation and blinds him to the universality of the Dionysian process, deluding him into the belief that he is seeing a single image of the world.

For Nietzsche, this delusion is neither right nor wrong but *necessary.* When he goes on to speak of the myth that controls every tragic story, he calls it "the glorification of the fighting hero."

Why, asks Nietzsche, should the suffering of such a hero have established itself as the preferred subject for tragedy? Its justification has sometimes been that it "transfigures" the raw suffering of actual life. "But what does it transfigure when it presents the world of appearance in the image of the suffering hero? Least of all the 'reality' of this world of appearance, for it says to us: 'Look there! Look closely! This is your life, this is the hand on the clock of your existence.'" Nietzsche concludes that the only possible justification for the ugly and discordant elements of art may lie in "an artistic game that the will in the eternal amplitude of its pleasure plays with itself." Stevens was working within the same argument, but from a point of view that ruled out every mediation *The Birth of Tragedy* had associated with the "image." He did not in fact want to consider the war as an aesthetic spectacle, or as a subject for the imagination. "The immense poetry of war," which he speaks of in a prose note written at this time, is not assimilable by poetry itself: it belongs to a different kind of making. Accordingly, "in the presence of the violent reality of war, consciousness takes the place of the imagination." And consciousness, here, is a consciousness of fact, of the bloody sacrificial work of the living hero, and not of the images he can be made to bear. Because the war never so much as enters into "an artistic game" of the will, it may be experienced as part of an act of mere consciousness. It has none of the complexities and none of the disharmonies that the world may reveal in the light of an imaginative transfiguration. So the usual relation between art and act is reversed; and Stevens can say of his hero, in section XIV:

> To meditate the highest man, not
> The highest supposed in him and over,
> Creates, in the blissfuller perceptions,
> What unisons create in music.

In consequence, this soldier appears as the poet's "civil" self, to whom, in the face of an overwhelming reality, the imagination must consent to be subdued.

The conditions of such a portrayal help to explain what can otherwise seem a moment of ironic understatement in section XIII. Stevens there observes that "the hero / Acts in reality, adds nothing / To what he does"; while he "is the heroic / Actor and act but not divided," he lacks every instinct of a creator. The passage means to connect tragedy with ethics and the *because* of fate, and it does so in the knowledge that suffering, on a sufficiently great scale, suspends our sense of mere being in the world as it is. The contrast between a fated suffering and mere being, like the contrast between tragedy and comedy which is another version of it, runs through all of Stevens's writing, and the "Examination" may be taken to stand for one extreme. Still, once we grant this much, Stevens seems to want a more than ordinary credence for his hero when he writes, in section XII: "We have and are the man, capable / Of his brave quickenings, the human / Accelerations that seem inhuman." How can one ask so much from a figure whose only claim is that he is nothing but an actor in reality? I have to cheat here and say that we get a confident answer only by looking at the epilogue to *Notes toward a Supreme Fiction.* The soldier, who for Stevens is the hero in a time of war, comes into his poetry there as the adequate sharer of the poet's work. The communion they realize together comes from "the bread of faithful speech" which the poet alone provides. Stevens says to the soldier, of his own "war between the mind / And sky," that "It is a war that never ends. / Yet it depends on yours." Thus their tasks are parallel. At the far reaches of imaginative and actual doing and suffering, they explore the diverse callings by which humanity may seek to survive.

Two final sections of the "Examination" look at the hero of the war as if in an elegiac afterglow. They try, in particular, to distinguish him from "the familiar man," who is the soldier's double or perhaps the soldier himself out of uniform. The hero, Stevens concludes, is a character of summer; the familiar man, serviceable in a crowd of others, is a character of autumn. These discriminations suggest that the title of his next volume, *Transport to Summer,* may have meant to revive a memory of his gift to the common hero: "transport" refers to a ship of war, as much as a passage of imaginative release; and the summer is still that of the closing lines of the "Examination."

> Each false thing ends. The bouquet of summer
> Turns blue and on its empty table
> It is stale and the water is discolored.
> True autumn stands then in the doorway.
> After the hero, the familiar
> Man makes the hero artificial.

But was the summer false? The hero?
How did we come to think that autumn
Was the veritable season, that familiar
Man was the veritable man? So
Summer, jangling the savagest diamonds and
Dressed in its azure-doubled crimsons,
May truly bear its heroic fortunes
For the large, the solitary figure.

The curious use of "discolored," to sketch the memories of the soldier once his season of action is done, links this hero's fortune with Stevens's own. The word had been used already in *Parts of a World*, to round off the personal credo of "Extracts from Addresses to the Academy of Fine Ideas"—

Behold the men in helmets borne on steel,
Discolored, how they are going to defeat

—where the patches of camouflage or faded colors belong to their helmets and fatigues. But in "The Motive for Metaphor," speaking only to himself, Stevens would confess the happiness he had felt at "the half-colors of quarter-things . . . Where you yourself were never quite yourself / And did not want nor have to be." In his work as a whole, such metaphors join with the sense of "a fading of the sun," or the house that "has changed a little in the sun," to propose, as a subject almost free of pathos, the warmth of the interest held by every intimation of the passage of time. The soldier, like no one except the poet, lives close to this subject, because he lives close to death.

What Stevens was most struck by during the war, and what he wrote the "Examination" to celebrate, was the wager the soldiers took in joining a task which, whether it succeeded or failed, would change the meaning of everything it touched. As to how we are to look on their human exercise of power, apart from conceding that it is, somehow, heroic, Stevens gives us little help until a poem written soon after *Parts of a World*, "Dutch Graves in Bucks County." He recognizes in that poem how different the fighters in a modern war are from the barbaric aristocrats he had once thought fitted for such work; yet, when he turns from the soldiers and thinks of their work in a distant perspective, his feeling evidently has more of wonder than of disdain. "And you, my semblables," he tells his readers, "know that this time / Is not an early time that has grown late." It is simply our time. And its battles are fought by

The much too many disinherited
In a storm of torn-up testaments.

They have altered a great deal from the disinherited of "Parochial Theme," whose cries were scarcely audible above the noisy shouts of the hunters. By the time Stevens wrote "Dutch Graves in Bucks County," he himself belonged to the life of "These violent marchers of the present," the crowds, and crowds of soldiers who, "in arcs / Of a chaos composed of more than order, / March toward a generation's centre." What caused an act of rejection to give way to an act of supposing was the experiment of thought and feeling that he sustained in *Parts of a World.*

IN ONE OF his greatest poems, "Chocorua to Its Neighbor," Stevens looked back on his own relationship to the hero he had created in these years. He reflected that "To say more than human things with human voice," as the religious poets do, "That cannot be"; and "to say human things with more / Than human voice," as Nietzsche aimed to do, "that, also, cannot be"; but "To speak humanly from the height or from the depth / Of human things, that is acutest speech." The figure who makes these truths come home to Stevens is no longer an allegory of consciousness against the imagination. On the contrary he seems to represent a pathos of distance that issues from every person's imagining:

> He was more than an external majesty,
> Beyond the sleep of those that did not know,
> More than a spokesman of the night to say
> Now, time stands still. He came from out of sleep.
> He rose because men wanted him to be.
>
> They wanted him by day to be, image,
> But not the person, of their power, thought,
> But not the thinker, large in their largeness, beyond
> Their form, beyond their life, yet of themselves,
> Excluding by his largeness their defaults.

The representative man of these stanzas is a fiction more strangely potent than any that he had yet discovered.

Yet Stevens never gave up his interest in the "accelerations that seem inhuman," the shifting sum of all the effects that belong to the Nietzschean hero. Even the mountain climber whose exhilarations the lonely peak, Chocorua, recounts to its neighbor, has something of the air of an earlier mastery. He, too, is a solitary figure. The difference is that he is closely attached to the changing life he shares with his fellows: it is not supposed that they are separated from him by their inability to know the change that they live. Nietzsche, in his pre-*Zarathustra* books, saw a possible good in attachments like these, but spoke of their uses distrustfully, because he thought them likely to serve the tyranny of a moral community over its distinct individuals. It seems fairest to conclude with his tentative view, in *Daybreak,* of a prospect Stevens's poetry helps to widen in a different way.

> *The brake.*—To suffer for the sake of morality and then to be told that this kind of suffering is founded on an *error:* this arouses indignation. For there is a unique consolation in affirming through one's suffering "a profounder world of truth" than any other world is, and one would much *rather* suffer and thereby feel oneself exalted above reality (through consciousness of having thus approached this "profounder world of truth") than be without suffering but also without the feeling that one is exalted. It is thus pride, and the customary manner in which pride is gratified, which stands in the way of a new *understanding* of morality. What force, therefore, will have to be employed if this brake is to be removed? More pride? A new pride?

Nietzsche for his part chose to build more pride, with more humiliations as well, for the sake of the more than human. Stevens, in the poems I have been concerned with, was building a new pride.

1987

SIX

Marianne Moore as Discoverer

Laurence Stapleton's book* is an example of what Marianne Moore would have called *sound propaedeutic,* and conducive to appreciation along three separate paths. It joins a study of Moore's development with a record of her whole activity as a writer, through six decades in poetry and prose, and at the helm of an extensive and interested correspondence. It claims much, and not solely in terms of "maturity," for the latter part of Moore's career: no other critic has and probably none will again attempt this so valiantly, and the effort is a happy one; fortunate for the author, and a pleasure for us to see. Finally, Stapleton throughout has appropriated something of both the savor and strength of her subject's prose. She praises, at one point, its "kinetic aptitude," and says precisely of Moore's precision: "she is sensitive to the slightest implication of words and even to the heft of syllables." With the aid of documents now available in the Rosenbach collection, Stapleton has also been able to quote variously from letters, journals, and drafts; what all this matter suggests is how far Moore's revisions have prodded us to forget, or to foreshorten in memory, the much fuller early versions in which many of her poems first made their effect; so that the study encourages and quietly exemplifies the attitude proper to a loyalist, which in this instance will end by demanding something better than a corrected reprint of the 1967 *Complete Poems* with five very slight additions.† What we want is a real *Collected Poems,* with everything Moore saw fit to publish, as far back as *Poems* and *Observations.* She was always a good self-critic, but specially and rather erratically austere in

---

* *Marianne Moore: The Poet's Advance,* by Laurence Stapleton.
† *The Complete Poems of Marianne Moore.*

the result of her longer backward looks. Any poem that she once called finished is good enough for us.

A fault of Stapleton's book, which it shares with every good criticism of Moore I have ever read, is the assumption of a generalized familiarity with the poetry, an atmosphere-of-Moore-ishness, which allows the quotations to be copious and admiring and yet seldom anchored in a parent poem. And perhaps we know the poetry well enough; but do we know the poems? Many readers will want to reply: "Oh certainly, I know what they're *like;* whimsical, helter-skelter; odds and ends, all in sharp focus; alive with incidental humor—every word an incident." Because I was tired of giving this answer myself, I made a list of poems. The following groups are neither exhaustive nor mutually exclusive; but they do make room for a different sort of answer.

Riddles, anecdotes, squibs: "To Statecraft Embalmed," "To Military Progress," "To a Steam Roller," "Silence"; with innumerable unrhymed epigrams, and divagations of a too-charitable satirist.

Prayers; calls to fortitude: "What Are Years?" "In Distrust of Merits," "By Disposition of Angels," and the bulk of the later poems (epitomized by "Blessed Is the Man," with its echoes of Eisenhower and Omar Khayyam).

Trials of ingenuity: "The Plumet Basilisk," "The Fish," "Peter," "England," "When I Buy Pictures," "The Labors of Hercules," "Snakes, Mongooses, Snake-Charmers, and the Like," "An Octopus," "Sojourn in the Whale," "The Student," "Spenser's Ireland," "Four Quartz Crystal Clocks," "Elephants," "His Shield."

Far-fetchers: "The Steeple-Jack," "The Hero," "The Jerboa," "The Frigate Pelican," "In the Days of Prismatic Color," "A Grave," "New York," "Marriage," "Virginia Britannia," "The Pangolin"; and, blameless outcast from the 1951 *Collected Poems,* "Melanchthon."

The most searching of her inventions belong to the last two groups. Wit, as *ingenium,* or the reasoning intelligence—as finder of hidden analogies, or master of the sociable challenge and repartee—here delights in testing its object for all uncharted incongruities, and a map showing every turn would be no help. Who, coming to the end of "Four Quartz Crystal Clocks," will say where we forget the smart touch of the colloquist, and find that we have learned something about science and the morality of play?

> The lemur-student can see
> that an aye-aye is not
>
> an angwan-tíbo, potto, or loris. The sea-
> side burden should not embarrass

the bell-boy with the buoy-ball
  endeavoring to pass
hotel patronesses; nor could a
  practiced ear confuse the glass
    eyes for taxidermists

with eye-glasses from the optometrist. And as
  MEridian-7 one-two
one-two gives, each fifteenth second
  in the same voice, the new
data—"The time will be" so and so—
  you realise that "when you
    hear the signal," you'll be

hearing Jupiter or jour pater, the day god—
  the salvaged son of Father Time—
telling the cannibal Chronos
  (eater of his proxime
newborn progeny) that punctuality
  is not a crime.

After such beautiful display one may still prefer the extravagant persuasion of the far-fetchers; and to justify the preference there is a decisive aphorism in "Armor's Undermining Modesty": "What is more precise than precision? Illusion." That poem more than any other was Moore's apology for her work, and to her its credo had an obvious application.

She was most satisfied, and hoped we would be, with poems that argued the necessity of some single illusion—poems in which, after enough scruples to disarm the skeptic, she could welcome the believing mind for its strengths, especially strength of sight. Any illusion that assisted life to its ends was perhaps another name for single-mindedness. In "The Steeple-Jack" this quality is what favors the not-native observer of a native place: the citizen for whom the author cares most is the one who may set "part of a novel" in the town she describes. Since Moore dropped the full title, "Part of a Novel, Part of a Poem, Part of a Play"—which covered two further poems in sequence, "The Student" and "The Hero"—"The Steeple-Jack" may now seem a more complacent piece of naturalism than it really is. But her decision was correct for other reasons. The three did not answer each other deeply enough, and "The Hero" had more in common with "The Jerboa" than with its companions. Like "The Jerboa," it bears witness to a personal ideal of ascetic heroism, some of whose elements Moore named in an essay on "Humility, Concentration, and Gusto."

As the "Too Much" section of "The Jerboa" concludes with the desert and its real animals, unenvyingly remote from civilization and its toy ones— "one would not be he / who has nothing but plenty"—so "The Hero" moves from the tourist laden with his collected wits to the different figure, rich without plenty, who can follow a personal liking: "He's not out / seeing a sight but the rock / crystal thing to see—the startling El Greco / brimming with inner light— / that covets nothing that it has let go." These poems make as right a pair as "The Frigate Pelican" and "The Pangolin," in which an animal at once upsets and submits to be measured by the human scale of custom and value; or "New York" and "Virginia Britannia," one poem each for the North and South, in which the dream of paradise is close-woven with the dream of plunder. But the foregoing are all well-known or at least much-recognized poems, and this late in the history of Moore's reputation I would rather concentrate on three that seem to me too little read: "A Grave," "Marriage," and "In the Days of Prismatic Color."

"A Grave" is propositional in structure, categorical in mood, shorn of even such heterodox exuberances as Moore sometimes allows to flourish within the parallel rows of a catalogue. It is a poem about death, as dry as life can make it.

Man looking into the sea,
taking the view from those who have as much right to it as you have to it
    yourself,
it is human nature to stand in the middle of a thing,
but you cannot stand in the middle of this;
the sea has nothing to give but a well excavated grave.
The firs stand in a procession, each with an emerald turkey-foot at the top,
reserved as their contours, saying nothing;
repression, however, is not the most obvious characteristic of the sea;
the sea is a collector, quick to return a rapacious look.
There are others besides you who have worn that look—
whose expression is no longer a protest; the fish no longer investigate them
for their bones have not lasted:
men lower nets, unconscious of the fact that they are desecrating a grave,
and row quickly away—the blades of the oars
moving together like the feet of water-spiders as if there were no such thing as
    death.
The wrinkles progress among themselves in a phalanx—beautiful under
    networks of foam,
and fade breathlessly while the sea rustles in and out of the seaweed:
the birds swim through the air at top speed, emitting cat-calls as heretofore—

the tortoise-shell scourges about the feet of the cliffs, in motion beneath them;
and the ocean, under the pulsation of lighthouses and noise of bell-buoys,
advances as usual, looking as if it were not that ocean in which dropped things
    are bound to sink—
in which if they turn and twist, it is neither with volition nor consciousness.

One sees the poem just as one hears it—a respectful monochrome, unflattering to man, of something larger than man: but how does it get this consistency of effect? One notes first the use of words at several removes from any lively particular, words like "unconscious," "volition," "characteristic," "contours," "repression," along with the careless drab music of the vernacular, "at top speed," "no such thing," "as much right to it," "the fact that," "as usual." T. S. Eliot would have had in mind words and phrases like these when he praised Moore for having heard, in "the curious jargon produced in America by universal university education," one of the possible languages of men in a state of vivid sensation. And yet there seems, at a glance, hardly one vivid feature in this poem; it seems almost wrong to call it a poem. Only on the return visit that it somehow compels, and a step or so back from its subject, do certain details emerge from the flat continuous statement; and then it takes on quite suddenly the answering bluntness and unanswerable severity of an Aeschylean chorus: nothing could be more direct, more like words meant to surprise and unenchant, than "it is human nature to stand in the middle of a thing, / but you cannot stand in the middle of this"; and, "the sea is a collector, quick to return a rapacious look. / There are others besides you who have worn that look"; down to the theoremlike and almost affectless "dropped things are bound to sink." It would be hard to imagine any poem that sustained a more uncanny gravity. Under its law we naturally reserve for ourselves the few stage properties of the sea, to make an interval of elation and release before the end: the sound of the bell-buoys and sight of the lighthouse, the "phalanx" of wrinkles beneath the foam, and birds swimming in the air, "emitting cat-calls as heretofore," with the ghostly tortoise-shell (no tortoise) moving among the cliffs below. Yet, much as these things may please us, the poem absorbs them without pleasure; and the detail we remember most irresistibly, a metaphor powerful enough to survive paraphrase, is also the most disquieting of all: the men, ignorant of death and of the figure they cut beside it, rowing quickly away from the thing they do not know is a grave, their oars "moving together like the feet of water-spiders as if there were no such thing as death." It is a long line without pause in which surely no reader has ever skipped one word. The entire poem must have been a favorite of Elizabeth Bishop's: some of it is still going in the background of "At the Fishhouses"; a smaller borrowing, but as gifted with appreciation and command as Bishop's use of a familiar Moore genre in "The Man-Moth."

By an impartial observer, "Marriage" might be described as a duel of quotations. But we are none of us impartial; so let it be a male critic who says, In this poem man holds the chains and one woman, the words; yet she is cunning as a whisper and makes it seem, almost to the end, a remarkably equal match. The contestants are Adam and Eve, or the virtues of Adam and Eve. And Moore's Adam is the same as Milton's, though she does not tell us so; he whose first recorded words, to the first of women, are "Sole partner and sole part of all these joys," dull, sententious, and good, the temple of a selfless mastery. Who else could be let down so gently but so finally by Moore's reference to "the ease of the philosopher / unfathered by a woman"? Many unkindnesses as well as (one feels) many liberties and general vexings, were required to move her to this. But steel against satire, Adam—the old and ever-renewed, in marriage—will be heard out; while Eve calmly wonders at "the spiked hand / that has an affection for one / and proves it to the bone, / impatient to assure you / that impatience is a mark of independence, / not of bondage." For, marrying, she has joined that locus "'of circular traditions and impostures, / committing many spoils,' / requiring all one's criminal ingenuity / to avoid"—and, crushed by his single stroke of wit, his "Why not be alone together," she now dwells in those circles, a listener. The poet comes confusingly near a gesture of sentimental homage when she speaks of

> This Institution,
> perhaps one should say enterprise
> out of respect for which
> one says one need not change one's mind
> about a thing one has believed in,

but she recoils by the end, and transposes even this tentative melody into a more dubious key, with a minefield of sharps and flats:

> What can one do for them—
> these savages
> condemned to disaffect
> all those who are not visionaries
> alert to undertake the silly task
> of making people noble?

But this is not quite the end; we see the wife a last time, still listening to her husband, whose eloquence now has something of "the statesmanship

/ of an archaic Daniel Webster," proclaiming "Liberty and Union / now and forever"; yet another man, husband, orator, in a poem that has featured everyone from Adam to Edmund Burke. There is more bitterness than affection in this windup; it is an unexpected tone, for which we are glad: suitable, after all, to a poet whose refusal to be assured about her impatience was the making of her. Besides, in the masterly orchestration of the thing, a great many other voices have been heard—Bacon, Shakespeare, Pound, Richard Baxter, Charles Reade, and at last a voice close to Moore's own, which turns out to be La Fontaine: "Everything to do with love is mystery; / it is more than a day's work / to investigate this science." There is in this more wonder than bitterness; and the quotations generally help Moore to keep her balance. "Psychology which explains everything / explains nothing, / and we are still in doubt." For every Adam there must be an Eve, who listens and smiles, and does not show her smile. The hurtful acuteness of some passages comes, notwithstanding the disclaimer, from the habitual care of a good and disturbing psychologist; and any writer who can describe Satan's investment in the serpent as "that invaluable accident / exonerating Adam," is none the worse for having a *parti pris*.

To square the account, she included in her *Selected Poems,* and reprinted ever after, a poem about Adam before Eve, "when there was no smoke and color was / fine, not with the refinement of early civilization art, but because / of its originality." The poem, "In the Days of Prismatic Color," is alert to the snares of its myth; it knows that this sort of aboriginal earliness can never exist as its own contemporary; it is not born but comes to be original, when later eyes have seen it so. History alone, with memory, can make those days, and Moore writes out the history that her poem seems to deny, by adopting an idiom she has employed at other times—refined, self-conscious, derivative, *and fine*—and pressing it beyond any known reach of the abstract. We arrive at originality by this curious route; so that she can say, of Adam's solitude and perfect vision, "obliqueness was a variation / of the perpendicular, plain to see and / to account for: it is no / longer that; nor did the blue-red-yellow band / of incandescence that was color keep its stripe." That is science not poetry, we may say, too stupid to read our myths deviously; but the image stops us short: it is the first poetic rainbow in half a century that one can admire without embarrassment. This poem is no friend of complexity, which it admits may not be "a crime, but carry / it to the point of murkiness / and nothing is plain"; nor of sophistication, which it suspects of being "principally throat," and "at the antipodes from the init / ial great truths." Yet it is wonderfully aware throughout that our originals though great can never be simple, except in their power to survive. We reduce them only from our need for something uncompounded to serve as the givens of thought and reliables of metaphor. But when they first appeared, before they could be remembered, there was always the stumbling, the obliqueness of the rude assault:

> "Part of it was crawling, part of it
> was about to crawl, the rest
>   was torpid in its lair." In the short-legged, fit-
> ful advance, the gurgling and all the minutiae—we have the classic
>
> multitude of feet. To what purpose! Truth is no Apollo
>   Belvedere, no formal thing. The wave may go over it if it likes.
> Know that it will be there when it says,
>   "I shall be there when the wave has gone by."

In those lines originality becomes one with the self-confidence of genius anywhere. Seeing the naturalness of the transition, from "the gurgling and all the minutiae" to "the classic / multitude of feet," we are educated in how originals make their way, and incidentally shown a distinction Moore keeps in view all the time, between the precisionist's dreaming with one eye open and the formalist's interrogation with both eyes closed.

So far I have said nothing about Moore's verse forms—and after all, too much has been said by others. To most readers they probably still convey, for a little while, the sense of an absorbing peculiarity, like a friend's midnight addiction to mango juice. One soon accepts them like any other convention, and once accepted they join the form of life with which the author has linked them permanently in our minds. Beyond that, what does anyone care about their appropriateness? They are uniquely suited, or unsuited, to the person who chose them, just as all poetry is; one can learn nothing more essential about Moore from her syllabic layouts than one can about Collins from the English-cucumber-shape of an irregular ode: the important thing about both is that they are products of a given age and climate, streaked by the weather that followed, but undesirable or obsolete only in the dimmest of short runs. Moore herself, in "The Past is the Present," says this best: "Ecstasy affords / the occasion and expediency determines the form." Yet an audience for whom modernism was never new may pass by her innovations unnoticing and therefore unalarmed; what they will want to have explained is her didactic freedom with aphorisms; for it is this that makes her remote not only from modernist practice but from all that has succeeded it. The causes of her uniqueness are rooted in what can sometimes feel like the land poetry forgot. I mean the Eighteenth Century—one of Moore's cherished haunts, and *not* her idea of the second fall of man, as it was to Pound and Eliot—when critics rashly spoke of "casting one's eye over mankind." Poems could then be praised for their sentiment. By this was generally meant the perfect utterance of a common feeling which no one could know was common until the poet made it so. Apart from poetry governed by the most relentless logical structure, sentiments might easily serve the purpose of classical sententiae: they were simply the best means by which the performer-with-words could recommend himself to the trust of his listeners. Moore's poems abound in wise feelings, which she often appears to set in place with an air of having left room for something of that sort, in case it should ask for admission. The reader who wonders at her daring must remember that among the writers she most admired were Pope, Johnson, Blake—and Shaw, a latecomer not at all strange to this company. She would have agreed with everyone who ever pointed out that a poem cannot be all poetry: only, she would have added, we ought in that case to change our definition of poetry. She did it more by example than precept, with "the physiognomy of conduct must not reveal the skeleton," and "Denunciations do not affect / the culprit; nor blows, but it / is torture to him not to be spoken to"; with "why dissect destiny with instruments / more highly specialized than components of destiny itself?" and "He can talk but insolently says nothing. What of it? / When one is frank, one's very presence is a compliment" and "The passion for setting people right is in itself an afflictive disease. / Distaste which takes no credit to itself is best."

Statements like these may look planted. But how different are they from those others, obviously at home in one place, which have a hardy existence on almost any soil? One does not need to know the title of the poem, "People's Surroundings," or the topic for discussion, the flats of Utah and Texas, to appreciate Moore's qualified love of "those cool sirs with the explicit sensory apparatus of common sense, / who know the exact distance between two points as the crow flies." In "Elephants," the relevant context can seem almost a pettiness to recall, after she speaks of one creature in particular as "too wise / to mourn—a life prisoner but reconciled." Again, how different are these in turn from the many celebrated passages of "straight" description, in which animal traits, refigured as man-mores, are esteemed as tokens of character and then of virtue?

> Make hay; keep
> the shop; I have one sheep; were a less
> limber animal's mottoes. This one
> finds sticks for the swan's-down-dress

of his child to rest upon and would
    not know Gretel from Hänsel.
    As impassioned Handel—

meant for a lawyer and a masculine German domestic
    career—clandestinely studied the harpsichord
    and never was known to have fallen in love,
        the unconfiding frigate-bird hides
in the height and in the majestic
        display of his art. He glides
    a hundred feet or quivers about
        as charred paper behaves—full
        of feints; and an eagle

    of vigilance.

The final phrase, tucked into a new stanza, nicely conceals its satisfaction at having found a witty way of obliging man to serve as a middle man— nothing but a German domestic could translate the eagle into a language the pelican understands: this done, the poem is done with Germany, Handel, and harpsichords. The perception starts from and returns to its formative sayings. In the meantime it has made havoc of our pedagogic aids, which read, in a march of progress, "From Abstract to Concrete" or "From General to Particular."

As a composer of words Moore's greatest affinities are with Francis Bacon, and the Baconian essay or prose-amble may be the least misleading analogy for one of her poems. To be curt, undeviating, end-stopped wherever a thought might enter, but at the same time vivid, striking, inventive in the highest degree conscionable, is the ideal of both writers. Like Bacon a despiser of ornament, Moore rejects with equal vehemence the aims of bringing conceit for a matter and matter for a conceit. She will frame no description that has any hint of the superlative, unless she can first set in the middle of it a skeptical gargoyle at least six syllables long: "Rare unscent- / ed, provident- / ly hot, too sweet, inconsistent flower bed!" She refuses to claim the literary exemption from syllogisms, dependent clauses, subordinate conjunctions, and everything that smacks of the uncraftily sheltered: she will submit with the worst of us, and discover poetry there besides. Bacon's untheatrical rigor would have found nothing wanting in her resolve to be literal, and for range of style he leaves her plenty. "Nature is often hidden; sometimes overcome; seldom extinguished," is a sentence one can imagine her writing, or quoting, as easily as "It is good to commit the beginnings of all great actions to Argos with his hundred eyes, and the ends to Briareus with his hundred hands; first to watch, and then to speed."

But Bacon's essays sometimes trail off in QEDs, whereas Moore was born to the stroke they call in tennis *a concluder*. An extraordinary number of her endings are extraordinarily beautiful. In "The Student," "Sojourn in the Whale," "The Hero," the first section of "The Jerboa," she lifts the errant thing to its resting seat, with a parental touch so quick and encircling that we come to rely on her in every playground, including Eden. Nor does she bring a particle of pomp to occasions that need a different sort of authority: "Spenser's Ireland" and "To a Steam Roller" are famous because they close with famous jokes. Yet above all these are the endings carried out in perfect earnest. First, "Elephants," which has warned us hardship makes the soldier, teachableness the philosopher, and then turns to Socrates, who

> prudently testing the suspicious thing, knew
> the wisest is he who's not sure that he knows.
> Who rides on a tiger can never dismount;
> asleep on an elephant, that is repose.

These lines once had and still deserve for company, the last of another elephant-poem, "Melanchthon," with their less reconciled note: "Will / depth be depth, thick skin be thick, to one who can see no / beautiful element of unreason under it?" However, Moore never outdid the description of man in "The Pangolin"—bringing him by chance to the fore ("To explain grace requires a curious hand"), keeping him there till he changed everything—and this she left standing.

>   Consistent with the
> formula—warm blood, no gills, two pairs of hands and a few hairs—that
> is a mammal; there he sits in his own habitat,
>   serge-clad, strong-shod. The prey of fear, he, always
>   curtailed, extinguished, thwarted by the dusk, work partly done,
>   says to the alternating blaze,
>   "Again the sun!
>   anew each day; and new and new and new,
>   that comes into and steadies my soul."

Felicities which here sound accidental the whole poem makes essential: man "curtailed," for instance, which takes us back to the pangolin "strongly intailed," a pun encouraging to all who if they pursue symbolic logic feel that they must do it on four legs.

In a memorable criticism, Kenneth Burke conceived of Moore's "objectivist idiom" as fostering "an appraisal or judgment of many things in and for themselves. They would be encouraged to disclose their traits, not simply that they might exist through the vicarage of words, but that they might reveal their properties as workmanship (workmanship being a trait in which the ethical and the esthetic are one)." Only the first part of this seems to me false. It brings her too much into line with Williams, whose work vaguely resembles hers in matters of the surface, but whose brittler temperament had much to do with his interest in programs like objectivism. Pound, who usually comes next in the effort to triangulate her, is just as wrong for comparison, in spite of their mutual loyalty. Irony like Pound's, of the nervous modern sort, which regards its object from an unsteady point of view but with an advanced degree of scorn, was never part of her armor or weaponry, and she could have written "Mauberley" without the quotation marks. Her intellectual virtues came from the enlightenment and protestantism; from the start, she had the concerns of a genuine moralist, as well as the ambition to be one; and she knew that the gesture of humility was to ask forgiveness from enemies rather than friends. These things help to make "In Distrust of Merits" a better poem than "Pull Down Thy Vanity."

Of all her contemporaries, the Stevens of *Harmonium* and the early Eliot, who also called his work "observations," seem closest to the spirit of her poetry. In one appreciation of Eliot she mentions "certain qualities" that he shares with Stevens—qualities she supposed would be sufficiently plain to her readers, though they were not so to the authors themselves "reticent candor and emphasis by understatement" being the two she cares for most. Some lines from "La Figlia che Piange" and "Peter Quince at the Clavier" are quoted as proof: a juxtaposition both strange and right, which it took Moore to imagine. And with those poems in view, one can understand how far she does belong to her generation after all, the generation of "Prufrock," "Le Monocle de Mon Oncle," and "Marriage." Eliot was alluding to their shared enterprise when in a letter to Moore he thanked her for writing poems that forced him to consider each word. Revolutions in taste cannot give us better monuments; but they may force us to work at the new ones slowly. Moore knew what she had done and what she had made possible, and nothing could be more emphatic than the reticence with which she told us so: "Know that it will be there when it says, / 'I shall be there when the wave has gone by.'"

1982

SEVEN

"That Weapon, Self-Protectiveness": Notes on a Friendship

In the following pages, I sketch what I take to be a deep affinity of poetic imagination between Marianne Moore and Elizabeth Bishop.* But it is a delicate subject, and, having announced it in this way, I have to add several qualifications. The affinity is temperamental. It shows in the poems that Moore and Bishop wrote. I will be saying nothing about the friendship they maintained outside of poetry. Also, affinity is not quite the same thing as influence. It goes both ways equally, as influence never does; or rather, it convinces us of the reality of some third thing. The effect of reading Moore and Bishop together, it seems to me, is that one can see aspects of their work as part of a shared predicament. Let me begin by saying what that is.

There is a tonality of self-assertion in Moore's early writing which her readers tend to forget. But Elizabeth Bishop never forgot it. Her own most powerful early poem, "Roosters," and the development that followed from it owe a great deal to a pattern of declaration and withdrawal which Moore was the first to exemplify. That poem indeed has a curious and instructive history. It came to Moore's attention just at the time when she herself had started to reject the side of her work to which Bishop was returning. I am not sure how far either poet was aware of this; and it does not matter much. What is suggestive is a certain coincidence of motives. At a crisis of their relationship, each poet was driven to attempt a full de-

---

* This essay draws gratefully on the correspondence housed at the Rosenbach Museum in Philadelphia. The interested reader will want to compare two other impressions of Moore and Bishop together: David Kalstone's in *Becoming a Poet* and Bonnie Costello's in "Marianne Moore and Elizabeth Bishop: Friendship and Influence" (*Twentieth Century Literature* 30: 130–49).

fense of her own work. And in the course of sustaining that effort, each came close to defining a path of self-revision that the other also would take. So the terms of a contest lead back to terms of mutual identity.

I do not know of another phenomenon like this in literary history. The relationship between Wordsworth and Coleridge feels different from the start, because it involves so clear a division of labor. One poet lives and feels, the other teaches a way to think about living and feeling. There was nothing resembling such an arrangement between Moore and Bishop. I offer this account, therefore, partly in a spirit of inquiry. It is, from one point of view, an anomalous record of the commerce that once existed between diverse minds; from another, it makes a general point about the sort of self-knowledge that poems may have—a knowledge both overt and perplexing, which may be another name for the knowledge of persons.

A poem by Marianne Moore in *Observations* is called "To Be Liked by You Would Be a Calamity." The phrase, written for Moore's voice, also bears the emphasis of an unsnobbish discrimination which one knows from certain comedies of the period, as in Cary Grant's line about a dull rival, "To hardly know him is to know him well." Moore's poem takes up the cue unflinchingly:

> "Attack is more piquant than concord," but when
>   You tell me frankly that you would like to feel
>   My flesh beneath your feet,
>   I'm all abroad; I can but put my weapon up, and
>   Bow you out.
> Gesticulation—it is half the language.
>   Let unsheathed gesticulation be the steel
>   Your courtesy must meet,
>   Since in your hearing words are mute, which to my senses
>   Are a shout.

The opening quotation, "Attack is more piquant than concord," comes, as the notes tell us, from Hardy, and it seems to say that for drama as for rhetoric, attack makes a more arresting *attitude* than concord. But the poem does not entirely keep the pledge of this beginning; it does something better.

We know there are occasions for which an attitude of attack will simply be improper. To judge by her most celebrated poetry and prose, Moore's writing was particularly adapted to such occasions. She armed herself with a shield, and it is her grace that we infer this to be a choice at once of feminine strength and feminine courtesy. So, by the end of this poem, her weapon is put up. But though no duel is fought, something striking has happened in its absence. The occasion was proper for a duel, and we are made to see the poet would have been equal to it. Her weapon is the sword after all. Only, she implies, her antagonist is unworthy. In the code of honor that is here invoked, a refusal to do battle is more aggressive than a challenge could possibly have been. It is the untoppable assault, disdaining even the clash of a fight—much as rhetorical silence may be more deadly than any question or answer. One might summarize the action of the poem by saying that, as speech moves from words to shouting to mere gesticulation, so action moves from courtesy to a challenge to the command of "Weapons up!" that calls off a challenge. The last move has great éclat since it both presumes and brings about the social nonexistence of one's antagonist.

Every reader, I think, will feel that the person addressed in this poem is a man. But how do we know? The main clue is "My flesh beneath your feet." It is true the form of that phrase is oratorical, almost like a description of heraldry, and to that extent neutral. Yet, together with the authority of "bow you out," it points to a sexual undercurrent that is apparent throughout the poem. For the restraint of "gesticulation" belongs to someone who can choose, and who wants us to see that she can choose, her weapons against his.

This poem represents a strength in Moore which she later kept from display; and she cut it from both editions of her collected poems. Her reason cannot have been solely an estimate of its worth. Among her poems of blame and praise, it has less distinction perhaps than "To a Steam Roller," but is more memorable than several others which she did choose to reprint. Anyway, the rank of the poem may be less interesting now than the quality in Moore that it helps bring to light. The whole look and feel of Moore's poems as they first appeared—the stance a reader would naturally have imputed to them—was quite different from what it has since been supposed to be. Many of the shorter and one of the long poems in *Observations* were cast in the form of compliments or satires, with a Popean discipline of raillery. These include "To an Intra-Mural Rat," "To Military Progress," "George Moore," "Novices," and "Marriage." All these poems were ranged near the front of *Observations,* where they would shape a reader's impression of what the author was up to. By contrast, Moore's 1951 *Collected Poems* moved them to the back; to start with, instead, it offered the genial topographical inquisitiveness of "The Steeple-Jack"; a little further on, with the poem that begins "In this age of hard trying," the poet would be found claiming a particular kinship with one whose

<pre>
                            by-
         play was more terrible in its effectiveness
            than the fiercest frontal attack.
          The staff, the bag, the feigned inconsequence
        of manner, best bespeak that weapon, self-protectiveness.
</pre>

By then, Moore had come to prize an ideal of intellectual capability in which imaginative or moral virtues shone most brightly from a hidden place of repose—"in an unhackneyed solitude." This is a reversal of emphasis from her satires and, at the same time, a further application of their tactics. Observation itself has now become half the language. The inconsequence may be feigned, the self-protectiveness may be a weapon, but they can be so only to the person who stays for a long look into them. To others, they have the surface charm of ornamental things. From those others, they are shielded.

In Moore's criticism as much as in her poetry, this stance is often associated with pairs of virtues. Reticence and candor, humility and gusto, are two famous instances, but the rule for them all is that a dominant trait may be known by its antithetical and recessive counterpart. Thus we are surprised (and it is a sort of surprise Moore connects with genuine imagining) to find that gusto should be an incidental accompaniment of humility; or, again, to find that reticence should sometimes imply a candor of its own. But Moore's interest in such pairs was a gradual and not an easy discovery. In *Observations,* she had been steadily concerned with the expulsion from genial life of certain pretenders to virtue; for, as William James understood, "Not the absence of vice, but vice there, and virtue holding her by the throat, seems the ideal human state." James had the good humor to feign that this view was not his own, but in the early Moore one will find no such pretense. Her predilections there went hand in hand with prejudices.

Elizabeth Bishop read *Observations* when she was a student at Vassar, and later said that it changed her sense of what could be done in poetry. This fact will mislead if we take it to disclose a source of her style. People who call Bishop a disciple of Moore, or "of the school of Moore," whatever that may mean, have got both poets wrong. But Moore did occasionally tease Bishop about the reviewers' cant of schools, sometimes with a rather anxious undertone; and in a letter of October 24, 1954, Bishop sent her a clarifying reply:

> I don't know what *Le Journal des Poetes* is, I'm afraid—you say it says I show your influence. . . . Well, naturally I am only too delighted to—Everyone has said that—I was going to say, all my life—and I only wish it were truer.

> My own feeling about it is that I don't show very much; that no one does or can at present; that you are still too new and original and unique to *show* in that way very much but will keep influencing more and more during the next fifty or a hundred years. In my own case, I know however that when I began to read your poetry at college I think it immediately opened up my eyes to the possibility of the subject-matter I could use and might never have thought of using if it hadn't been for you.—(I might not have written any poems, I suppose.) I think my approach is so much vaguer and less-defined and certainly more old-fashioned—sometimes I'm amazed at people's comparing me to you when all I'm doing is some kind of blank verse—Can't they *see* how different it is? But they can't, apparently.

This is considerate praise that does not strike a false note of self-deprecation. But it deflects the original question by passing quickly from Bishop's style (which she knows she did not get from anyone) to her subject matter (where she can admit an uncomplicated debt to Moore). If one looks at Bishop's own subjects, however, one finds that they are nothing at all like Moore's. What resemblance there is occurs in lighter pieces—"Seascape" and "Florida" are the only ones that really seem close.

But suppose one has in view the sort of stance I described in *Observations:* something less pervasive than style, and less foursquare than subject, yet a thing as pronounced as either in its results for poetry. Here one can start to see a cause of Bishop's absorbing interest in the poems of *Observations.* Certainly the depth of her interest was exceptional. Moore was the first and would remain the only celebrated person whom Bishop ever sought as company. With her, Bishop overcame an ingrained shyness sufficiently to introduce herself; to renew a favorable first acquaintance by suggesting many subsequent meetings; and to attend faithfully to one side of a lifelong correspondence, in the early years by writing as much as a letter or postcard a week. When, in her late twenties, some years into their friendship, she was first invited to address Miss Moore familiarly, as Marianne, she put "Marianne" at the top of her next letter with a fringe of magic lights.

I now want to tell a story about the genesis of "Roosters." It is a story I believe to be true, though the evidence for it is merely interpretative. But it is apt anyway for the present occasion because it connects an important poem by Bishop with the satirical impulse of *Observations.* Imagine, then, Bishop's reading of another poem in that book, "To a Prize Bird":

> You suit me well, for you can make me laugh,
> nor are you blinded by the chaff
>   that every wind sends spinning from the rick.

You know to think, and what you think you speak
with much of Samson's pride and bleak
    finality; and none dare bid you stop.

Pride sits you well, so strut, colossal bird.
No barnyard makes you look absurd;
    your brazen claws are staunch against defeat.

The prize bird's qualities fit the poet, as salamander skin would later do; they are right for her, as a chosen suit is right. Seen in this way, her subject here makes an oddly masculine emblem. Yet the bird's eloquence is hampered by inconsequence, for what he holds fast to is the bar inside the cage, and he can be colossal only in that cage, his temple. As for his power as a figure of imagination, it is chiefly negative. He is *not blinded* by the chaff he hears and repeats, in the sense that, being indifferent, he can seem superior to dull words or syllables. This mention of blindness leads by association to Samson's "pride and bleak / Finality." I do not think the allusion is meant ironically, and anyone who does think so faces contradictory evidence from the daughter of John Milton Moore. Yet the bird is impressive only in being unconformable. He struts, is colossal or brazen, in the manner of heroic statuary. If he is staunch against defeat, that is not the same as being assured of conquest. Nevertheless, this is the only place I can recall in Moore where pride is allowed to show itself as a virtue without qualification.

The adjectives *brazen, strutting,* and *colossal* will have caught the ear of any reader familiar with "Roosters." Still, a brief summary may be helpful. Bishop's unforgettable poem begins as the poet is awakened from sleep by the first grating cries of roosters before the dawn. She treats this daily disruption as an annoyance; as the poem goes on, it comes to seem more like an assault. The roosters are fancied as presiding over every bedstead, invading every privacy of the town she inhabits. They strut and swagger, and fight each other for dominance, in a heedless and brutal spectacle, all for the sake of projecting a "senseless order" over the town. But here the poem breaks off, and the poet considers a revised image of the scene, which she calls "the pivot." A cock crowed to signal Peter's betrayal of Christ; yet this brought the recognition that saved him: he saw only then that he was guilty. Thinking of her own betrayals, the poet wonders if the dreadful cries may not be a reminder of sin and therefore a blessing in the end. Her meditation closes with dawn realized, in what now seems, more plainly than it did before, the setting of an aubade. *How can the night have come to grief?* The conventional question addresses her love and what it has done to itself, as much as it laments the ruin of her dreams by the harsh noises of the morning. But the roosters no longer dominate her thoughts. Instead, there is a gentler bird, the swallow, its belly touched by the pink light; and there is the possibly hopeful image of the sun climbing in her window: a male, like the roosters that heralded him, rather more pagan than Christian, but "faithful as enemy, or friend."

Bishop wrote "Roosters" early in 1940. Until then, she had submitted most of her work to Moore for comment or revision. This was an arrangement of deference, well understood on both sides, and with decorums carefully observed by Bishop, even when she chose not to take the advice. But I can give a better idea of the implicitness of their friendship by recounting a curious incident. When, without consultation, Bishop sent her story "In Prison" to *Partisan Review* and told Moore she had done so, she received a jesting, maybe only half-jesting, reproof. It had been independent of her, said Moore, to try to publish the story alone, and if it was returned with a printed slip that would be why. The tenor of the comment may suggest a sort of preceptorial gravity from which any sane beneficiary would plot to escape. Yet I think that Bishop for her part sometimes overestimated Marianne Moore's conventionality—or tended to heighten, in her own conception of it, the severity of Moore's sense of imaginative virtue. The story "In Prison," for example, she did eventually show to Moore, after a lot of disclaimers. Moore did not deprecate its modernist and psychological procedures, as Bishop had feared she would, but wrote a letter full of subtle and discriminating criticism, in which she announced that "you and Dr. Niebuhr are two abashing peaks in present experience for me." The same letter of May 1, 1938, goes on to say that she feels a scruple in praising Bishop, from a fear of spoiling her; and there follows this extraordinary paragraph:

On the other hand,—Dr. Niebuhr says Christianity is too much on the defensive, that it is more mysterious, more comprehensive, more lastingly deep and dependable than unsuccessfully simpler substitutes which objectors to it offer; and I feel that although large-scale "substance" runs the risk of inconsequence through aesthetic impotence, and am one of those who despise clamor about substance—to whom treatment really *is* substance— I can't help wishing you would sometime in some way, risk some unprotected profundity of experience; or since no one admits profundity of experience, some characteristic private defiance of the significantly detestable. Continuously fascinated as I am by the creativeness and uniqueness of these assemblings of yours—which are really poems—I feel responsibility against anything that might threaten you; yet fear to admit

such anxiety, lest I influence you away from an essential necessity or particular strength. The golden eggs can't be dealt with theoretically, by pre-
sumptuous mass salvation formulae. But I do feel that tentativeness and
interiorizing are your danger as well as your strength.

What most compels notice in this judgment is the warning it gives against
self-protectiveness and inconsequence—even "that weapon, self-protectiveness" and the power of "feigned inconsequence"—and the encouragement it gives to "some characteristic private defiance of the significantly
detestable." For *significantly* we may read *publicly* detestable. Hence
Moore's reiterated emphasis on the strength such a gesture would require.

"Roosters" seems to me an answer to this letter, and to the imperative it
contained: so much so that the poem carries a special authority for
Bishop's career as a whole. Any reader, but especially a male reader, is
bound to think of it as a strong utterance, in something like an objective
sense. From beginning to end it covers the whole range from satire to
prayer—from, if a parallel is wanted in Moore's work, the register of "To
Be Liked by You Would Be a Calamity" to that of "In Distrust of Merits."
I can point a moral by saying it is a poem of significantly characteristic private detestation, against all the acknowledged and audible legislators of
the world whom the poet finds arrayed against herself, and whom she explicitly identifies as male. Bishop remarked in a letter to Moore that she
had written the poem with thoughts of the recent Nazi invasions and the
overrunning of small towns in Norway and Finland. Just a glimpse of that
motive appears in the fantastic interlude of "Roosters" in which the fighting cocks become fighter planes vying to outmaneuver each other for a
kill:

> Now in mid-air
> by twos they fight each other.
> Down comes a first flame-feather,
>
> and one is flying,
> with raging heroism defying
> even the sensation of dying.
>
> And one has fallen,
> but still above the town
> his torn-out, bloodied feathers drift down;
>
> and what he sung
> no matter. He is flung
> on the gray ash-heap, lies in dung

with his dead wives
with open, bloody eyes,
while those metallic feathers oxidize.

It is this repulsive image that will prompt the transition, "St. Peter's sin /
was worse than that of Magdalene," and lead to the poet's suggestion that
the revenge she takes in this poem is short-sighted; that "deny" is not all
the roosters cry; that, in her own denials, she resembles them more nearly
than she had supposed. But the stanzas above are worth dwelling on a
little longer.

Something of their animus came, I believe, from Bishop's reading of
another poem by Moore, the satirical ode "To Military Progress." Though
the creature it addresses is never specified, we do know that he grinds
chaff, unlike the prize bird who was oblivious to "the chaff / that every
wind sends spinning from the rick"; and again, that he is a petty creature
or contrivance, with a good deal of just that barnyard absurdity which the
prize bird had scorned. Here is the poem:

You use your mind
like a millstone to grind
   chaff.
You polish it
and with your warped wit
   laugh

at your torso,
prostrate where the crow
   falls
on such faint hearts
as its god imparts,
   calls

and claps its wings
till the tumult brings
   more
black minute-men
to revive again
   war

at little cost.
They cry for the lost
   head
and seek their prize
till the evening sky's
   red.

A striking feature of the poem's movement is the effect of sudden magnification and miniaturization, whereby a gigantic torso that is seen close up yields, without quite fading or dissolving into, the tumult of "black minute-men" who swarm as if framed in an aerial perspective. The same kind of shift occurs in "Roosters," but in a reverse direction: from the distant, small, and merely irritating first crow of the rooster out of the "gunmetal blue dark," to the swelling into the foreground of "protruding chests / in green-gold medals dressed."

The similarities between a minor poem by Moore and an ambitious poem by Bishop would be trivial if they did not somehow catch a resonance from the larger aspirations of both poets. Yet one feels the propriety of the echo when one places "To Military Progress" alongside "Marriage," a poem of a comparable scale with "Roosters"—with its knowledge of

> the spiked hand
> that has an affection for one
> and proves it to the bone

and its testimony "that men have power / and sometimes one is made to feel it." Here we come back to the life described in "Roosters," with all those

> many wives
> who lead hens' lives
> of being courted and despised.

So when she wrote "Roosters," Bishop was, for once, moving close to the overt subject matter for which Moore's writing was famous. An early and intelligent critic, Randall Jarrell, was not quite right to classify it as an "animal-morality poem" in the vein of Moore; in procedure, it is closer to the severe poems of *Birds, Beasts, and Flowers*, such as "Tortoise Shell" and "The Ass." Yet in relation to all of Moore's early work, "Roosters" feels like a gesture of solidarity, and Bishop could reasonably have expected a sympathetic response. What she got was not exactly the opposite of that. But Moore's dealings with the poem were so characteristic, private, public, and strongly self-protective that the facts had better just be recited.

To test her scruples, Moore sent Bishop a rewritten version of the poem, entitled "The Cock," a word by comparison with which *roosters* must have seemed to her ear coarse and unclassical. She broke up some of the triple rhymes into twos or ones and elsewhere cut and rephrased—the kind of heavy revision she had occasionally tried when editing the *Dial,* as, for example, with the text of Hart Crane's "Wine Menagerie." But her minor objections, to what she took to be the poem's faults of impropriety or sophistication, were mixed up in her comments with a partly facetious, partly earnest running disputation between the two poets, concerning the permissibility of Bishop's ever using the word *water-closet*. Moore seems to have been conscious that in this instance her prudence might be taken for prudishness.

In reply, Bishop gave solid reasons for her choices in the poem; and that provoked from Moore a spirited self-defense, in a letter of October 16, 1940:

> Regarding the water-closet, Dylan Thomas, W. C. Williams, E. E. Cummings, and others, feel that they are avoiding a duty if they balk at anything like unprudishness, but I say to them, "I can't care about all things equally, I have a major effect to produce, and the heroisms of abstinence are as great as the heroisms of courage, and so are the rewards." I think it is to your credit, Elizabeth, that when I say you are not to say "water-closet," you go on saying it a little.

The heroisms of abstinence that Moore speaks of would find their proper aphorism near the end of "Armor's Undermining Modesty": "A mirror-of-steel uninsistence should countenance / continence." But her paradox in the letter I have quoted is still more decisive. The men whom she names are convicted of priggishness from having been too timid to avoid the duty of appearing unprudish. She cannot be bothered with their athletic moralism, having a "major effect to produce" for herself. This peculiarly felicitous act of exclusion is carried off in a mood of independence which Bishop would have understood well.

On the face of things, Moore's response only points to an accidental difference over manners. Why then did the major effect of "Roosters" so elude her intelligence? The answer, I believe, is connected with her gradually changing view of her own career, which I mentioned at the start. Throughout the thirties and forties, she was withdrawing from a style of polemical irony which had been vital to her early poems, just as it had been to Eliot's (an analogy she herself might have drawn, for she admired the gusto of *Sweeney Agonistes*). "Roosters," therefore, was calculated to bring to mind a part of her imagination that she wanted to be finished with. And in Moore's later work, the commanding moments frequently seem to occur as effects of *revised* satire. These are moments in which an act of moral exclusion does not show the risk of its having been ventured first as an attempt at personal derision. I have in mind, for example, the monstrous setting she built for the apparently pleasant remark, at the end of "Four Quartz Crystal Clocks," that "punctuality is not a crime." The motto, in context, refers back to the salvaged days that may come of minutes saved here and there, and it appears in that light as a warning given by "Jupiter or jour pater, the day god" to

> the cannibal Chronos
> (eater of his proxime
> newborn progeny).

This says that every inching forward of the hand of the clock, past punctuality, is an inversion of nature, on a par with the cannibal father devouring his sons. A lot of her milder-sounding jokes are coded warnings of a similar kind.

The design of passages like this, as Moore came to understand them, was finally to "attain integration too tough for infraction." By contrast, "Roosters" was all infraction, all assault, most of the way through. Yet it was following a course marked out by Moore herself, which she was only then beginning to turn away from. It chose the very weapon that she was in the process of surrendering.

What can one learn about "Roosters" from the perspective opened up by its relationship to Moore? Like "Marriage," it is a protest against the people who most fiercely threaten the poet's imaginings, and who do so with the practical sanction of worldly authority. Those people are statesmen, businessmen, soldiers, husbands. The poet, who alone can displace them, is a woman not a wife. The grotesque feeling of the poem comes from the impression it makes of accurate hatred—an emotion only to be missed by those who have been tricked into insensibility by its rhymes. The pretense which the rhymes signal, of a satisfied striving for the minor effect, is, in fact, crueler in the end, as its ironies return upon the reader, than any comparable "undermining modesty" in Moore's early writing. Yet, for the reasons I have been tracing, this was an experiment which Bishop's reading of Moore led her to try. The strange thing about the partial retraction on which "Roosters" closes is that it touches just the note of humility that would become familiar above all in Moore's later work. And yet it does so before one can point to a movement as definitive in a single poem by Moore.

Humility itself may have a tactical value, as both of these poets recognized. Moore showed what that could mean in the way she chose to rewrite the last stanza or "Roosters." "The sun," Bishop had written,

> climbs in,
> following "to see the end,"
> faithful as enemy, or friend.

Moore changed it to

> And climbing in to see the end,
> the faithful sin is here,
> as enemy, or friend.

That version is weaker than Bishop's as poetry for the same reason that it is clearer as morality (incorporating, as it does, the Peter-Christ parable, which Bishop left implicit at the close). Moore's revision, however, seems to me in line with the poem's argument in the last several stanzas. For by that point it has become a petition for forgiveness. It is the nature of roosters, Bishop concedes, to annoy, hector, tear, and fight for command. Though they break in to the poet's sleep and the dreaming life that comes with sleep, their denials are not unlike hers; as, for that matter, their "active displacements in perspective" are not unlike hers. One may recall the sound like the grating of a wet match that first brings their cries to consciousness, and then recall "The Bight," "At the Fishhouses," "The Armadillo," and "The End of March," where a similar sensation always seems to be closely linked with the work of a powerful imagining.

As for Bishop's reasons for seeking forgiveness, they will remain obscure only so long as we look at her as a citizen and not a poet. Like the creatures she denounces, she is a reshaper of things in the world, and others will live with what she makes. There is one kind of poetry in an inventive reading of maps, another kind in the overrunning of actual places on a map of conquest. Either way, the aim is to make a senseless order prevail. So Bishop's allusion to "marking out maps like Rand McNally's" is not the innocent detail it seems. It is carefully placed in this poem, by an author for whom "The Map" would become a kind of signature. Her sense, in allying herself with the roosters, of a complicity in all that she hates, may suggest that the withdrawal from satire here allowed Bishop to escape from a graver turning against herself. A corresponding shift from invective to prayer would enter Moore's work with "In Distrust of Merits." The black minute-men of "To Military Progress" are still there ("O small dust of the earth / that walks so arrogantly"), but the poet goes on to observe, "There never was a war that was not inward." It is a fine summing-up of everything Bishop wanted us to feel at the statuary scene that makes "the pivot" of "Roosters":

> Christ stands amazed,
> Peter, two fingers raised,
> to surprised lips, both as if dazed.

For betrayal haunts all language and all gesticulation, from the most personal acts to those that implicate a whole society.

I have been speaking of the parallels between Moore and Bishop, and the mutual loyalties of their poetry, as if Bishop's own judgment of the essential difference between them ought to be taken for granted. So it ought to be by the reader who aims to value them as individuals. Yet there remains a sense in which Bishop, toward the end of her career, drew closer to Moore's pattern than might have been predicted of the author of "Roosters." She, too, came to "dominate the stream in an attitude / of self-defense," to borrow Moore's words from "Critics and Connoisseurs." There is a feeling both of loss and of tenacious reserve in the way she reveals her consciousness of this fact. It will come out plainly, I suspect, when we can read her letters to Robert Lowell, whose self-exertion was as foreign to her and as marvelous as her imagination was to him. Within her own poetry, Bishop left a clue to her path of development in the latest of her poems that may still be read as an homage to Moore. I mean "The Armadillo," of which the unusable title must have been "Another Armored Animal."

Bishop's personal emblem in that poem has become *"a weak mailed fist / clenched ignorant against the sky."* No longer staunch against defeat like Moore's prize bird, this creature in its retiring way is successfully blind to the prospect of destruction. As a fable about both poets, "The Armadillo" makes a more poignant tribute than the more explicit "Invitation to Miss Marianne Moore." But the lovely and underminingly modest later poem—begun as a prose encomium for the "Moore issue" of a quarterly— may be taken to round off the story. Bishop there salutes as characteristic properties of Marianne Moore's writing her "dynasties of negative constructions" which, she says, go to form "a long unnebulous train of words." My aim has been to show that the words are unnebulous because they protect the mind of a poet without mass salvation formulae; that the constructions are negative because they often have at heart the purpose of bowing someone out.

1990

Elizabeth Bishop's Dream-Houses

In a very striking passage of "Roosters," Elizabeth Bishop turns to address the shiny, gloating, and definitively male creatures whose cries disturb her sleep:

> each one an active
> displacement in perspective;
> each screaming, "This is where I live!"
>
> Each screaming
> "Get up! Stop dreaming!"
> Roosters, what are your projecting?

The sleeper, as she tells us in another poem, eventually recovers from these assaults and continues to inhabit "my proto-dream-house, / my crypto-dream-house, that crooked box / set up on pilings." She has taken in enough of the roosters' admonitions to concede, "Many things about this place are dubious." But the force of her rhetorical question—"What are *you* projecting?"—suggests a reserve of personal strength. Bishop's own poems are active displacements of perspective. They too project a warning about where she lives, and they have the authority of dreams rather than awakenings.

That she was praised throughout her career for a humbler kind of success is doubtless just as well: charitable misunderstandings help an artist to go on working quietly. Yet it is worth recalling the standard terms of this praise, for they reveal how little had changed in the years that separate Bishop's first appearance from that of Emily Dickinson. Admirers of "Success is counted sweetest" (who thought it probably the work of Emerson) were replaced by encouragers of the best woman poet in English. And a sure ground of appreciation for so special a performer was taken to be her "accuracy." What did that mean? Not, evidently, that she adapted the same style to different situations, and not that she changed all the time, with a relentless originality. It was an aesthetic compliment, difficult to translate into English. Similarly, Bishop was prized for her "charm." In the sense of a warm sociability, she certainly was not charming, least of all when she meant to be, as in her poems about the poor. In any other sense, charm is a tedious virtue for a poet, just as conventional accuracy may be a vice. And yet, in spite of their evasiveness, both words converge on a trait which all of Bishop's readers have felt in her poems: the presence of an irresistible self-trust. To her, art is a kind of home. She makes her accommodations with an assurance that is full of risk, and, for her as for Dickinson, the domestic tenor of some poems implies a good-natured defiance of the readers she does not want. The readers she cares for, on the other hand, are not so much confided in as asked to witness her self-recoveries, which have the quality of a shared premise. Her work is a conversation which never quite takes place but whose possibility always beckons.

My point of departure in testing what this feels like in practice is an early poem, "The Monument." Bishop appears to have conceived it as an oblique eulogy for herself, and she frames it deferentially enough to suit a posthumous occasion. The poem's authority and weight have less in common with modern inventions like Joseph Cornell's boxes than they do with an older tradition of immortality—"Not marble, nor the gilded monuments / Of princes, shall outlast this pow'rful rhyme." We are well-advised at the start not to measure a sure distance between those lines and these:

> Now can you see the monument? It is of wood
> built somewhat like a box. No. Built
> like several boxes in descending sizes
> one above the other.
> Each is turned half-way round so that
> its corners point toward the sides
> of the one below and the angles alternate.
> Then on the topmost cube is set
> a sort of fleur-de-lys of weathered wood,
> long petals of board, pierced with odd holes,
> four-sided, stiff, ecclesiastical.

Irony, in one of its meanings, is a pretense of concern in a speaker, for the sake of revising a listener's whole structure of concerns; the pretense here is that Bishop's listener, in order to cherish the monument, need only hear it described just so. She patiently adjusts the description ("It is X. No. Like several X's . . . ") to anticipate any complaint, as later in the poem she will give the listener a more official embodiment by composing speeches for him. All this self-qualification is a gravely enacted farce. When it is over we will find ourselves still staring at the monument and rehearsing what she has said about it, until we see that the object of the poem was to compel our attention without giving reasons.

In the course of the one-woman narration, with its imagined interruptions, we listeners are permitted exactly four objections to the monument. These may be summarized abstractly: I don't understand what this thing is trying to be; I've never seen anything hang together like this; It's just too makeshift to succeed; and, What are you trying to prove, anyway? In short, museum-boredom ("Big deal; take me somewhere else"), which the poet meets at first with a curatorial delicacy. But her final speech, which takes up almost a third of the poem, overcomes all defensiveness and simply expands the categorical authority of her earlier statement, "It is the monument."

> It is an artifact
> of wood. Wood holds together better
> than sea or cloud or sand could by itself,
> much better than real sea or sand or cloud.
> It chose that way to grow and not to move.
> The monument's an object, yet those decorations,
> carelessly nailed, looking like nothing at all,
> give it away as having life, and wishing;
> wanting to be a monument, to cherish something.
> The crudest scroll-work says "commemorate,"
> while once each day the light goes around it
> like a prowling animal,
> or the rain falls on it, or the wind blows into it.
> It may be solid, may be hollow.
> The bones of the artist-prince may be inside
> or far away on even drier soil.
> But roughly but adequately it can shelter
> what is within (which after all
> cannot have been intended to be seen).
> It is the beginning of a painting,
> a piece of sculpture, or poem, or monument,
> and all of wood. Watch it closely.

This ending allies "The Monument" with other American appeals to the power of metaphor to shape a life, particularly Frost's "A Star in a Stone-

Boat" and Stevens's "Someone Puts a Pineapple Together." Even in their company, Bishop's poem keeps on growing as one thinks of it. It has perhaps less invention than they have; but then, it presumes a questioner suspicious of all that is new; and its persistent skepticism is a grace equal to any exuberance.

Earlier in the poem, still explaining the look of the monument itself, Bishop had composed a diagram of the viewer's relation to what he sees, which may also be read as a geometric proof of her own power over her readers.

> The monument is one-third set against
> a sea; two-thirds against a sky.
> The view is geared
> (that is, the view's perspective)
> so low there is no "far away,"
> and we are far away within the view.

I take the first five lines to mean that our eye is placed just above horizon level, so that the whole sky and sea appear as a flat vertical backdrop, without depth and therefore without any far or near. But in what sense can we be said to be "far away within the view"? It must be that the view looks out at us too, as through the wrong end of a telescope, from a perspective capable of absorbing everything: it takes us in as it pleases. Indeed, the monument can contain the world, by implication. That is the sense of the listener's disturbed question, "Are we in Asia Minor, / or in Mongolia?"— site of "Kubla Khan," where a kindred monument was decreed by imaginative fiat. So the poem says here, with the metaphor of perspective, what it says at the end by the rhetoric of conjecture: an active mind alone makes the world cohere, as "Wood holds together better / than sea or cloud or sand could by itself, / much better than real sea or sand or cloud." The flat declaration, "It chose that way to grow and not to move," only seems to announce a faith in the autonomy of art objects; Bishop returns us to the human bias of the thing, by her emphasis on those features of the monument which "give it away as having life, and wishing; / wanting to be a monument, to cherish something." Before it can be, it must want to be something. And we read it for whatever spirit it communicates; we cannot do more than watch. But we are accompanied by the prowling sun which also keeps watch—a casual sublimity, the reward of the poet's discovery of a shelter uniquely right for herself. It is an image to which Bishop will return in "The End of March," where the "lion sun . . . who perhaps had batted a kite out of the sky to play with," is mysteriously connected with the wire leading out from her dream-house "to something off behind the dunes."

The monument will do for a figure of a poem, which turns out to be an allegory of what it is to *make* anything in the optative mood. A figure of a poet appears in the more straightforward allegory called "The Man-Moth." In a brief note, Bishop traces the title to a newspaper misprint for "mammoth," but the reason for its appeal to her is plain when one remembers the man-moth of Shelley's *Epipsychidion:*

> Then, from the caverns of my dreamy youth
> I sprang, as one sandalled with plumes of fire,
> And towards the loadstar of my one desire,
> I flitted, like a dizzy moth, whose flight
> Is as a dead leaf's in the owlet light,
> When it would seek in Hesper's setting sphere
> A radiant death, a fiery sepulchre.

Part of Bishop's aim is to translate this image of the poet to a less radiant climate—that of the modern city—where his quest can take on the shape of an almost biological compulsion.

> Up the façades,
> his shadow dragging like a photographer's cloth behind him,
> he climbs fearfully, thinking that this time he will manage
> to push his small head through that round clean opening
> and be forced through, as from a tube, in black scrolls on the light.
> (Man, standing below him, has no such illusions.)
> But what the Man-Moth fears most he must do, although
> he fails, of course, and falls back scared but quite unhurt.

Where the monument chose a certain way to be, the Man-Moth acts without a will: his quest is merely a condition of existence. It is as if he were born knowing *there is a creature (and you are he) who does all of this*—climbs skyscrapers because he "thinks the moon is a small hole at the top of the sky"; travels backward in underground trains, where he dreams recurrent dreams; and through all his risks, looks on mortality as a "disease he has inherited the susceptibility to." He is defined not by his activity but by the contrast he makes with man, who

> does not see the moon; he observes only her vast properties,
> feeling the queer light on his hands, neither warm nor cold,
> of a temperature impossible to record in thermometers.

Man's shadow is no bigger than his hat; the Man-Moth's is almost palpable, trailing "like a photographer's cloth behind him"; and one is reminded that "shadow" is still our best English word for *figura*. In a way that can be shown but not said, the Man-Moth, by being what he is, interprets man to himself. But the poem makes a lighter fable of this. Like any other second-storey artist, the rogue hero abstracts a few choice possessions from his victim and flees the scene.

How his theft may be retrieved is the subject of Bishop's final stanza, which is addressed to man, still "observing" and coldly utilitarian.

> If you catch him,
> hold up a flashlight to his eye. It's all dark pupil,
> an entire night itself, whose haired horizon tightens
> as he stares back, and closes up the eye. Then from the lids
> one tear, his only possession, like the bee's sting, slips.
> Slyly he palms it, and if you're not paying attention
> he'll swallow it. However, if you watch, he'll hand it over,
> cool as from underground springs and pure enough to drink.

The Man-Moth's eye is "an entire night itself," a complete image of the world of the earth's surface, where he seeks what is most different from himself. The object of his quest he calls a tiny hole of light; man, less interestingly, calls it the moon. To reach it would mean suffusion by the light and hence, to an eye all pupil, destruction. The Man-Moth, however, is sustained by the fantasy of an ascent through "that round clean opening," and of being forced "in black scrolls on the light." In this dream of consummation he would become his writing.

One may interpret the dream as expressing and concealing a hope that some principle of self will survive the dissolution of the body. Of course, the fallacy is easy to expose: immortality is not a form of health to which one can inherit a susceptibility. Yet this analysis gives no comfort to man, about whom we have heard it said that "Man, standing below, has no such illusions"; for the compliment holds in reserve a fierce irony: "Man, standing below, has no such ambitions." Nor does Bishop herself want to dismantle our illusions. She is interested in the use we make of everything the illusion-bound creature brings back from his journeys. This is figured in the poem as a hardly calculable refreshment, with the character almost of a bodily secretion. The Man-Moth's "one tear, his only possession, like the bee's sting," may be his gift to us. The image comes close to a hackneyed sentiment about perfection and pain, and hovers near an allusion to Keats's "Ode on Melancholy," but it slips free of both. One may easily feel an unintended poignancy—the reader, like the map-printer in another of Bishop's poems, "here experiencing the same excitement / as when emotion too far exceeds its cause." But the tear is not really a possession, the light that produced it after all was man's, and both parties seem amenable to the exchange. Our acceptance of every curiosity in the poem owes something to its conscious urbanity: the opening line even gives us the "battered moonlight" of a cityscape—battered by too much jingling in the pockets of too many songwriters, but still salvageable by one poet. In other poems by Bishop, the same word evokes a larger freedom with imagery that looks worn or already found: the fish that is "battered and venerable / and homely"; the big tin basin, "battered and shiny like the moon." "The Man-Moth" and "The Monument" go beyond the dignity of statement—the somewhat ponderous naturalism—that such diction has usually aimed to license and keep honest. They stand apart from the poems of Bishop's generation in the stubbornness with which they try ingenuity by the test of prosaic heft.

TO AN EXCEPTIONAL degree in modern poetry, Bishop's work offers resistance to any surmise about the personality of the author. One reason is that the poems themselves have been so carefully furnished with eccentric details or gestures. These may seem tokens of companionability, yet a certain way into a poem the atmosphere grows a little chill; further in, as the conversation strolls on, one senses the force field of a protective ease. On rereading Bishop's work, the question likeliest to recur is: what are the poems concealing? It helps, I think, to frame this as a question about a difficult passage—for example, the pathos of some lines near the end of "Crusoe in England," in which Crusoe describes the objects that recall his years of solitude.

> The knife there on the shelf—
> it reeked of meaning, like a crucifix.
> It lived. How many years did I
> beg it, implore it, not to break?
> I knew each nick and scratch by heart,
> the bluish blade, the broken tip,
> the lines of wood-grain on the handle . . .
> Now it won't look at me at all.

Like many comparable passages of her work, the description is weirdly circumstantial. What does it mean for a poet who is a woman to write, as a man, of an object so nearly linked with masculine assertion, with this mingling of tenderness, pity, and regret?

The poetic answer, which has to do with the cost of art to life, does not exclude the sexual one, which has to do with an ambivalent femininity. The poet's own weapons in art as in life have been more dear to her than she can easily confess. The punishment for deserting them is that they refuse to return her gaze; they lose their aura and she ceases to be a poet. A similar recognition is implied in other poems, where a wish to conquer or dominate—resisted at first, then acted on—darkens the celebration of having come through every challenge. Thus "The Armadillo" moves from horror of a creature, quite distant from the poet, to wonder at the same creature, which in the meantime has been implicitly identified with her. She devotes a poem to the armadillo because it is a survivor, forearmed against any catastrophe. Like her, it watches in safety a dangerous and beautiful spectacle, the drifting of the "frail, illegal fire balloons" which at any moment may splatter "like an egg of fire / against the cliff." As for the poet herself, the poem is proof of her armor. In the same way, in "Roosters" she is a second and unmentioned crier of the morning; the poem, with its "horrible insistence" three notes at a time, announces exactly where she lives.

These identifications go deep. Such poems are not, in fact, animal-morality pieces, in the vein of Marianne Moore. They more nearly resemble Lawrence's "Fish," "The Ass," "Tortoise Shell," and "Tortoise Family Connections"—protestant inquests concerning the powers of the self, which have the incidental form of free-verse chants about animals. Bishop writes without Lawrence's spontaneous humor, and without his weakness for quick vindications. Indeed, there is something like self-reproach in a line that begins the final movement of "Roosters": "how could the night have come to grief?" By a trick of context, this phrase opens up an ambiguity in the cliché. It warns us that there has been matter for grieving during the night, before the first rooster crowed, at a scene of passion which was also a betrayal. "The Armadillo" too reveals the complicity of love with strife, in its italicized last stanza; here the last line and a half make a chiasmus, in which strength is surrounded by a yielding vulnerability.

> *Too pretty, dreamlike mimicry!*
> *O falling fire and piercing cry*
> *and panic, and a weak mailed fist*
> *clenched ignorant against the sky!*

"Weak" and "ignorant" are meant to temper the surprise of the "mailed fist clenched," and they cast doubt on those three central words: the fist, emblem of contest, is defended by weakness and ignorance, its only outward fortifications. The gesture of defiance, however, becomes all the more persuasive with this glimpse of a possible defeat. The way "The Armadillo" comes to rest has felt tentative to some readers, and yet the only question it asks is rhetorical: "See how adequately I shelter my victory." In other poems just as surely, an elaborate craft gives away the poet as always present, at a scene she has painted as uninhabitable. The repeated line in a well-known poem, "One Art," will declare her control by rhyming "disaster" with "The art of losing isn't hard to master"; as if we could expect her endurance to be taxing of course, but no more doubtful than her ability to pair off the words in a villanelle.

Sexuality is the most elusive feature of Bishop's temperament—before writing any of the poems in *North & South,* she had learned to allegorize it subtly—and the reticence of her critics alone makes its existence worth noting. Like other habitual concerns, it interests her as it joins a care for what she sometimes calls the soul. This is an argument carried on from poem to poem, but its first appearance, in "The Imaginary Iceberg," is startling.

> Icebergs behoove the soul
> (both being self-made from elements least visible)
> to see them so: fleshed, fair, erected indivisible.

Until these concluding lines the poem has been a light entertainment, a "Convergence of the Twain" told from the iceberg's point of view. The lines shift our perspective on everything that came before—in effect, they translate a poem which did not seem to need translation. "Fleshed, fair, erected indivisible": the words, we see at once, belong to the human body rather than the soul. They are monstrously beautiful because they are a lie. For in the metaphor about the soul which has been perfectly built up, the comparison demands instead: cold, white, immense, indestructible. This yields a pleasant description of an iceberg which, when we ponder it, is replaced by a sublime representation of the soul.

It is characteristic of Bishop's wit that she should have begun the same poem fancifully: "We'd rather have the iceberg than the ship, / although it meant the end of travel." Translating, as the poem suggests we do, this becomes: "We'd rather have the soul than the body, / although it meant the end of life." Yet for Bishop travel is not a chance metaphor. It stands for all that can divert the soul from its prospects. To hold fast to what it knows, may mean for the soul to remain always "stock-still like cloudy rock"; or like a mariner, curled asleep at the top of a mast or seated with his eyes closed tight, untouchable by the charms of the voyage. This is the condition of "the unbeliever" in the poem of that title: believing only in himself, he knows "The sea is hard as diamonds; it wants to destroy us all." With his intensity perhaps, the soul may be equal to the imaginary iceberg which "cuts its facets from within. / Like jewelry from a grave / it saves itself and adorns / only itself." The phrase "from a grave," as it finally seems, is not fanciful at all but descriptive. It says that a guarding of the soul's integrity may also be a defense against death. The sense in which this is especially true for a poet is the sense that matters to Bishop.

THE TITLES of three of Bishop's volumes *(North & South, Questions of Travel, Geography III)* show how far she accepted—at times rather flatly—the common opinion that travel was her distinctive subject. Yet few readers are likely to know even a single region as intimately as she knew two hemispheres; and to make her geography poems interesting we have to read them as poems about something else. With this need of ours, a whole tract of her writing refuses to cooperate: poems about squatters and other half-cherished neighbors—efforts of self-conscious whimsy (like "Manuelzinho") or of awkward condescension (like "Filling Station"). I think these are the only poems Bishop ever wrote that dwindle as one comes to see them more clearly. One has to move away from these in order to learn what must have been clear to her from the first: that geography carries interest as a figure of the soul's encounter with fate (or as she puts it, with "what we imagine knowledge to be"). Occasionally, in the terms she proposes for this encounter, Bishop echoes the hero of Stevens's *Comedian as the Letter C,* who sought

> an elemental fate,
> And elemental potencies and pangs,
> And beautiful barenesses as yet unseen,
> Making the most of savagery.

But the poems I have in mind all end in a distrust of these things. In them, the dream of freedom, under the aspect of a perpetual self-renewal, is interpreted as a helpless revolt against the conditions of experience. The poet, however, offers no hope that we shall ever escape the enchantment of the dream.

"Brazil, January 1, 1502" marks the conquistadors' first step into a trap, a vast mesh of circumstance disguised as a jungle, and cozily misnamed "the new world." The poem starts off, innocuously, with an epigraph from Sir Kenneth Clark, "embroidered nature . . . tapestried landscape."

> Januaries, Nature greets our eyes
> exactly as she must have greeted theirs:
> every square inch filling in with foliage—

> big leaves, little leaves, and giant leaves,
> blue, blue-green, and olive,
> with occasional lighter veins and edges,
> or a satin underleaf turned over.

It is all, she goes on to say (confirming her epigraph) "solid but airy; fresh as if just finished / and taken off the frame." Courteously artful, we are like the conquistadors in supposing that we can make nature over in a language we know—for them, the language of tapestry, for us that of naturalistic description. In either case we reproduce the nature prized by a Western connoisseur of art; and the poem is about how we cannot ever effect the conversion without loss. Nature will always take its revenge by drawing us still farther in, and suspending our knowledge of the thing that claims our pursuit.

So, in the next stanza, the tapestry is described as "a simple web"—a moral text, its foreground occupied by "Sin: / five sooty dragons near some massy rocks." Even after these have been naturalized as lizards, Bishop tells us "all eyes / are on the smaller, female one, back to, / her wicked tail straight up and over, / red as a red-hot wire." Between then and now, the allegorical and the natural, the poem admits no disparity— none, anyway, to compete with the similarity implied by such imperial habits of seeing. Hence the appropriateness of the poem's grammatical structure. "*As* then, *so* now." This structure is completed only in the third and last stanza, which reverses the order of the comparison. As we find it now, not unfamiliar,

> Just so the Christians, hard as nails,
> tiny as nails, and glinting,
> in creaking armor, came and found it all,
> not unfamiliar:
> no lovers' walks, no bowers,
> no cherries to be picked, no lute music,
> but corresponding, nevertheless,
> to an old dream of wealth and luxury
> already out of style when they left home—
> wealth plus a brand-new pleasure.
> Directly after Mass, humming perhaps
> *L'Homme armé* or some such tune,
> they ripped away into the hanging fabric,
> each out to catch an Indian for himself—
> those maddening little women who kept calling,
> calling to each other (or had the birds waked up?)
> and retreating, always retreating, behind it.

In the light of this ending, the poem may be read as a colonial dream of all that seems infinitely disposable in the colonized.

But it is also about something that evades our grasp in every object that appeals to the human love of conquest. The Indian women, "those maddening little women who kept calling, / calling to each other"—but not to their pursuers—only repeat the attraction of the female lizard, "her wicked tail straight up and over, / red as a red-hot wire." Both alike appear to beckon from behind the tapestry of the jungle fabric. They entice, and bind their spell. Another retreat will always be possible to them, since the jungle has gone opaque to the men hunting them, who believe at every point that it is transparent. This is another way of saying that the invaders have become victims of their own conquering perspective. They recreate here "an old dream of wealth and luxury"; yet the dream was "already out of style when they left home"; and the new place, as disclosed to other eyes, has seemed far from homelike. In the end their crossing of this threshold, "hard as nails, / tiny as nails," says most about their sense of home, which was equally marked by a failure of knowledge. What they take to be an act of possession is not, therefore, even a successful repossession, but the enactment of a familiar ritual of self-deception.

This poem shows Bishop moving well outside the limits of the travel sketch. By itself, it is almost enough to persuade us that she exploits the genre elsewhere chiefly to break with it, from an impulse comparable to Dickinson's in revising the poem of "home thoughts." At any rate the sketch that goes furthest to appease the worldly taste of her readers carries a suspicious title, "Over 2,000 Illustrations and a Complete Concordance," and the steady mystification of its narrative seems bent on protracting our suspicion. The poem, with an unsettling confidence, treats worldliness as a form of literal reading that is death—but the title is worth pausing over. What is a concordance? A system of reference to all the uses of every important word in the Bible, or for that matter in any sacred book, including the work of a great poet. The illustrations accompanying it may be pictures—the picture-postcard atmosphere of much of the poem will toy with this—yet they are as likely to be passages longer than a phrase, which give a fuller context for the entries. When reading a concordance, we do not look at individual words to be sure of their reference, but to satisfy ourselves of a fateful pattern of choice. From the sum of an author's repetitions, we may learn a tact for whatever is irreducible in his character. "Over 2000 Illustrations" owes its force to the propriety with which one can substitute both "reader" and "traveller" for "author," and view a place in the world as denoting a place in a text.

The thought that troubles Bishop at the start is that the book of nature and history may not be either a clean text or an already canonical one, whether Bible or secular fiction, but something more like just such a concordance, with occasional glimpses into its depths coming from the illustrations alone.

> Thus should have been our travels:
> serious, engravable.
> The Seven Wonders of the World are tired
> and a touch familiar, but the other scenes,
> innumerable, though equally sad and still,
> are foreign. Often the squatting Arab,
> or group of Arabs, plotting, probably,
> against our Christian Empire,
> while one apart, with outstretched arm and hand
> points to the Tomb, the Pit, the Sepulcher.
> The branches of the date-palms look like files.
> The cobbled courtyard, where the Well is dry,
> is like a diagram, the brickwork conduits
> are vast and obvious, the human figure
> far gone in history or theology,
> gone with its camel or its faithful horse.
> Always the silence, the gesture, the specks of birds
> suspended on invisible threads above the Site,
> or the smoke rising solemnly, pulled by threads.

The broken, randomly spliced rhythm of this opening, the discreteness of its sentences, as well as the words "often" and "always," suggest the episodic quality of the moments chronicled in the illustrations. They tell a story, apparently senseless, and in no particular order, which the poem later calls the story of "God's spreading fingerprint." Only the Christians in the illustrations make a connection from place to place; and in the margin, everywhere, are faintly sinister Arabs, plotting or "looking on amused": together, these figures give it the unity it has. But as the account moves on, it grows still more oddly inconsequential: "In Mexico the dead man lay / in the blue arcade; the dead volcanoes / glistened like Easter lilies. / The jukebox went on playing 'Ay, Jalisco!'" The blare of the jukebox comes in when the story's meaning appears to have been surely lost, and it signals a transition. Now the tone of the illustrations (which somehow have become cheap guidebook images) drifts toward the hallucinatory:

And in the brothels of Marrakesh
the little pockmarked prostitutes
balanced their tea-trays on their heads
and did their belly dances; flung themselves
naked and giggling against our knees,
asking for cigarettes. It was somewhere near there
I saw what frightened me most of all:
A holy grave, not looking particularly holy,
one of a group under a keyhole-arched stone baldaquin
open to every wind from the pink desert.

By the last five lines of this passage, every worldly fact has been rendered exchangeable with every other, and the loss is of nothing less than the history and the pathos of the things one may come to know.

Bishop is frightened "most of all" by the suddenly exposed grave in the desert because it reminds her of a life emptied of causes and consequences, with "Everything only connected by 'and' and 'and.'" The conclusion of the poem brings together author, reader, and traveller a last time, and envisions a sort of text that would return attention to something beyond it.

Everything only connected by "and" and "and."
Open the book. (The gilt rubs off the edges
of the pages and pollinates the fingertips.)
Open the heavy book. Why couldn't we have seen
this old Nativity while we were at it?
—the dark ajar, the rocks breaking with light,
an undisturbed, unbreathing flame,
colorless, sparkless, freely fed on straw,
and, lulled within, a family with pets,
—and looked and looked our infant sight away.

Much less than everything is restored by this ending. Though the holy book, once opened, confronts us with an ideal representation of our origins, we have to read it uninnocently. We know how thoroughly we have revised it already by our later imaginings, by every arrangement which makes the end of a life or work distort its beginning. To deny our remoteness from the scene would be to cancel the very experience which permits us to pass through "the dark ajar." So we stand with the poet, both in the scene and outside it, uncertain whether pleasure is the name for what we feel. Her wishfully innocent question—"Why couldn't we have seen / this old Nativity while we were at it?"—has the tone of a child's pleading, "Why couldn't we *stay* there?"—said of a home, or a place that has grown sufficiently like home. Some time or other we say that about childhood it-self. The book, then, is hard to open because it is hard to admit the strength of such a plea; harder still, to hear it for what it says about our re-lationship to ourselves. Any place we live in, savage or homely, dream-house or rough shelter, we ourselves have been the making of. And yet, once made, it is to be inherited forever. Everything may be connected by "because" and "therefore," and every connection will be provisional. The last line accordingly yields an ambiguous truth about nostalgia: to look our sight away is to gaze our fill, but also to look until we see differently—until, in our original terms, we do not see at all. The line, however, war-rants a more general remark about Bishop's interest in the eye. In common with Wordsworth, she takes the metaphor of sight to imply the activity of all the senses, and these in turn to represent every possibility of conscious being. Sight is reliable because it can give no account of itself. We make it mean only when we look again, with "that inward eye / Which is the bliss of solitude" (words, incidentally, which the hero of "Crusoe in England" tries reciting to himself on the island, but can remember only after his res-cue). It is in the same poem that Wordsworth says of the daffodils, "I gazed—and gazed"; and the action of "The Fish" turns on this single con-centrated act: "I stared and stared," and the colors of the boat change to "rainbow, rainbow, rainbow," and she lets the fish go.

In passing from sight to vision, or to "what is within (which after all / cannot have been intended to be seen)," Bishop always respects the claims of unbelievers different from herself. Her mood is almost always generous, in its readiness to inquire into not-yet-habitable truths; and I want to con-clude with an especially full expression of that mood, from "Love Lies Sleeping." She writes there of a dawn in a city, with eleven lines of a soft introductory cadence, good enough for the opening bars of a Gershwin tune; with a memory of the waning night and its "neon shapes / that float and swell and glare"; with a panoramic view and a long tracking view that ends in the window of one dwelling, where the poet asks the "queer cupids of all persons getting up" to be mild with their captives:

> for always to one, or several, morning comes
> whose head has fallen over the edge of his bed,
> whose face is turned
> so that the image of
>
> the city grows down into his open eyes
> inverted and distorted. No. I mean
> distorted and revealed,
> if he sees it at all.

The words are as serious and engravable as an epitaph. At the same time, with a doubt exactly the size of a comma, they point to a revelation that may have occurred, and, for the sake of its distortion as well as its truth, keep it living in surmise.

1984

NINE

The Making of the Auden Canon

This is the Auden canon as planned by Auden.* The poet who was apt to deride "accurate scholarship" would nevertheless have been pleased with the editorial job: the *Collected Poems* supplies dates and variant titles, but otherwise keeps the apparatus to a helpful minimum, and is good to the eye and the touch. We shall have to wait for a promised second volume, *The English Auden,* if we want to read the canon as a palimpsest, compare the rubbed-out edges with the bold outline laid over them, and arrive at some conclusion about the poet's character. In the meantime Auden's literary executor, Edward Mendelson, wisely cautions us to regard Auden's final change of dress as indeed final. It is. But a few intractable spirits ought to remain on the scene to ask if this was not after all another disguise. In his foreword to the *Collected Shorter Poems* (1965), Auden defended revisions "as a matter of principle" by quoting Valéry: "A poem is never finished; it is only abandoned." The allusion is not quite candid. Valéry, who was by no means of Auden's party in these matters, saw the work of a poet as forming an activity of unbroken meditation. To decide what the public should see of the meditation was a secondary worry: a fragment might be as important as a completed poem. What could a poem be for Auden, on the other hand, if not the finished expression of feeling on a given occasion?

Auden generally revised for sentiment rather than sound and, without being an exponent of "pure sound," one may raise a simple enough objection. To play the sage or pedant, and chasten the record of an earlier renegade self, is never good for the character; the results, when it is a poet who

* *W. H. Auden: Collected Poems,* ed. Edward Mendelson.

does this, are seldom happy for the poetry; and Auden is an exception to neither rule. Poetry survives, he said in his elegy for Yeats, "In the valley of its making where executives / Would never want to tamper." Poets are the first to tamper. Consider the following inconspicuous change in "Paysage Moralisé":

> It is the sorrow; shall it melt? Ah, water
> Would gush, flush, green these mountains and these valleys,
> And we rebuild our cities, not dream of islands.

The altered version gives "It is our sorrow. . . ." It is an emphatic bit of scoring, and what is gained is emphasis. But the loss is very great: the poem has given up something of its tacit strength. "Our sorrow," it insists, "yes; all of us." What was implication is now statement. *Our* and *sorrow*, by the way, do not mix well as sounds. And *our* slows down the cadence, where, in the first version, it was slowed and then halted, as if stunned, only at *sorrow*, the last word of the first sentence of the envoi.

More painful and harder to miss is a change in the Yeats elegy itself. "O all the instruments agree / The day of his death was a dark cold day" has become "What instruments we have agree. . . ." Granted, we do not have all the instruments: to say so is perhaps a stroke for moderation and truth. But the poem has stopped singing. "This Loved One," a very early poem which Yeats anthologized, used to address a "Face that the sun / Is supple on." We are now to favor "Face that the sun / Is lively on." Here it is surely sound and sound alone that disturbs the revising poet. And we did hear a slight drone in the short vowel sounds: yet it seemed right for the mostly drowsy mood of these lines. The hopeless correction is a fine flower of poetic diction.

In the mid-1940s Auden began, in bracing moral tones and on every possible occasion, to lay down the laws of modesty proper to the poet. Poetry, he had said, makes nothing happen. Nothing, that is, in particular, nothing right away, nothing to bet on: so one might have gathered too from Robert Frost's perfectly balanced appeal for the poetry of griefs against the poetry of grievances. But Auden went considerably further than this. In prose and in verse, he gave perhaps the most limited description of the aim and use of poetry that has ever come from a major poet: in his ideal world poetry is among the more harmless indoor pastimes. And of course there is a matter-of-fact equability in this view of poetry; and it made a pleasant change from the climate of Yeats and Eliot. Very successfully, Auden became the virtuoso of modesty. In art as in life, however, modesty must never be confused with sincerity. There is something bullying in Auden's desire to ingratiate, and he is out to bully himself as well as others. Here one reaches the heart of his impulse to revise. For, more than most poets, Auden in every phase was concerned to be the useful man, the man society cannot dispense with: first as the voice from the tripod, then as the licensed jester. There was an element of pathos in his quest. And if one holds the full career in mind, one will see how pervasive was his fear of isolation: the revisions are issuing, not from a conflict between one manner and its successor, but from an anxiety, which has become almost a ruling passion, about manners in general.

"Human beings," announces the narrator of *The Age of Anxiety*, "are, necessarily, actors who cannot become something before they have first pretended to be it; and they can be divided, not into the hypocritical and the sincere, but into the sane who know they are acting and the mad who do not." What a strange generalization. Play-acting, one might object, simply does not have so central a place in the lives of most of us. But to Auden the dictum seemed self-evidently true. Baudelaire writes somewhere of "the aristocratic pleasure of giving offense": equally aristocratic is the pleasure of having it in one's power to offend but holding back. And Auden's earliest role, in which he sought to offend all, and his latest, in which he offended none, were not markedly different in the demands they made on the player. Both entailed a steady awareness of the risks and attendant rewards of authority. The paradox that the word frames, with its rival connotations of power and trustworthiness, was not lost on Auden. Of his own uneasy stance he made his poetry.

The mark of his best early poetry is the widely distributed shock.

> Others have tried it and will try again
> To finish that which they did not begin:
> Their fate must always be the same as yours,
> To suffer the loss they were afraid of, yes,
> Holders of one position, wrong for years.

We once read of a similar defeat in "History to the defeated / may say alas but cannot help or pardon." But there it does not work. Auden's self-criticism as usual is disingenuous: "To say this is to equate goodness with success. It would have been bad enough if I had ever held this wicked doctrine, but that I should have stated it simply because it sounded to me rhetorically effective is quite inexcusable." In fact, the sentiment is consistent with everything Auden believed about history. The trouble is rather that these lines resist any historical context. They are brilliantly anonymous, the feeling they impart is far from local, and they should not have been kept for the end of "Spain."

Who are the "old gang" that must be killed off in Auden's early poems? Those, the poems continually assert, who have been possessed by a bad motive. The behavior they are denounced for extends from the sinks of personal cowardice to the summits of political oppression. The drawing together of two vastly different sorts of corruption, that which comes of power and that which comes of fear, is an astonishing feature of Auden's ideology. In forty years it has not ceased to be a puzzling human lapse. Yet none of the poems connected with this lapse is without canonical status. So we can still read the ballad of "Miss Gee"—Miss Gee, who, being too meek to live and too thwarted, grows a cancer and dies—and we can applaud the flat pitiless gaze of the poet.

> They laid her on the table,
>   The students began to laugh;
> And Mr Rose the surgeon
>   He cut Miss Gee in half.
>
> Mr Rose he turned to his students,
>   Said, "Gentlemen, if you please,
> We seldom see a sarcoma
>   As far advanced as this."

Or perhaps we will shudder a little, and not for the reason the poet intended. It is such an odd choice of targets for an exercise of *nil admirari*.

Courage, or the courage of these particular convictions, together with an unworried pertinacity in the campaign to disgust, Auden learned from D. H. Lawrence. To disgust on behalf of the truth, as Lawrence taught, was often in bad taste. The reader who wants a key to the attitude of Auden's early work and finds himself resisting those enjoyable but esoteric psychologists, Groddeck and Homer Lane, can do no better than to look up Lawrence's *Psychoanalysis and the Unconscious* and its sequel, *Fantasia of the Unconscious*. There he will come upon the Leader, the Group, the Wrecked Society, the Disease-Growing Neurotic, the War to the End of the Pure-in-Spirit. "The Wanderer" has its source in one of Lawrence's characteristic improvised arias, about the peace that belongs to the hero returning home. "Consider," with its celebration of the hawk's-eye view in which an absence of compassion is notable and to be admired, looks back to several passages loaded with *frisson:*

> We can see as the hawk sees the one concentrated spot where beats the life-heart of our prey. . . . Love is a thing to be *learned,* through centuries of patient effort. It is a difficult, complex maintenance of individual integrity throughout the incalculable processes of interhuman polarity. . . . Who can do it? Nobody. Yet we have all got to do it, or else suffer ascetic tortures

of starvation and privation or of distortion and overstrain and slow collapse into corruption.

But Auden can touch us as Lawrence's crank manifesto cannot. And his
moods of disgust take from the surrounding poems or lines a resonance
not merely of disgust. One sees the moods, in the end, as frank confes-
sions of weakness, of failure, of his own indebtedness to the system of illusions he hates and would dispel. For the band of heroic conspirators that
dominate his work are plainly shadowed rather than shadowing, among
the watched not the watchers. They as surely as Miss Gee are headed for
defeat; but they of all others cannot accept it. Their fate reads out its sentence, simple and laconic like the end-stop of a line of verse, in poems that
do not strike the tragic note yet have the tragic need to step quietly.

> For to be held as friend
> By an undeveloped mind,
> To be joke for children is
> Death's happiness:
>
> Whose anecdotes betray
> His favourite colour as blue,
> Colour of distant bells
> And boys' overalls.

Few of Auden's grateful readers have been tempted to solve the paradox
of an angry poetry which is most confident and most beautiful where it is
most cautious. The gratitude seems enough.

> I, decent with the seasons, move
> Different or with a different love,
> Nor question overmuch the nod,
> The stone smile of this country god
> That never was more reticent,
> Always afraid to say more than it meant.

Here at least one ought to trust the tale. Auden's poetry knows what its author sometimes forgot: that what it seeks to join—life and death, isolate
heroism and the sense of community—must remain forever parted.
There is nothing to be done. And this knowledge brings to Auden's early
poetry its unique dignity and its air of self-sufficient and unappeased lone-
liness.

Much of what Auden wrote between "The Letter" (1927) and "On This
Island" (1935) has kept its original vigor. The best of these poems, untitled
at birth but eccentrically christened in their after-years, come back to the
memory whole from the sound of their first lines: "From scars where

kestrels hover"; "Again in conversations / Speaking of fear"; "Before this loved one / Was that one and that one"; "The strings' excitement, the applauding drum"; "Will you turn a deaf ear / To what they said on the shore"; "Since you are going to begin today / Let us consider what it is you do"; "It was Easter as I walked in the public gardens"; "This lunar beauty / Has no history"; "'O where are you going' said reader to rider"; "Consider this and in our time"; "Doom is dark and deeper than any sea-dingle"; "Hearing of harvests rotting in the valleys"; and the terrifying and unforgettable refusal to forgive a happy childhood, called "Through the Looking-Glass," which begins: "Earth has turned over; our side feels the cold, / And life sinks choking in the wells of trees." On these poems rests Auden's claim as one of the great inventors of modern poetry. Leafing through Robin Skelton's anthology, *Poetry of the Thirties,* and hearing Auden in poems as individually realized as MacNeice's "Sunlight on the Garden" and Henry Reed's "Hiding beneath the Furze," one feels his influence as an invigorating fact.

Auden is at his height perhaps only in *Paid on Both Sides,* the one verse drama of our time that is really verse and really drama. The Nower-Shaw feud gives Auden a sustained glimpse of the individual operating within the group, and the flaw at the heart of all human action is laid bare. We fight others in the name of ancestors whom we are fighting to escape. This is the trap. Our loyalty to all "Whose voices in the rock / Are now perpetual" is always necessary and always destructive. The self-imposed ailment is here treated humorously, and tellingly, as an appropriate emblem of sick ancestor-worship: the Doctor cures the wounded Spy by removing from his body an enormous tooth, which "was growing ninety-nine years before his great grandmother was born. If it hadn't been taken out today he would have died yesterday." And the final chorus is our nearest approach to an Auden credo.

> Though he believe it, no man is strong.
> He thinks to be called the fortunate,
> To bring home a wife, to live long.
>
> But he is defeated; let the son
> Sell the farm lest the mountain fall;
> His mother and her mother won.
>
> His fields are used up where the moles visit,
> The contours worn flat; if there show
> Passage for water he will miss it:
>
> Give up his breath, his woman, his team;

No life to touch, though later there be
Big fruit, eagles above the stream.

To move from this to the aggressive middle style of the forties is a bewildering drop. Auden has become the good poet of responsibility: the vagueness is in the role, not the phrase, and no number of capital letters would save it. The style now is Dryden plus contemporary journalism. Stretches of *For the Time Being,* especially Herod's speech, are in the mode of Jean Anouilh's updating of Greek tragedy. Yet Auden's conspiratorial phase hints directly enough at his later courtship of the social muse: the progress has its logic. The missing link is *The Orators,* which one may hope *The English Auden* will reprint in full. The Airman of that story makes his sacrifice not from strength but from weakness, and the drama reaches its climax in the "Letter to a Wound," where the wounded man's love for his own limiting defect allows it, after endless cossetting, to establish complete domination over his mental life. In Auden's view the case is representative—he printed the "Letter" separately in his first collected volume. And in the mid-1930s his poetry shows him growing steadily convinced that society is itself a conspiracy of weaknesses from which the individual cannot secede. By 1942 his conversion is wholehearted.

We must all live in a world that is the sum of all those things we cannot do. This is what Auden says, tirelessly, in every possible context. But his diagnosis has not altered. It is only that the prognosis has turned pessimistic. With a curious fidelity to his old beliefs, he was able to change sides without ever changing his mind. The lesson he discovers in Melville belongs properly to himself.

> Evil is unspectacular and always human,
> And shares our bed and eats at our own table,
> And we are introduced to Goodness every day,
> Even in drawing-rooms among a crowd of faults;
> He has a name like Billy and is almost perfect,
> But wears a stammer like a decoration:
> And every time they meet the same thing has to happen;
> It is the Evil that is helpless like a lover
> And has to pick a quarrel and succeeds,
> And both are openly destroyed before our eyes.

Society, the family, have triumphed, with all their capacity for evil: we can only give them our pledge. Sympathy is the gift Auden has come most keenly to desire in his poetry, and it is, he seems to think, a quality more nearly allied to prose than to poetry. In the run-on lines of his elegy for

Freud he brings the which-side-am-I-supposed-to-be-on theme to a final resolution.

> But he would have us remember most of all
> to be enthusiastic over the night,
>   not only for the sense of wonder
>   it alone has to offer, but also
>
> because it needs our love. With large sad eyes
> its delectable creatures look up and beg
>   us dumbly to ask them to follow:
>   they are exiles who long for the future
>
> that lies in our power, they too would rejoice
> if allowed to serve enlightenment like him,
>   even to bear our cry of "Judas,"
>   as he did and all must bear who serve it.

Of Auden's fellow-traveller phase nothing need be said, since, according to his wish and the present volume, it never happened. In *Letter to Lord Byron* and *New Year Letter* we are overhearing a charming conversational wit who will doubtless be equally charming to readers a century from now. *The Age of Anxiety* is a long forced amusement dedicated and devoted to Betjeman. But there remain three poems, in a wholly new manner, in which one feels that Auden is writing at the top of his powers. The manner is that of the oracle who unhappily knows too much; the poems are "The Fall of Rome," "Under Sirius," and "The Shield of Achilles." The first of these has something of the spirit of Dryden's *Secular Masque*. For technical precision over a short distance it scarcely has a rival in Auden's work or in anyone else's. The American rhyme of *clerk* with *work* is cunning, and identifies the empire whose careless largesse Auden was elsewhere at pains to celebrate.

"Under Sirius" is a rhetorical flourish, executed in a single stroke, which warns the lazy epic poet Fortunatus of his coming disaster. "Improve the man," Auden says, here as elsewhere, "by giving him a good fright." This poem makes the grandest of all his gestures of veiled menace.

> How will you look and what will you do when the basalt
>   Tombs of the sorcerers shatter
> And their guardian megalopods
>   Come after you pitter-patter?
> How will you answer when from their qualming spring
>   The immortal nymphs fly shrieking,

And out of the open sky
The pantocratic riddle breaks—
"Who are you and why?"

For when in a carol under the apple-trees
The reborn featly dance
There will also, Fortunatus,
Be those who refused their chance,
Now pottering shades, querulous beside the salt-pits,
And mawkish in their wits,
To whom these dull dog-days
Between event seem crowned with olive
And golden with self-praise.

"The Shield of Achilles," written perhaps under the influence of Simone
Weil's "The Iliad, or The Poem of Force," mingles the gray world of the
death camps with the thriving civilization depicted on the shield, until
neither is quite recognizable and both seem appalling. Only Auden would
play Cassandra to Achilles in this way. The anachronistic details are deftly
managed and the poem is a careful tour de force.

Apart from these poems, *Paid on Both Sides,* and some lyrics in his first
three volumes, Auden can be seen to best advantage in his songs. "Fish in
the unruffled lakes"; "Now the leaves are falling fast"; "Underneath an
abject willow"; "Make this night loveable" and, the poem to which it is
sequel and counterpoint, "Lullaby": these are intent on themselves as
true poetry must be. Yet the faithful reader of Auden will find such a list
ungenerous, and he is right. A poet is someone who invents a new tone of
voice. Early, middle, and late, Auden was busy doing so: in "Herman
Melville," in parts of the Freud and Yeats elegies, in the calm equipoise
and tact of *The Sea and the Mirror,* and in "Bucolics" and "Horae Canon-
icae," which are his unofficial farewell to his art. One may watch him
"doing" Graves or Frost in poems as late as "Limbo Culture" and "Objects" (1957); but what was closest to him he learned early, most of all
from Hardy; and his typical poem like Hardy's starts from a meditation
which must be idiosyncratic on a landscape which must be difficult.
Hardy's "Where the Picnic Was" and Auden's "From scars where kestrels
hover" are employing remarkably similar methods to remarkably different ends. "In Praise of Limestone," if not for its poetry, then for its criticism, survives as a testament of the healing power of things beyond the
human thrall.

Auden frequently lacks the sounded or line-by-line concentration that
one associates with the greatest modern poetry. But he has a subject

uniquely to himself. This is the skeleton-key quest, the quest without a goal. The conventional detective story, he wrote in *The Dyer's Hand,* assumes a world in which "it is certain that a crime has been committed and, temporarily, uncertain to whom the guilt should be attached; as soon as this is known, the innocence of everyone else is certain." A work of art such as *The Trial,* on the other hand, assumes a world in which "it is the guilt that is certain and the crime that is uncertain; the aim of the hero's investigation is not to prove his innocence (which would be impossible for he knows he is guilty), but to discover what, if anything, he has done to make himself guilty." There are critics who will prefer to call this the Kafka theme or the Childe Roland theme. But, of our contemporaries, it was Auden who appropriated it most thoroughly and self-consciously.

It is the subtle and artful form of the confidence game which he plays artlessly in his revisions. It gives his anxiety free rein, without the indecencies of simple exhortation, or the idiocies of confession. It presents in full figure the threat of his nervous sense of duty and isolation: yet we feel the threat as something named, informed by dramatic energy, and mastered. In a poem of 1956 Auden received a definitive last word from his accuser. Society, the Group, the Superego, the Other, had long since become the "they," impenetrable and unreflecting and never to be questioned, whom Auden shares with Kafka and Edward Lear. From "moonless absences you never heard of" they, who have seen everything, are now asking for total surrender. And Auden, helpless in their sight, wants the battle to continue and calls the poem "There Will Be No Peace."

> There will be no peace.
> Fight back, then, with such courage as you have
> And every unchivalrous dodge you know of,
> > Clear in your conscience on this:
> Their cause, if they had one, is nothing to them now;
> > They hate for hate's sake.

But he had answered himself two decades earlier. The choice of weapons is really no choice. It is mere reflex. At last, as one of Auden's few inspired revisions makes clear, we are the victims of our own survival.

> Clear, unscaleable, ahead
> Rise the Mountains of Instead,
> From whose cold cascading streams
> None may drink except in dreams.

We must make ourselves at home with whatever illusions of independence we can salvage: hence the cheerful welcome accorded to belief as a value in itself. The poems let one see how shrewdly and yet precariously, like the rest of us, Auden built the church of self-knowledge on the rock of his own all-too-human nature. While remaining an altogether distinctive moralist, he was himself in this sense a representative case.

1976

TEN

Answer, Heavenly Muse, Yes or No

" Give me *tact*," said James Merrill, at a very young age, to the enchantress who shared the servants' quarters with a cook, a governess, and a tutor. (The enchantress was a one-time guest; the others were regulars, and had been instructed to provide their charge with "local color" from the streets of Istanbul or any of the rich, too rich Eastern cities over whose fallen glamour the poems he wrote as a grown-up would hover comically, elegiacally.) "And—isn't it the same thing—give me a *perfect ear.*" The enchantress hesitated a moment, sensing in the faintly ridiculous expression a not quite distinct opportunity for a joke or a lesson; but she thought better of it, glanced doubtfully at a list of her other petitioners, and with a sigh, whose meaning none of the servants could possibly have interpreted, granted him both wishes. Since then, the joke she never made has lingered in the poet's mind, side by side with puzzles and puppies; and it is his fate to gaze long at the disappearing Cheshire Cat's grin of all questionable phrases, including his own, and show a half-raised eyebrow as a pledge of his self-consciousness. It is a minor wit's habit, the only such habit in Merrill's possession. He knows this very well, but loyalty to the enchantress forbids him from altering any detail of what he takes to be her legacy. Besides, he might observe (were he at all inclined to argue), certain of his poems have moved a generation of readers by making it hard to draw the line between manner and mannerism—with their calm deflections, their articulate wish to make something "Out of the life lived, out of the love spent," their brilliant and serious assurance that every claim they permit themselves is justified, because depths last longer than heights.

Merrill finds all images of himself absorbing: to be lost in the endless refinements of speculation is a destiny full of charm, which he firmly rejects. But the received styles of our period are autobiographical, or "confessional," and this is the poet in whom the more durable of those styles were unified. Lowell and Jarrell hardly touch the perfect surface of "The Broken Home" or "Lost in Translation"; their first steps seem the relics of an earlier and obsolete technology. In general, Merrill is undervalued by readers who care too much about the obvious fact that he is himself an inventor with a following. His poems are strangely adaptable. They abolish the debts they incur, and shrug off their burdens lightly in the only place where it ought to be done, between the first line and the last. Indeed, his poems do everything lightly; most disputes about them would center on this. He chose, as a mythological subject, not Faustus and Helen but Cupid and Psyche, for whom knowledge cannot go beyond velleity. His sensibility appears to have formed itself wholly on the pains of *curiosa felicitas,* and he is happy to have it appear so.

Our sense of an achieved composure at the center of Merrill's work has tended to divert attention from the occasionally insensitive passages in which he seeks, in the record of his own memories, some reflection of the public life of the age. Sudden glimpses, of the Kennedy funeral train in "In Nine Sleep Valley" or of a newspaper photo in "An Urban Convalescence," have come near to ruining at least two fine poems. What Merrill needed was a way to house his public meditations in a sufficiently grand private vehicle. With *The Book of Ephraim* he seemed to have found it, and now we have the sequel, *Mirabell,** and still a third volume is promised to complete the long poem that borrows its scheme of ascent from Dante. This review is accordingly an interim report. It assumes that there is such a thing as poetic character (a different thing from *the* poetic character); that as Merrill looms larger for us it is to this element in him that we are chiefly drawn; and that his character is not, like Stevens's, a journeying from strength to strength, or like Hart Crane's, a kind of human miracle that we would prefer not to see in perspective even if we could, but rather the compound we recognize in the best of our contemporaries, of weaknesses we can easily ignore with a single emphatic strength we can never forget.

Ephraim and *Mirabell* are about the structure of the universe, and answer the questions Whence? Whither? and How? Two generic voices dominate each of the two parts of the poem. Their names, we feel, ought to be Here and There, but at this point Merrill subdivides. Here may be JM

* *Mirabell: Books of Number,* by James Merrill.

(James Merrill) or DJ (David Jackson, friend and housemate). There was originally Ephraim, a Greek Jew born in A.D. 8 "a favorite of TIBERIUS." It may now be Mirabell, or Maria Mitsotaki, or W. H. Auden, but with no strict rule against Chester Kallman, Marius Bewley, and any number of others. The truth is that as soon as a friend of the poet's has parked his car to the side of *our* busy thoroughfare, he knocks on the table at Stonington and is affectionately recycled into the poem: all are clubbable. The characters are sufficiently differentiated as to humor but not as to idiom, so that a few simple theatrical cues have to identify them: Auden says "MY DEARS," Maria "MES ENFANTS." Whether the spirits or "patrons," as Merrill calls them, actually used these eminently decipherable salutations, we are never told, but the result is convenient for following the story and only a little tiresome. There appears to be exactly one line of communication from There to Here, and Merrill's interlocutors now and then have the frantic air of collegiate disk jockeys wrestling for a microphone. This, however, is his only *donnée.*

The poetry is of two sorts. First, news of the universe, set up entirely in uppercase lettering, spoken by the voices There. Then, Merrill's observations on the bearing of all this upon his own life. In *Ephraim* the latter predominated, but in *Mirabell* the news itself has become all-important, at the confessed sacrifice of what we would ordinarily call poetry. Most of the book is written in telegraphic capitals which bear the mark not so much of Merrill's poetry as—with many *Yrs* and *Us* and *Wds* and *Shds*— of an accidental effusion by a ticker tape, a crazed linotypist, several traffic signs, and Ezra Pound in one of the more imposing phases of his correspondence. Twenty or thirty pages into the poem, the eye grows accustomed to its new habitat, and we come to feel that the wits There are as sure-footed as Here, though more wearing. But granting *Mirabell* its typographical liberties, and reserving all our disappointment at having so much made of Mirabell's turning himself into a peacock out of infatuation with his new friends, which is something everyone has seen happen at a party, we may still suspect that the powers now divide almost too neatly into fancy and imagination. Maria, Auden, Mirabell, perhaps even DJ, who is too dimly seen for us to believe that he subsists entirely on this side of the ouija board, all are clever beyond our abilities and our needs, but none could have written the little poem beginning "No, no! Set in our ways / As in a garden's," the crown jewel of *Ephraim*. Nor could they have imagined the sonnet about Avebury from the notably this-wordly first book of *Mirabell.*

Within a "greater circle" (the whole myth
Dwarfed by its grass-green skyline) stand
Two lesser, not quite tangent O's
Plotted monolith by monolith.

Two lenses now, whose once outrippling arcs
Draw things back into focus. Round each stone
(As Earth revolves, or a sheepdog barks)
Rumination turns the green to white.

It's both a holy and a homely site
Slowlier perfused than eye can see
(Whenever the stones blink a century
Blacks out) by this vague track
Of brick and thatch and birdsong any June
Galactic pollen will have overstrewn.

It might be said that without the larger fiction of the entire poem this
moment would be lost, and quite impossible to place. And it is true that a
phrase like "galactic pollen" withholds its proper meaning unless we have
kept up with JM's eccentric discoveries about Akhnaton, nuclear energy,
the Bermuda Triangle, and the acquaintance of an immortal patron with
his *First Poems,* any of which on its own merits we would gladly tie to a
stone and sink deep in the Euphrates. Our regret, however, has nothing to
do with the argument of the poem, by which only camp-followers or
pedants would pretend to judge it, but everything to do with its gradually
narrowing sympathies, and the consequent tendency to allow fewer and
more modest occasions of human eloquence, while the prattle of patrons
increases in both volume and ambition. Merrill is by nature suggestible to
the point of simple faith, and in *Mirabell* he takes his full swing. Part of
this is of course the buoyancy of Wilde, but we could wish it had been
tempered, as for Wilde it generally was, with a little more of the heritage
of Wordsworth. As it is, a voice from There burbles "Leave for Cape
Wrath tonight!" and the auditor Here does leave, without ruffling a map
or consoling his neighbors.

Like its predecessor, *Mirabell* is centrally furnished not only with the
ouija board and makeshift indicators, but also with a mirror. The board
and mirror by themselves, we remember, generated two impressive poems
in an earlier volume, *The Country of a Thousand Years of Peace;* and both
poems now make curious reading, for what they tell of the inward evolution and specialization of Merrill's interest in the esoteric. The mirror
once refused to *teach us how to live,* but still felt a tug of vulnerability in the

voices of the world's children, which could be heard wondering aloud, *If not you, who will?* Refusing a mirror's responsibilities in their full Elizabethan sense, it knew what help could come of arrangement alone and kept up appearances with a partly moral purpose of instruction. But the mirror has now become merely an adjunct to the board; and the board, loved at first (in "Voices from the Other World")

> Because, once looked at lit
> By the cold reflections of the dead
> Risen extinct but irresistible,
> Our lives have never seemed more full, more real,
> Nor the full moon more quick to chill

—this capricious medium is now to be loved in itself, and perhaps all the more because it makes our world *less* real. Throughout *Ephraim* the voices were overheard as splendid possibles, which drew from Merrill a luminous attentiveness to the particulars of "Our life, our life, our life." The pathos of skepticism having departed, we are left with the dark religions of the wandering teacup, a long way from "the very world, which is the world / Of all of us."

> —This outside world, our fictive darkness more
> And more belittles to a safety door
> Left open onto light. Too small, too far
> To help. The blind bright spot of where we are.

Even more grimly chastened, later in the poem, Merrill confesses: "Dear Mirabell, words fail us. But for you / How small our lives would be, how tedious." It is the photographic negative of the poem written twenty years earlier. In between, the autobiographical quest which looked as if it would yield the story of a supreme fiction, several times as long as Stevens's poem and miraculously no less personal, has, with its longueurs, its trial-and-error cosmogony and important messages from important friends, come more and more plainly to resemble the typical long poems of our time, *Paterson* and *The Cantos*.

Where, in *Ephraim*, the wish for systematic salvation was the gentlest rustling of an angel, candid and calm, never bent on giddy transcriptions, in *Mirabell* there is a panic rush and waste, an earnestness that is really the reverse of "might half slumb'ring on its own right arm." Everything must be set down immediately. This urgency is akin to that of the tabloids, with the same profusion of uppercase lettering. Once, Merrill had a store of negative capability; now, his spirits do not—and they are running the show. It would be less troubling if the mirror did something other than duplicate. It cannot. Merrill looks up there and finds—exactly what he has down here: a very cosy, comfy place for a seventy-year layover, filled with the gossip of friends, the vigilance of easy and uneasy relations; a little by-chamber of infinity, built by Time and Matter and the God Biology, but upholstered in the finest taste. Johnson thought the good and evil of eternity too ponderous for the wings of wit. Merrill's wit is a little flattering, a little light, and airy, to be employed on the good and evil of eternity. He is in fact everything he calls Auden, and derides him for (less gently than he evidently supposes). He reveals *sub specie aeternitatis* that Auden's besetting flaw was "THE MIS-MARRIAGE / OF LYRIC TO BALD FARCE." No patron was required to tell us this—yet before passing it on, Merrill should have heeded the admonitions of an *un*familiar ghost, named Tu Quoque. The boldest uppercase sections of *Mirabell* are farce too far advanced to admit the lyric impulse. The most moving, on the other hand, like number 8.9 beginning with "WE MET ON THIS FAIR FIELD & SEEM BY ITS EASE TO BE/IN CONVERSE"—are pure Auden.

All objections to the symbolism of *Mirabell* Merrill has nicely met by anticipation. Robert Morse, "closest of summer friends in Stonington," reminds the by then thoroughly indoctrinated and cauldron-stirring players that "Everything in Dante knew its place. / In this guidebook of yours, how do you tell / Up from down? Is Heaven's interface / What your new friends tactfully don't call Hell? / Splendid as metaphor. The real no-no / Is jargon, falling back on terms that smell / Just a touch fishy when the tide is low." An equally telling criticism was floated in *Ephraim,* where an analyst hearing the adventure of DJ and JM unshockably classified it as folie à deux, and asked the poet himself to supply the motive. To which JM replied: "Somewhere a Father Figure shakes his rod / At sons who have not sired a child? / Through our own spirit we can both proclaim / And shuffle off the blame / For how we live." Merrill can be, when he chooses to be, not less exquisite in sobriety than in extravagance. But this turns out to be one of the ruses by which from time to time he recites an unflattering sentence against himself, in order to be freed for further indulgences; and in *Mirabell* we are invited to share, with who knows what mingled emotions, an especially awkward siege of aesthetic bigotry: DJ wonders, "Are we more usable than Yeats or Hugo, / Doters on women, who then went ahead / To doctor everything their voices said?" And JM replies, in a great many punning words, Yes: reproductive man has squandered his mind on sex, so that only "the docile takers-in of seed" remain as undissolved intellect. We leave it to the archangel Michael, in part 3, to say why the metaphor is corrupt.

The ouija board ought to be regarded as an object of experience rather than belief. We would then criticize its products not on scientific grounds but because, in *Mirabell,* they represent an arbitrarily selective range of experience. These table rappings have become what schoolchildren call a *closed game*—something they get when all the players are there and nobody else can join. Almost any irregularity can still be introduced without bringing the game to an end; on the contrary, this is when the playmakers really take control; it ceases to be a game and becomes a ritual of identification. *Mirabell* exhibits the obscure but powerful system of hierarchies proper to any such ritual. Because the rules are secret, Merrill's patrons are always divulging more than they realize, and getting into trouble.

> Peacock, what's wrong?
>> I AM HERE   I AM MORE CAREFUL
> Poor darling, were you punished?
>> WE MUST GO ON

The poem grows more exacting of its ceremony in proportion as it grows more distraught in the pursuit of mystery. But the resolve that William James found a condition of genuine belief—"It favors gravity, not pertness; it says 'hush' to all vain chatter and smart wit"—is as far from the scene as Ephraim's poignant irony: "Must *everything* be witty? AH MY DEARS / I AM NOT LAUGHING   I WILL SIMPLY NOT SHED TEARS." Memories from actual life, like the dog hit by a car at number 9.5, are put into the poem as honest encumbrances, but they are not understood. We have stayed too long in the theater.

In much of his enterprise Merrill resembles Cocteau's Orpheus, who writes down the numerical sequences broadcast by the "unknown station" of the car radio, and keeps Eurydice in check with the words "How does one know what's poetry and what isn't?" (But it is Cegeste, the inferior poet, too clumsy to be entrusted with walking through mirrors, who has been inventing the messages all along and transmitting them from Eurydice's bedroom.) This review may nevertheless be the work of a peevish empiric: it certainly omits the charm of *Mirabell,* especially in the first half, on which others have preferred to dwell. On one point the poem as we have it is consistent throughout. It is radiant with self-confidence. Merrill may have a surprise for us at the bottom of his cup, and anything is possible to the author of a dozen small masterpieces and an unclassifiable but perfect something, *The (Diblos) Notebook.* His example, in spite of the jungle of complications, is invigorating; and there are other signs that we are entering a period congenial to the long poem: Daryl Hine's *In and Out* and John Hollander's *Reflections on Espionage* both come to mind. These poets have nothing in common except genius and an editor—together with the ability to make irritables melt away, and perhaps the suspicion that the language of the cultural entrepreneur may no longer be adequate to the demands of a poem. Merrill's enchantress incidentally brought him the gift of apt quotation, and, confronted with the familiar thought at the end of the last paragraph, he might respond with one as familiar and as true. "For if a man can be partaker of God's theatre, he shall likewise be partaker of God's rest."

1979

ELEVEN

Geoffrey Hill and
the Conscience of Words

Three decades ago, in the first poem of his first book, Geoffrey Hill made this beginning: "Against the burly air I strode, / Where the tight ocean heaves its load, / Crying the miracles of God." The poem, "Genesis," recounted the first days of the world, in the language of the last days. With creation itself represented as a fall, the poem seemed to embody an apocalyptic conception that was far from Christian. But its ending was different: "And by Christ's blood are men made free / Though in close shrouds their bodies lie / Under the rough pelt of the sea." The opposition in "Genesis" between the poem's mood and its resolution could be discerned elsewhere in *For the Unfallen* (1959). In his later volumes, *King Log* (1968), *Mercian Hymns* (1971), and *Tenebrae* (1978), Hill continued to write a poetry of strife, with a wish to end in conciliatory prayer. Because he is the most powerful living poet, it has been natural for readers to suppose that his chief aim was power. Hill does not understand himself so. What seems to his admirers a vigilant self-command, he would prefer to regard as an expiatory self-denial. This restriction was noticeable in a recent sonnet sequence, "Lachrimae." It comes out more plainly and insistently in his critical essays.

Hill's earlier books are out of print here, and his work is not yet familiar to American readers. Invidious comparison may therefore be helpful. He stands out now as the British poet who can be read beside the masters of the high style. He is, to suggest more precisely the traits in question, the poet of exemplary conscience that Robert Lowell aspired to become. Hill's writing, however, feels unfamiliar in another sense as well. It has none of the unction of geniality; does not weaken itself with whimsies, or otherwise truckle for patronage; never says, brightly, "These oysters remind me of starlight!" or, gravely, "Forgive me this weak trespass." He does not want to be loved for his poems, or search out ways of being likable in his poems.

This distinct negative appeal—a charmless personal integrity—is a source of Hill's endurance thus far. And it has encouraged him to try for an uncommon success, and write a long poem about another poet.[*] Like no other poem of the age, *The Mystery of the Charity of Charles Péguy* sustains a partly public meditation with continuous personal intensity. Its motive may be described as an attempt to hold poetry and history in a single thought. Yet its eloquence is direct, chaste, and declarative, checked only by the thought that all eloquence terminates in action. In theme, it recalls earlier poems by Hill: "Ovid in the Third Reich," "Annunciations," and "Funeral Music." In style it is original, and widens the range of modern poetry.

Péguy himself may need some introduction. He began his literary career as a polemicist for the Dreyfusard party, underwent an extreme but not unnatural conversion from socialism to the France of "the old republic," and died in 1914, a patriotic soldier in the war he had urged his country to fight. Attachments like Péguy's resist translation. He loved the soil and the folk of his native Orléans, as he imagined them, and wrote of their heroine as he imagined her, in *The Mystery of the Charity of Joan of Arc*. These things were connected for Péguy with his own childhood, and with the passions and haunts of childhood. At the same time, they had the character of sympathies radically chosen. He said of a more detached intellectual, whom he respected but could not cherish: "When I am with M. Benda, I am with a man who has been reading forever; when I am by myself, I am with a man who has been reading since my mother and me." France was thus bound by impalpable links to the singular life that had nourished him.

IN POLITICS, though he held some views in common with a systematic reactionary like Charles Maurras, Péguy's own beliefs derived from no abstract source. Personal experience was always his guide, and not least when he clamored for the death of his former comrade, Jean Jaurès. Believing in the solidarity of working men of all nations, Jaurès opposed France's entry

---

[*] *The Mystery of the Charity of Charles Péguy*, by Geoffrey Hill.

into the war, and to Péguy this represented a final betrayal. The true France, he wrote, the France of the National Convention, requires "Jaurès in a tumbril and that great voice drowned in the beating of drums." Soon after these words were published Jean Jaurès was assassinated—by a madman who, as Hill remarks in a prose afterword, "may or may not have been over-susceptible to metaphor." "Tout commence en mystique," wrote Péguy, "et tout finit en politique": everything begins in mysticism and ends in politics. Yet this was not less true of himself than of those whom he condemned.

Hill's poem turns upon the event in which the logic of Péguy's epigram came to include its author:

> So much for Jaurès murdered in cold pique
> by some vexed shadow of the belle époque,
>
> some guignol strutting at the window-frame.
> But what of you, Péguy, who came to "exult,"
> to be called "wolfish" by your friends? The guilt
> belongs to time; and you must leave on time.

This, then, is a poem about the complicity of words with their foreseeable and unforeseen consequences, in the world of action that exists for the writer like a fate. That world, Hill says (borrowing a phrase from Auden), "is different, belongs to them— / the lords of limit and of contumely." Though limiting, they have their proper claim, for (to borrow another phrase that Hill has pondered), "The words of a dead man / Are modified in the guts of the living."

The Mystery of the Charity of Charles Péguy is written from the perspective of the lords of limit, who sometimes do speak on behalf of the living.

> Did Péguy kill Jaurès? Did he incite
> the assassin? Must men stand by what they write
> as by their camp-beds or their weaponry
> or shell-shocked comrades while they sag and cry?

Evidently there are two answers to these questions. *En mystique,* no: words are not binding on their author, they are germs of thoughts that he cannot know. *En politique,* yes: and not only bonds, they are shackles or grappling irons, that connect his name forever with the things he has described and changed. In short, the implications of words may be utterly distinct from the conscious motives that produced them; and yet, once they have issued in action, words may rightly be charged with having the force of such motives. The saying acquits as mere word, the doing convicts as absolute deed. What defense then remains for Péguy?

A USUAL exemption for writers who happen to be poets is that "poetry makes nothing happen," but Hill does not believe this. His purpose is indeed to explain Péguy's fate as that of all who use language with conviction. Poet and soldier at once, Péguy stands as a figure for the contest from which eloquence arises: his valor and cunning were at home in both vocations; and his apology belongs to all writers, whose words are liable to persuade. Their attachments, that is, are liable to be translated by readers who take them over as programmatic beliefs:

> Rage and regret are tireless to explain
> stratagems of the out-manoeuvred man,
> the charge and counter-charge. You know the drill,
> raw veteran, poet with the head of a bull.
>
> Footslogger of genius, skirmisher with grace
> and ill-luck, sentinel of the sacrifice,
> without vantage of vanity, though mortal-proud,
> defend your first position to the last word.

Stanzas like these suggest an irony in the relation between eloquence and the author who utters it. From this, Hill does not move on to the dilemma of guilty action and guiltless immobility—the terms in which some other modern poems, Tate's "Ode to the Confederate Dead" for instance, entirely reframe the problem. Hill's poem on the contrary is an impassioned homage to Péguy, even if it presumes an attitude of chastened recognition.

Large tracts of the poem, especially toward the end, are given over to an allusive sketch of Péguy's "dream of France, militant-pastoral." These passages are essential to the view of Péguy's character that Hill proposes, and also to the scheme of cinematic montage on which the poem depends throughout. Yet they seem more uncertain in tone than the rest of the poem. How far can such a pastoral draw credence from a poet whose national mystique, if he has one at all, is not the same as Péguy's? The descriptions are carefully poised, and never reflect a borrowed nostalgia. But their insistent presence implies a less suspicious understanding of historical myth than appeared in Hill's earlier long poem *Mercian Hymns.* There the archaic details were relished for their anachronism, and often touched by a grotesque humor. Here, with a foreign rather than a native subject, the landscape becomes very nearly a retreat, secure against the hostilities of the cenacle or the battlefield:

> Hedgers and ditchers, quarrymen, thickshod
> curés de campagne, each with his load,
> shake off those cares and burdens; they become
> in a bleak visionary instant, seraphim

> looking towards Chartres, the spired sheaves,
> stone-thronged annunciations, winged ogives
> uplifted and uplifting from the winter-gleaned
> furrows of that criss-cross-trodden ground.

These peasant figures, drawn as they are from Péguy's writing, allow Hill to compose an affirmation, "uplifted and uplifting," for which his own language is not quite answerable. When, in moralizing the vision, he writes "Landscape is like revelation," the word *like* is a very small qualification to cover the whole distance from critical sympathy to sympathetic appropriation.

The poem's concluding note is a good deal more skeptical, without any loss of power to its eulogistic bearing-of-witness. The length of Péguy's career, from his opening "J'accuse" to his death "outflanked again" in a beet-root field, here receives its summing up in a trope that brings together custom and ceremony, militant rhetoric and military discipline:

> Low tragedy, high farce, fight for command,
> march, counter-march, and come to the salute
> at every hole-and-corner burial-rite
> bellowed with hoarse dignity into the wind.

> Take that for your example! But still mourn,
> being so moved: éloge and elegy
> so moving on the scene as if to cry
> "in memory of those things these words were born."

The last quotation is adapted from a sentence of Marcel Raymond, but it comes into the poem inevitably, a matter-of-fact marker of the choice to inherit Péguy's work as an ambiguous legacy.

THE ESSAYS collected in *The Lords of Limit** present themselves as interrogations of the moral life of literature. The evidence that they judge

---

* *The Lords of Limit: Essays on Literature and Ideas,* by Geoffrey Hill.

comes from the use of language—what others would simply call, but Hill does not consent to call simply, style. In different ways they analyze betrayals (that is, treasons) of the moral intelligence, which leave their mark in the betrayals (that is, disclosures) of language. The heroes of the book, as much as its antagonists, are looked at in the light of such failures. Thus, when T. H. Green says that "the 'Treatise of Human Nature' and the 'Critique of Pure Reason,' taken together, form the real bridge between the old world of philosophy and the new," Hill brings him up short: the verbal formula "'real bridge' here preempts its own verification. . . . And this strategy itself is crucial in certain forms of nineteenth-century bridge-building." Apparently Green's metaphor is most evasive just where it pretends to be most edifying: we cannot know what to think of the bridge unless we know what lies on either side of it. But his faults do not disqualify him as a hero: "There are triumphs," writes Hill, "that entrap and defeats that liberate." Green's life, as Hill sees it, was a defeat that liberated. So too was the life of Robert Southwell. But there is another sort of failure that concerns Hill almost as much: "It is not only the 'bad artists' who are cruelly judged. The good are too."

A twenty-page essay called "Redeeming the Time" surveys the entire nineteenth century, by the analysis of certain phrases that seem to Hill either to exhibit an admirable rigor or to conceal a deplorable laxity of purpose. T. H. Green, Coleridge, and Hopkins are quoted favorably, to expose the deficiencies of Arnold, Mill, and George Eliot. Of all these writers, Hopkins was the least engaged in questions of language and conduct, and his reputation was posthumous to the last possible degree. What can it mean to play him off against Arnold and Mill, who were active participants in the public debates of the time? Doubtless the standards of contemporary reputation are parochial. But someone who seeks to displace them ought to produce evidence that is convincing and imaginative rather than coaxing and ingenious. What are we to make of Hill when his case for Hopkins is clinched by a special construal of the punctuation of the phrase "(my God!) my God," and this is held to establish the shallowness of George Eliot's secular sense of vocation in *Felix Holt?* The truth is that Hopkins, revealed here "in his intense selfhood and in his most frightful splintering," defines a subject for interrogation very different from any subject that George Eliot proposes. Taken at her word, she does not suffer by comparison with Hopkins taken at his.

"Our Word Is Our Bond" is the most subtle and ambitious essay in the book, and the most interesting for what it says about Hill's own sense of vocation. Its aim is to place the aesthetic view of poetry in a tense opposition with the conception of language as performative utterance. The rival terminologies are drawn from romantic and modern criticism on one side, and from J. L. Austin's *How to Do Things with Words* on the other. To test how far the opposition may be sustained or made to collapse under pressure, Hill examines the record of Ezra Pound's wartime broadcasts for Mussolini and his subsequent court hearing on charges of treason. As the case developed, a plea of insanity allowed Pound to escape the usual punishment for traitors, at the price of being confined for several years in St. Elizabeth's Hospital. This result satisfied no one then, and it has satisfied no one since.

But Hill is not, in fact, concerned with the details of the case, or with the reasonableness of the accusation of treason. Rather he finds Pound guilty of a subtler *trahison* against language, so that there appears an ironic justice in his fate after all. And yet, the language of Hill's condemnation itself is puzzling: "The moral offence," he remarks, "of [Pound's] cruel and vulgar anti-semitism does not call into question the integrity of his struggle; neither does the integrity of his struggle absolve him of responsibility for the vulgar cruelty." Now what has *vulgarity* to do with it? Had he been less vulgar, Pound would not have been less cruel, nor indeed less culpable. Yet Hill repeats the word: "vulgar anti-semitism," "vulgar cruelty." Let us be clear about what is at stake. The anti-Semite Charles Maurras, who had more refinement than Pound, used the pages of his paper *Action Française* to publish the names of members of the French resistance, in the hope that it would ease the way to their capture by the Gestapo. This was cruel but was it vulgar? It is questionable whether an act of naming, as distinct from an act of rhetorical persuasion, can appropriately be described as vulgar, apart from the obvious instances of coarse expressions. Still, supposing it to be cruel merely, how does that alter the judgment?

A criticism of Hill's prose may be suggested by his poetry. These essays often argue against a narrow definition that would confine poetry to a special domain of aesthetic beauty. They likewise argue against a narrow definition that would confine it to the domain of persuasive speech or propaganda. What Hill wants instead, he says, is "an atonement of aesthetics with rectitude of judgment." The profession of such a need is not aesthetic—it is ethical also, as it has to be. But when Hill comes to assess the miscarriage of poetic command in a writer like Pound, he falls back on something very like a purely aesthetic viewpoint: "poets are not legislators." If this meant that poets should be read scrupulously, so that their assertions do not wrongly persuade, one might endorse the sentiment, and not only as applied to poetry. Yet Hill seems to be pointing to a world of speech in which poetic assertions, if rightly framed, will never be liable to persuade—as if poetry might succeed at last in making nothing happen. So, having once scrutinized the assertion by Pound that "all values come from our judicial sentences," he decides that the formulation is truer in reverse: "all values go into our judicial sentences." Can they be expected to remain there, once they have gone in?

The faith that Hill's poems consider and that his prose affirms is that moral intelligence may be embodied and contained in poems. His word for such incorporation of ethical judgment in an aesthetic object is "atonement"—a word Coleridge used to similar effect. This belief seems the counterpart of another, to which Hill gravitates in opposite moods, when he wants words to have both a more acknowledged and a more precise effect than they practically can. In such a mood, he praises an utterance of Robert Southwell's, under interrogation by the Privy Council. Asked why he was more responsive to their questions than to those put by his torturer, Southwell replied: "Because I have found *by experience* that the man is not open to reason"; and Hill finds this praiseworthy for something beyond its human grace: "Southwell's retort, in an instant, both judges the travesty and redeems the word." Taking the last clause slowly: to say that the retort judges, as a defendant may judge his accusers, is paradoxical but just. The reply also restores a true and deep sense to two words, *find* and *experience*. And evidently, for Geoffrey Hill it calls to mind with inescapable vividness a human possibility of moral attention and courage. But to say that it "redeems the word" is portentous and evasive. When the spirit of the same words is mistaken by a different kind of reader, the redemption will prove to have been, as it always is, only provisional.

Judged by his own uncompromising standard, Hill's essays are unsettled half-arguments for the moral act that his poems exist to perform. They would feel stronger if they had more charity—if they did not condemn Iris Murdoch for once speaking unguardedly of a century as if it were a character ("the nineteenth century . . . could think itself a single world") and go on to commit the same fault ("the nineteenth century preferred a half-remorseful majesty in its great apostates"). Nor is their readiness to judge quite matched by an answerable style: the prose, with its involutions, its performed hesitations and sideways flights, is as remote from ordinary speech as it is from public eloquence. Yet this obstruction placed in the path of a fluent commerce with the reader is characteristic, and what Hill says of Ben Jonson's Catiline will never be said of him. "We know that he takes himself too seriously and humanity too lightly." It is the opposite with the author of *The Lords of Limit* and *The Mystery of the Charity of Charles Péguy.* He takes himself seriously, and this seems a condition of his not taking humanity lightly.

1985

POSTSCRIPT

One of the brave acts of poetic speech in our time was the publication in 1998 of Geoffrey Hill's long poem *The Triumph of Love.* The poem is a confession—of impotence, and faith—by a writer and citizen of the twentieth century. A work of exhortation and satire, it is also, with a clarity Hill's early work had only begun to touch, a celebration of love. But love here becomes another name for gratitude: so we are confronted by an oddly public prayer of thanks in no way public—for the admonishments as well as the memories that have upheld a thinking being. Intimations of a self and the recognitions of justice that build up a living conscience are presented side by side in the narrative. Some of the reviews seemed thankless, and largely taken up with challenging the poet's authority to address the politics and history of the age he lives in, but their worst mistake was to treat it as a collection or a sequence of lyrics, vaguely interrelated. It would be impossible to read the poem this way and understand what it is aiming at. From the first naked perception of the poet as a child to the last self-reproach of the proud man out of key with his time, *The Triumph of Love* marks a natural resting place in Hill's lifelong meditation on the need to reconcile the power and command of words with an act of moral testimony.

This is a poem of many mutterings, and if it sustains a hope, it does so in the face of a besieging fear: that the things one has cared for and learned to cherish are vanishing, not only from the system of life but from the possibility of human recollection.

LI

Whatever may be meant by *moral landscape,*
it is for me increasingly a terrain
seen in cross-section: igneous, sedimentary,
conglomerate, metamorphic rock-
strata, in which particular grace,
individual love, decency, endurance,
are traceable across the faults.

> Admittedly at times this moral landscape
> to my exasperated ear emits
> archaic burrings like a small, high-fenced
> electricity sub-station of uncertain age
> in a field corner where the flies
> gather and old horses shake their sides.

Hill's life began under a threat of destruction to Europe and its culture, a threat he believes is now being fulfilled by the conduct of the benign victors. Among the memories he counts at once public and private are bewildered glimpses of photographs of the burning of the Jewish ghettoes and later the photographs and documentary evidence of the death camps. "Do we indeed not know ourselves?" he asks—a question that is rhetorical but bound to remain unsolved. "If / witness meant witness," a reply comes back some pages later, "all could be martyrs." But memory runs out faster and faster, and for the sake of what? To usher in not a reign of cruelty now, but a cult of efficiency and supine luxury and "savage torpor" (Wordsworth's phrase, quoted here, and its affinity with Hill's way of feeling is evident). "They," as he calls the masters of art and commerce—they "are vassal- / lord-puppet-strutters, not great scourges of God. A simple text would strike them / dumb, and is awaited." He speaks perhaps as a lesser prophet in the hope of a greater to come.

Adorno wrote two famous sentences about poetry and the Holocaust, which if one could trust some of his critics would seem to have been: "The Holocaust is so awful a subject that no poetry can or should be written about it." What he actually said, in the first essay of *Prisms,* was this: "To write poetry after Auschwitz is barbaric. And this corrodes even the knowledge of why it has become impossible to write poetry today." One is tempted to put the second sentence in italics since it marks not just a qualification but an expansion of the thought. The last totalitarianism did not die in 1945 or in 1989. Totalitarianism is the desire to make the world all one thing—to simplify the human image in the name of a more-than-human ideal. The Thousand Year Reich was one of these; so was the dictatorship of the proletariat. What to say of a worldwide ethic, "global" as never before, turning solely on consumption and demand, where every desire is anticipated and custom-built, where imagination is rendered unintelligible before the fact?

> I am saying (simply)
> what is to become of memory? Yes—I know—
> I've asked that before.

The new costume of totalitarian power—of human experiment on the human creature—is so shallow and savorless it has become impossible to hate. And this is part of its poison. To the extent of his abilities, Hill has made *The Triumph of Love* a poem also of hate: deprecation must go with the prayer it intends. His misanthropy has much of the tenor of Swift's, driven back by revulsion and pity to a resourceless simplicity. But most of all, this prayer and exhortation is a moral essay that happens to be written by an artist. Its anger is deflected only now and then, to mockery, by the author's compulsion to respond to a clutch of dotard agents with names like MacSikker and Croker, whom he has imagined inheriting his posthumous text and trying to market it while he is still alive. They dislike him as much as possible, and show it by their interpolations: "For definitely the right era, read: deaf in the right ear." Hill speaks, in turn, of a larger negligence, of which they are only the accidental reminders:

CXIX

And yes—bugger you, MacSikker et al.,—I do
mourn and resent your desolation of learning:
Scientia that enabled, if it did not secure,
forms of understanding, far from despicable,
and furthest now, as they are most despised.
By understanding I understand diligence
and attention, appropriately understood
as actuated self-knowledge, a daily acknowledgement
of what is owed to the dead.

What does this leave for the poet himself? A temporary reprieve, arrived at late, owing everything to a self-knowledge that advances as blindness recedes, with a glacial slowness: "vulnerable, proud / anger is, I find, a related self / of covetousness. I came late / to seeing that. Actually, I had to be shown it."

Here then is a prophecy, two generations after the European war that nearly ended humanity, at a time of unexampled prosperity and the triumph of commerce from day to day. Yet at this time, unfeeling is being taught again, in the name of the self-informing of the human creature for its own good by a restless and perpetual entertainment. The doctrine that seduces through self-love will make anything eventually possible. To this final threat, the poet responds only by a defiance in the cause of sheer memory, with a serenade of treasured things.

CXXX

Milton—the political pamphlets. Blake
in old age reaffirming the hierarchies.

Péguy *passim,* virtually. Bernanos,
if only for having written *la colère
des imbéciles remplit le monde.* Radnóti
at Bór. The great self-recovery of Wat.
ta-Rah ta-Rah ta-rarara Rah

Only this, against the dread that what thou lovest well does not remain. Yet there is nothing for it but to shout the names to the sky: the names mean something, may mean more than any description to those who have the clue. *The Triumph of Love* is full of inflections that have been familiar in Hill's work before, but it has a new skill of modulation—the pedant's grimace and self-prodding for sanity, reminiscent of Berryman's dream songs, but with a resonance pitched deeper than grousing irritability and panache. The voice, the movement, even the pauses that constitute so much of the poem, betoken a genuine discovery, remarkable as coming so late and as a thing in itself so complete. The book cannot be mastered— the author would not claim to have mastered it—but the character of its achievement is plain enough. An act of witness, as it wants to be, but more personal than it knows, it is a halting but unmistakable tune hummed in snatches by the poet to himself and for some who may be listening.

TWELVE

Ted Hughes's *River*

Yeats's hawk of the mind offered masterful images to poetry, but only when *it* was mastered, "hooded or caged, / Till the yellow eye has grown mild." Until then (so the fable implied), it disarmed the poet, and left him with a pretense of wit. Ted Hughes's hawk in the rain was a different thing. Its master, who had never supposed wit among his native weapons, could imagine the creature's exploits as a sensational satisfaction, and its wreck as no less a satisfaction. With an inhuman sympathy, the poet himself strained

> towards the master-
> Fulcrum of violence where the hawk hangs still.
> That maybe in his own time meets the weather
>
> Coming the wrong way, suffers the air, hurled upside down
> Fall from his eye, the ponderous shires crash on him,
> The horizon trap him; the round angelic eye
> Smashed, mix his heart's blood with the mire of the land.

"The Hawk in the Rain," it may seem in retrospect, laid out very accurately Hughes's favorite way of situating himself. This involves, first, awestruck reverence for a creature, glimpsed when its artfulness and poise make it seem remote from man; and, second, an excited daydream of the same creature's submission to instinct, reaching a climax as its appetites are pursued catastrophically.

The hawk of Yeats's poem was—to use an old word in an old way—symbolic: it told a truth about the mind. Significances of this sort Hughes apparently regards as intrusions. At any rate he does his best to disclaim them in certain poems, and his assurance here may have helped him to command the still-extant audience for nature poetry. Seventy years of modernist practices, together with the overt expressionism of much of Hughes's work since *Crow,* have not been enough to shake the remnants of this audience, whose taste coexists with an irony it cannot acknowledge. Nature transfigured is always nature described with respect to something—an unconfessed mood or interest, or some earlier description. Looked at in the terms that poetry demands, therefore, nature ceases to be the object required by nature poetry. Hughes understood this well two decades ago, when he wrote the opening stanza of "Pibroch":

> The sea cries with its meaningless voice
> Treating alike its dead and its living,
> Probably bored with the appearance of heaven
> After so many millions of nights without sleep,
> Without purpose, without self-deception.

It is a summary attempt, the poetic naturalist's attempt, to "see life steadily and see it whole," and what it shows is a chaos.

But the last two lines are interesting for another reason. They echo, perhaps involuntarily, a strange poem of the First World War, Edward Thomas's "The Gallows." Like Hughes, in a few poems Thomas felt drawn to compose transcriptions of nature-as-fact; but in the end he drew back, and "The Gallows" partly tells why. It is the tale of a keeper who shot all the trespassers on his land, and hung them up on a tree: a weasel, who "lived in the sun"; a crow, "who was no sleeper"; a magpie with "a long tongue and a long tail."

> And many other beasts
> And birds, skin, bone, and feather,
> Have been taken from their feasts
> And hung up there together,
> To swing and have endless leisure
> In the sun and in the snow,
> Without pain, without pleasure,
> On the dead oak tree bough.

This is the ur-Hughes poem, and one phrase of it particularly seems to haunt him. Thomas says of the keeper's execution of the crow, that he "Made him one of the things that were." All natural facts end in this. But, where Thomas recoiled from a scene of unvaried annihilation, Hughes continues to look on, with a respect for propriety that stops short of relish. His poems concern existence as it is, from the perspective of what it would be to become one of the things that were.

To the animals this means being without pain and without pleasure. But for us it implies something more: to be without sleep, without purpose, without self-deception. Hughes, as his poetry advances, appears increasingly to cherish the idea of such a state. This looks like a perversion of the will until one realizes that for him the end of life has two separate aspects. It is a rejoining of nature in a disanimate form, but it is also a parting from nature that may bring revelation. At the end of "Pibroch," more explicitly than in any of his later poems, Hughes sees nature as affording both views at the same time.

> Minute after minute, aeon after aeon,
> Nothing lets up or develops.
> And this is neither a bad variant nor a tryout.
> This is where the staring angels go through.
> This is where all the stars bow down.

A doing and undoing without end, it is the end that is always happening. Because Hughes treats it not only as a subject for consciousness but as a stimulus to the nerves, his poems sometimes have an air of primitivism. But that is a surface effect. Sustained as it has been, through several volumes of poetry, Hughes's inquisition into pleasure and pain must be supposed the undertaking of an adept. The risk of protracted work in this line is a displacement of imagination by mere consciousness.

IN WORKMANSHIP, *River* is the most nearly perfect of Hughes's books. The landscape it dwells on is a scene of wreckage, and, equally, of the scattering of new life. The theme that pervades the sequence is energy—energy, as it is formed by necessity and trapped by necessity. Thus "Salmon-Taking Times" surveys the river after a flood, when shreds of once-living matter coat the water and catch on the river's salient points:

> a gauze
> Struggles tenderly in the delighted current—
> Clambers wetly on the stones, and the river emerges
> In glistenings, and gossamer bridal veils,
> And hovers over itself—there is a wedding
> Delicacy—
>   so delicate
> I touch it and its beauty-frailty crumples
> To a smear of wet, a strengthless wreckage.

Here as elsewhere in the sequence, a strengthless delicacy appears as the afterimage of mindless exertion. In this case Hughes spoils the effect a little,

with a pair of similes which restore just the comfort that the poem has resisted: "It is like a religious moment, slightly dazing. / It is like a shower of
petals of eglantine." The curious word *strengthless* is more evocative than
either of these phrases; and it suggests a general truth about Hughes's fascination with power. His tender intimacy with dead things, or with things
void of all impulse, is the repose of a spent aggression.

Boundary emotions like these give Hughes's poetry its atmosphere of
diffusive shock: something well worth distrusting when it is offered by
critics (including, at times, Hughes) as a tough-minded antihumanistic
therapy in the service of life. It is not that. Still, it was the need for an
abrasive and vigorous style—answerable to just such emotions—that
opened the way for Hughes to invent one of the original idioms of our
period. *River* differs from his earlier books mainly in the thoroughness
with which it welcomes nature's violences as a premise for invention. In
the alternation of day with night and of life with death, among the creatures inhabiting a river and the valley alongside, the poems find an easy
balance by discovering alternations of their own. Some are occupied with
a modest notation of creature traits, others with exploring the valley's re-
cesses for emblems of the self. These distinct emphases correspond to
Hughes's sense of art as a form of discriminating attention and as a
record of the defeat hidden in every conquest of power. As for the poet's
motive, it remains what he declared it to be in a characteristic passage of
Wodwo:

> There's no reason why I should not last quite a long time yet. I seem to have
> an uncommon reserve of energy. To keep my mind firm, that is the essen-
> tial thing, to fix it firmly in my reasonable hopes, and lull it there, encour-
> age it. Mesmerize it slightly with a sort of continuous prayer. Because when
> my mind is firm, my energy is firm. And that's the main thing here—en-
> ergy. No matter how circumspect I may be, or how lucid, without energy I
> am lost on the spot. Useless to think about it. Where my energy ends I end,
> and all circumspection and all lucidity end with me.

Hughes does not strictly identify the speaker as himself. But the conditions that obtain here may be recognized as those of his native landscape.
The "sort of continuous prayer" describes his attitude of attention, and he
draws it out for the sake of a sustaining "energy."

This sounds like a point of view whose outmost limits are defined by
the self. Yet a few of the acts of attention in *River,* by absorbing the poet
entirely, rob him of the wish to lend a personal tincture to his subjects. In
"An Eel" this reticence seems a kind of grace:

> Eerie the eel's head.
> This full, plum-sleeked fruit of evolution.
> Beneath it, her snout's a squashed slipper-face,
> The mouth grin-long and perfunctory,
> Undershot predatory. And the iris, dirty gold
> Distilled only enough to be different
> From the olive lode of her body,
> The grained and woven blacks. And ringed larger
> With a vaguer vision, an earlier eye
> Behind her eye, paler, blinder,
> Inward.

The epithets, nicknames that shape little allegories, estrange even as they humanize. "Squashed slipper-face" is a bold cartoon stroke to come so near the start; in its softer way, "the olive lode of her body" has been carefully measured with the neighboring color tones; while "undershot predatory" seems a miracle of oblique description. Even an improvised touch like the mouth "grin-long and perfunctory" is no less precise. It is a token of the mastery here that the poem should have built a defense for *vaguer*, a word that as a rule signals the poet's having only vaguely seen what he wants to say.

"An Eel" continues its naming to the end without any loss of resourcefulness: with "the amazement of her progress," incorporating a well-earned pun; and the fin that "secretes itself / Flush with her concealing suit"; and, as befits a suited thing, a last fixing of identity that follows from a verbless sentence.

> Her whole body
> Damascened with identity. This is she
> Suspends the Sargasso
> In her inmost hope. Her life is a cell
> Sealed from event, her patience
> Global and furthered with love
> By the bending stars as if she
> Were earth's sole initiate. Alone
> In her millions, the moon's pilgrim,
> The nun of water.

Apart from the total impression, which succeeds, many of the individual details strive to be individually fine, and do succeed in themselves: "damascened," "suspends the Sargasso," the etymologically rich use of "hope" (prying out the implicit *hoop,* and all that the undershot predator expects to grasp by springing forward); above all, the train of thought that the final metaphor presupposes, by which the moon's pallor is associated with self-denial, and its influence on the ocean tides with pilgrimage. Only one phrase stands out as a routine extravagance: "furthered with love / By the bending stars." But this is a small defection from a work of remarkable patience.

In intensity of character and variety of rendering, some of these animals call to mind the animals of *Birds, Beasts, and Flowers*. Also, less gravely, certain of Hughes's lines recall to the ear certain of Lawrence's. His nicknaming a mink "jolly goblin, realist-optimist" seems an obvious instance; as does this picture of "An August Salmon":

> A holed-up gangster,
> He dozes, his head on the same stone,
> Gazing towards the skylight,
> Waiting for the time to run out on him.

One occasionally feels a trace of overdetermination in the effort. Of the foregoing lines, Lawrence would have trusted the first enough to leave out the fourth, and the second enough to leave out the third. It may be that Hughes has more design, with less spontaneity. Some such sacrifice was probably necessary to assure a regular texture for the sequence.

THE TROUBLE is that the more facile stretches of *River* often have to be read as irresolute amplifications of whole poems by Lawrence. In a critical passage of "Last Night," for example, Hughes only half realizes the dramatic point of the recognition he describes.

> I stood in a grave
> And felt the evil of fish. The strange evil
> Of unknown fish-minds. Deep fish listening to me
> In the dying river.

The same recognition is pursued less mysteriously, and yet more scrupulously, in the comparable passage of Lawrence's "Fish":

> I left off hailing him.
>
> I had made a mistake, I didn't know him,
> This grey, monotonous soul in the water,
> This intense individual in shadow,
> Fish-alive.

I didn't know his God,
I didn't know his God.

Which is perhaps the last admission that life has to wring out of us.

What Lawrence says throughout this poem he says best in three words, "He outstarts me." Meaning: wherever I look to begin again, in a search for things before my knowing, I find him there already. Meaning also: he startles me back into the unsolved part of myself, as I could not do merely by looking inward. Lawrence, every reader must have felt, knows that he has to return to the creatures, even against his will.

An opposite impression of conscious returns may temper one's admiration for Hughes. More than the deliberateness of his writing, what confirms the impression is the literalism of his concern with sensations. In the end these creatures are all used for a purpose. To Hughes, they represent the zero level of existence: the condition from which man derives, which he is trying to forget, and to which he must therefore be continually exposed. One comes to this moral cumulatively in reading and rereading the poems of *River;* but it will be plain to anyone familiar with Hughes's earlier work; and it warrants illustration from another of the prose sketches in *Wodwo.* The sketch, called "Sunday," is, in fact, a Nick Adams–ish story, about a violent experience that marks a transition from youth to manhood. The hero watches from the street outside a local pub, where a caged rat, held tight by a rope, is set free into the waiting jaws of Billy Red, a geek. He goes on watching, to see Billy Red "spin half round and drop smack down on his hands and knees on the cobbles. . . . A dozen shakes, and Billy Red stopped, his head lowered. The rat hanging from his mouth was bunching and relaxing, bunching and relaxing. He waited. Everyone waited. Then the rat spasmed, fighting with all its paws, and Billy shook again wildly, the rat's tail flying like a lash. This time when he stopped the body hung down limply." So, at this lower limit of humanity, man is a conquering beast; and for the boy, to bear witness across the boundary is a rite of passage. One poem in *River,* "That Morning," contains a similar moment. The poet looks on as "Two gold bears came down, / And swam like men." Is it, then, as men that he describes them, "Eating pierced salmon off their talons"? Anyway the recognition follows unmistakably: "So we found the end of our journey. / So we stood, alive in the river of light / Among the creatures of light, creatures of light." The last two phrases are to be read, not as a repetition, but as an antithesis that has been surmounted. We are asked to see the human predator as one more creature of light.

Yet for Hughes every image of strife is also potentially an image of re-birth. He has written an essay that explains his belief in the analogy; and his comments there on another poet apply with added force to himself. In an introduction to Slyvia Plath's journals, Hughes observed that her "real creation" was "that inner gestation and eventual birth of a new self-conquering self"; but this new self, "who could do so much, could not ul-timately save her," any more than a new poem can alter a poet's fate: "the moment of turning one's back on an enemy who seems safely defeated, and is defeated, is the most dangerous moment of all." In the case of Plath, a sense of the dangers of this strife impelled him to destroy some of her journals, in order to spare her children from reading them. "In those days," he says, he "regarded forgetfulness as an essential part of survival." Both the impulsive gesture and the reasoned apology have a purposeful in-tegrity. By contrast, his own poems show very little respect for forgetful-ness as a principle of survival. They expose the reader to an exhaustive remembering of violence. And rather than efface, they dwell most perti-naciously on scenes of frustrated birth. In a metaphor that hardly any other careful poet would test, Hughes writes of a cormorant:

> Level your eye's aim and he's off
> Knocking things over, out through the window—
>
> An abortion-doctor
> Black bag packed with vital organs.

The cormorant is not, one sees, what Hughes calls him—"A Rival"—but rather a double of the poet's self, practitioner of expert flayings.

Such figures deserve praise for being far-fetched, even if they can be too quickly fetched. Some of the details of Hughes's landscape belong to the world of the tabloid shocker—just as some of the details of his language belong to the poetry of the confessional shocker. But in this book, as has not always been the case in his recent work, the second-rate materials that surface from time to time are eventually used with genuine power. "New Year" revolves around a metaphor, but a controlled one, concerning another fatal birth:

> Snow falls on the salmon redds. Painful
>
> To think of the river tonight—suffering itself.
> I imagine a Caesarian,
> The wound's hapless mouth, a vital loss
> Under the taut mask, on the heaped bed.

The silent to-fro hurrying of nurses,
The bowed stillness of surgeons,
A trickling in the hush. The intent steel
Stitching the frothing womb, in its raw hole.

And walking in the morning in the blue glare of the ward
I shall feel in my head the anaesthetic,
The stiff gauze, the congealments. I shall see
The gouged patient sunk in her trough of coma—

The lank, dying fish. But not the ticking egg.

The *frisson* of the third line is vindicated by the rest of the poem; and one respects the tenacity with which both sides of the comparison are held in view: the hospital emerging strikingly, but never so as to obscure the snow falling on the salmon redds. This fidelity in turn is rewarded by the truth of two smaller details. "The blue glare of the ward" captures very finely the quality—a penetrating, clean, not-yet-brightened coldness—of a certain sort of morning light; while, in a passing phrase—"The silent to-fro hurrying of nurses"—the snow drifts are as nearly suggested. With the detached last line, the elastic rhythm of the whole is tightened to an aphorism.

The kinds of poems that give *River* its movement and pattern are either, like "New Year," allegories of self-discovery or else, like "An Eel," sketches of the characters that may later join such an allegory. There are also topographical poems—"River" and "In the Dark Violin of the Valley" are the best—in which Hughes imagines the flux of the river's life, "like a needle sewing body / And soul together, and sewing soul / And sky together and sky and earth." In an antithetical mood, he may imagine the river issuing from heaven, and rising "at a rending of veils." This sewing and this rending are the underplot of the sequence: because they oscillate steadily, the shape of the quest does not vary much; its end, in more than one sense, may be known from its beginning. But an exception ought to be made for the longest poem in the book. "The Gulkana" follows the course of a river in Alaska, and, by speaking of the things that compelled the poet to a different journey, it summarizes the themes of the shorter poems. *Gulkana,* as Hughes reminds us, is also a word for "a pre-Columbian glyph." From the start of the poem, we are made aware of the inscriptions of an archaic savagery: these are what the explorer has to decode, and what the poet has to translate.

The embarkation here is presented as still another birth: "We moved, not properly awake / In a weird light—a bombardment / Of purplish emptiness"; and, as he listens to the wilderness, the poet seems to hear "a stone voice." Beneath his boot soles, he can feel the "subsidence" of the ground—a sinking, but also an upwelling—and with it a sensation of "nearly a fear / Something I kept trying to deny." The poem, evidently, will be a bowing to compulsion. Having noticed a similar movement in other poems, one may surmise that the pursuit of earlier life-forms will be connected with a hunt for traces of a repressed self. The poem cooperates with this surmise: the fear, Hughes remarks, is of "one inside me, / Of a bodiless twin, some disinherited being"—or again, "a larva from prehistory / Whose journey this was." The poet feels that he, too, is a hunted thing. He propitiates the unseen creature, with notations of everything he does see: an Indian village; a fish eye; egg sacs, and all the "drugged, ritual victims" of the river's surge after winter; in short, the properties made familiar throughout *River*. At last he turns to a thought of the aboriginal Americans, to whom the hieroglyph-river is supposed to have been an apprehensible complex of life and death. Yet the poem's concluding image is as illegible to the reader as the Gulkana is to a modern traveller. It shows the face of an old Indian headman, "A whole bat, that glistened and stirred."

As such phrases attest, Hughes does not care for irony as a tone of voice. Rather, he is interested in irony as a disruption of perspective. That he can exhibit its effects within a space of two lines seems a measure of how far the book is possessed by his single story. One thinks of "*Only birth matters* / Say the river's whorls" (the whorls making a watery grave); and of "Where sun rolls bare, and earth rolls, / And mind condenses on old haws" (haws being the membranes that reduce "mind" to brain-stuff). These last are the final words of the book; and they have a message. Search out every trope as he will, the poet finds only these animal tropisms—in every aspiration to the ideal, only a reflexive symptom of the physical. Didacticism of a kind has prompted his writing from the first, so that, to commentators not preoccupied with the morality of violence, the selection of Ted Hughes as poet laureate was wholly intelligible. It has to be added that his first official production is a characteristic one. A river poem for the christening of Prince Harry, it pictures the ceremony as a drenching rainstorm which nobody can go indoors to avoid. One is partly impressed by the dexterity: without apparent compromise, this "Rain-Charm for the Duchy" brings a subject of state into the precincts of Hughes's work. As an afterthought one wonders if his poetry may not have grown a little regular in its own ceremonies, to yield such a pleasant, handsome, rousing compliment to a prince, from a slight redeployment of the original poetic stock.

SOME WAY into a poet's career, each new invention may seem to belong rightly with his earlier inventions. It sorts out well; every time, it seems a success. But this belonging is always a trap. Lawrence knew why better than any other poet, because he was interested in transitions of the self, that is, successes that could not be repeated. Hughes has been concerned with just such transitions, in a more methodical way. For him, they are changes that may be cultivated, like a journey with a few marked stages. He continues to write of the passage from energy to energy, through a catastrophic descent to the instincts. Indeed, all his work is a dispassionate record of the descent, and of the renewal that it brings. Confident as his poems are of their usual plot, how can they escape familiarity? The truth is that neither Hughes's poems nor his creatures have aimed steadily for the response Lawrence gave to the fish:

> I said to my heart, *who are these?*
> And my heart couldn't own them.

Hughes for his part has kept trying to own them. Often they have escaped, and he has gone on saying to his heart that the poet is a creature as strange as any. It is a sound admonition. The comfort that may prove hardest for him to elude is the praise Lawrence offered to a lesser creature: *"He's a rare one, but he belongs."*

1985

A Poet and Her Burden

What Is Found There takes its title from some lines by William Carlos Williams: "It is difficult / to get the news from poems / yet men die miserably every day / for lack / of what is found there."* In his attempts at thought Williams was often silly, and it is possible that he meant this literally; but it comes from a late poem ("Asphodel, That Greeny Flower") written after the Second World War, and the mood of hope qualified by anxiety could be heard about that time in poets of the most disparate tendencies. Wallace Stevens, in the middle of the war, writing a coda to *Notes toward a Supreme Fiction,* wheedled with his audience uncharacteristically: "How simply the fictive hero becomes the real; / How gladly with proper words the soldier dies, / If he must, or lives on the bread of faithful speech." The poet was doing his job in the war, as the soldier did his, or so the metaphor implied. The poet anyway offered "the bread of faithful speech"; and more honor was in the gesture than may have appeared. Both Stevens and Williams were too old then to serve as actual soldiers, and their hopes for poetry were uneasily linked to a distant pride in those who risked their lives.

Adrienne Rich goes in for a more consistent sort of poetic soldiering. Since 1968 or so, she has seen herself as a bringer of news in verse, the news that men and women require as much as their daily bread. Her work still bears her signature and yet it has been, where possible and as far as possible, work on behalf of the deprived and disesteemed: lesbians, gays, African Americans, Latin Americans, the poor, the unemployed and the ill-employed, the undervalued. Whether or not people are dying for want

* *What Is Found There: Notebooks on Poetry and Politics,* by Adrienne Rich.

of poetry—a suggestion that Rich entertains, but not too literally—she has found it a fertile premise to suppose that poetry might help people to live more completely.

It is a high-minded wish; and the poet who never felt its appeal was probably never a poet. The last systematic-looking attempt to keep the wish alive was the early critical program of I. A. Richards, in *Principles of Literary Criticism* and elsewhere, but the idea goes back to the second generation of utilitarians—to Mill under the influence of his reading of Wordsworth and his friendship with Carlyle. Educationally, much good can come of a hypothesis that people, in some quasi-organic sense, need poetry. It may not hold every cynicism at bay, but at least it keeps one idealism alive. Difficulties start to intrude, snags of detail and definition, when the soldier/poet/provider/bringer-of-news innocently asks: "How do I put into my poems 'what is found there'?"

The answer in *What Is Found There* begins with the epigraphs, all drawn from the subcritical, rhetorical, hortatory world of feeling that these notebooks easily inhabit. Muriel Rukeyser is quoted as saying:

> Dead power is everywhere among us—in the forest, chopping down the songs; at night in the industrial landscape, wasting and stiffening the new life; in the streets of the city, throwing away the day. We wanted something different for our people: not to find ourselves an old, reactionary republic, full of ghost-fears, the fears of death and the fears of birth. We want something else.

The style of continuous approximate eloquence, lending itself to mixed metaphor almost as a weary duty, is a distinct idiom mostly heard in left-wing literature (though not only there, as many country-western lyrics are alive to attest). Casually as it comes, a phrase like "throwing away the day" is bad poetry, and therefore not good prose. Still, one is apt to feel "Yes, I've known those moods, pretty much—that same feeling of waste," and the vague melodrama of thrown away sentences works on you as if it were a deep-lying confirmation of the waste. Another epigraph, from Audre Lorde—"new combinations, extrapolations and recognitions from within ourselves"—follows soon after to give the positive side.

Much of Rich's book is composed of quotations like these—some of them quite long, with whole poems by poets who are little-known. (I enjoyed one discovery, a poem by Lynn Emmanuel, but have seldom read a book that quoted so much bad poetry.) Not since Auden's *A Certain World* has a living author been treated by a publisher with this degree of indulgence. But Auden's commonplace book was an exuberant anthology, and skipping the obiter dicta you could work out a reading list for several winters. *What Is Found There* is more like the clippings of an average summer, with captions that grew, with a little prodding, into little clumps of essays. The message is flat and predigested. The peoples of North America have been maimed, trodden under, anesthetized by the culture of capitalism, even as they have been cheated of their thoughts and sensations by the relentless march of technology.

I wrote that last sentence very fast, as Rich wrote the book, and trusted it to turn out looking like a random passage from the book. I was not quite fast enough. Here is an *almost* random passage, except that it comes at the end of a chapter:

> And perhaps this is the hope: that poetry can keep its mechanical needs simple, its head clear of the fumes of how "success" is concocted in the capitals of promotion, marketing, consumerism and in particular of the competition—taught in the schools, abetted at home—that pushes the "star" at the expense of the culture as a whole, that makes people want stardom rather than participation, association, exchange and improvisation with others. Perhaps this is the hope: that poetry, by its nature, will never become leashed to profit, marketing, consumerism.

Apart from the trick of reiteration—("perhaps this . . . ")—a comfortable pitcher's mound that sinks to a sand trap for the writer overstimulated by public speaking—this is about as resourceless as fluent prose can get. The threadbare catalogues are not heightened by a trace of precision: the *tions* and *ings* and *isms* are put through their paces one more time and then one more; so that when a slight shift occurs (*promotion* becoming *profit*), it seems an afterthought without consequence for logic or tone. The practical criticism in these notebooks is written with a different diction, but the mental processes that led up to it have not been appreciably different. Rich can quote a long stretch of contemporary free verse that ends in a Whitmanlike catalogue of events and place names, and then ask, or rather intone:

> Is this lesbian poetry? Yes—and most potently—because it is grounded in and insistent to grasp the poet's own white Southern Christian culture with its segregated history and legacy of contradictions, the beauty and sorrow of its landscape, its sexual codes and nightmares. She knows the region's living creatures, how they move and unfold, how wild country and gardens coexist, she pays attention to people; she tries to "remember, and failing that, invent" (Monique Wittig) where a white woman can stand in that heritage. Is this "Southern poetry?" Yes—in a new way: the white woman

turned outsider as lesbian connects differently with the white southern literary tradition, Agrarians and Fugitives, required reading in college, Allen Tate, John Crowe Ransom, their loyalties and affinities with the Confederate dead.

It is certainly well for a writer to pay attention to people, and to herself and to the things around her. Most of the encomium would hold true for all good poetry at all times in all places; the attempts at specification are as loose and optional as the spliced grammar of the final sentence: woman turned outsider as lesbian, outsider turned lesbian as woman, lesbian turned woman as outsider. All the possibilities sound immensely fruitful, and a good critic of course need never do more than point, but the intent here is not to point (*what* loyalties? *what* affinities?) but to commit oneself excitedly, quotably, in the breathless manner peculiar to literary and literary-political advertisements on the run.

Even by the ad hoc rules of the partly autobiographical journalistic genre that Rich has here devised, she does one thing very questionable. She condescends to herself. The young Adrienne Cecile Rich is made to appear so typically illusioned—so artless and thoughtless an example of the aesthete as fifties cold war imperial beneficiary and exploitee—that one wonders out of what unglowing cinders the formidably confident prophet of the notebooks could have arisen. Because I was so silly yesterday, I am so wise today: it is a contemptible theory, when you think about it, and more observed as a convention of a therapeutic culture than believed by anyone in private. *My* younger self was more demanding and more given to admirations than his successor. Is the comparison all to the advantage of the successor? The disabused, the gender-fortified, solidarity-seeking and solidarity-finding Adrienne Rich of the present gives a thorough trouncing to the Yale Younger Poet of 1951—a too-academic success as she now thinks her then self, honored but not honorable; the success being possible only within constraints half understood and less than half acknowledged. Doubtless the mature person who bears the same name has one degree more right to make such a judgment than anyone else.

But what if the tables were turned? What if the author of "Living in Sin"—a memorable poem written in the fifties and full of Rich's best qualities: anecdotal ease and nervous energy, poignancy free of self-pity and wit that could pour itself calmly into every detail—what if that author could judge the conscience-stricken reviser who snipped a word from a passage that once mildly deplored

> that morning light
> so coldly would delineate the scraps
> of last night's cheese and three sepulchral bottles;
> that on the kitchen shelf among the saucers
> a pair of beetle-eyes would fix her own—
> envoy from some black village in the moldings . . .

altering the last line to read:

> envoy from some village in the moldings . . .

That revision, canonized in the *Collected Early Poems*, was not done for sound or sense, and the young author would just possibly have found absurd the state of mind of the politic elder who enforced the change.*

THE REVISIONS in this large volume for the most part are remarkably light. The author has not been at pains to modify the impression of her early work; and in her generation no other apprenticeship was at once so gifted and so ingratiating. There are good poems in *A Change of World* (1951) and *The Diamond Cutters* (1955), where the manner still seems eclectically imitative: Auden and Frost are the main influences, but the author's retrospective note confesses to many others, "even English Georgian poets." (Some day, in the same way, people will confess to "even American Black Mountain poets.") But all of her work in this phase passes the test of holding your attention line by line. A personal sting and zest come into her writing in the third and fourth books, which seem to me her best, *Snapshots of a Daughter-in-Law* (1963) and *Necessities of Life* (1966). The poems have become irritable in a positive sense, with the readiness of someone awake to every elusive stimulus. Gone are the sonnets about buildings at Harvard or Oxford, about the art of the past and the lesson it teaches; though a line from one of those poems stands as a warning over the door of Rich's next phase: "A too-compassionate art is half an art."

Compassion was a late result. It was preceded by tormenting self-doubt, a sense of grief or grievance to which the poems of the sixties offer motives only partly digested from personal experience. The rhetoric is high and tense now, not tentative, with a confidence in the need for political engagement much in advance of the author's information. The turmoil of moods comes out in the titles of these years: *Leaflets* (1969), *The Will to Change* (1971), and *Diving into the Wreck* (1973), the last being the immediate successor to the volumes collected here. The final two sections

* *Collected Early Poems, 1950–1970,* by Adrienne Rich.

of *Leaflets* and all of *The Will to Change* are really notations—strident and untethered, beyond any expectation that a reader should supply the missing connections. Frayed as they are, and split off from any imaginative discipline, the poems are also oddly free of personal posturing. But the style has begun to be stereotyped.

The change, from her poetry of the late fifties and early sixties, looks now as if it were a deliberate refusal of poise, as if the author slammed down the piano lid: "No more of *those* songs." The puzzle is that her conversion should have been so complete over so short an interval. When you read "Peeling Onions," a poem of 1961—which begins "Only to have a grief / equal to all these tears"—you are in a world of rueful wit: "There's not a sob in my chest. / Dry-hearted as Peer Gynt / I pare away, no hero, merely a cook." The self-mockery and lament are intimate with each other, and the claim of neither is compromised. Grinding frustration, the neighbor of grief, lies somewhere in back of the poem, but it declares its interest with a fit of free verse against the endless rhyming of domestic waste. The poem closes on a headlong one-line paragraph: "These old tears in the chopping bowl." One wonders first at the subtlety of feeling, then at the economy and above all the speed. As late as 1966, in "The Demon Lover," Rich was deepening this vein of her work to take in hauntings quite unsusceptible to irony.

The year 1968 was the crossroads. It is fairly represented here by the prose conclusion of "The Burning of Paper instead of Children," a meditation on the trial of Daniel Berrigan.

> I am composing on the typewriter late at night, thinking of today. How well we all spoke. A language is a map of our failures. Frederick Douglass wrote an English purer than Milton's. People suffer highly in poverty. There are methods but we do not use them. Joan, who could not read, spoke some peasant form of French. Some of the suffering are: it is hard to tell the truth; this is America; I cannot touch you now. In America we have only the present tense. I am in danger. You are in danger. The burning of a book arouses no sensation in me. I know it hurts to burn. There are flames of napalm in Catonsville, Maryland. I know it hurts to burn. The typewriter is overheated, my mouth is burning, I cannot touch you and this is the oppressor's language.

The voice of seven years earlier had been credible and agile—wry, you may call it, but that is a poor way of saying that it had found a tone for attacking the smaller demons across a surprisingly wide range of experience. The new voice is ominous, as it aims to be, but that turns out to mean it belongs to nobody's life. This dry litany of crimes and recriminations, drained of apparent affect, was part of the metaphysical-moral climate of Godard's movies of the time, but the movies had pictures and it made a difference. The comparison of the writer's "heat" to the agony of children burned by napalm will not bear comment.

Rich was turned about in the late sixties, driven from crisis to crisis, threshed by every storm and prompted to the full-throated utterance of every plausible, half-pondered slogan, all with the same relentless, experimental, impersonal air. The poems start to have titles like "To Frantz Fanon" and lines like "LeRoi! Eldridge! listen to us, we are ghosts / condemned to haunt the cities where you want to be at home." The image of the poet as bloodless revenant, one of the white Undead (the sort of assertion that gladly takes a *we* where an *I* would resist): this casual allegory bears no resemblance to the portrait that Rich had associated with herself in "By No Means Native," from her first book.

> As for himself, he joined the band of those
> Who pick their fruit no matter where it grows,
> And learn to like it sweet or like it sour
> Depending on the orchard or the hour.
> By no means native, yet somewhat in love
> With things a native is enamored of—
> Except the sense of being held and owned
> By one ancestral patch of local ground.

Under the pressure to change, the memory of moods that had once been real to her is liable to sudden distortions, but it is her memory of poetry that most betrays her. "What are you doing here at the edge of the death-camps, Vivaldi?" she writes, in a solemn challenge so self-absorbed as to forget its source in Allen Ginsberg's "A Supermarket in California," with the cheerful salute: "And you, Garcia Lorca, what were you doing down by the watermelons?"

A revealing word that comes up more than once in Rich's early work is "pedagogues." The pedagogues are always on the scene before we arrive—Rich cannot bring herself to despise them; their trusted ironic wisdom is one step ahead of her—but her poetry seems to say: if the juice is gone, it is because of them. Later the pedagogues turn into "*conservateurs*": "I have learned to smell a *conservateur* a mile away: / they carry illustrated catalogues of all that there is to lose." Now, on the jacket flap of the *Collected Early Poems,* the same figure appears under a more familiar name: "With more than 700,000 copies of her books sold, Adrienne Rich's work is unequalled today in reclaiming serious poetry from scholars and returning it to the lives of general readers." I wonder how many of those sales are owed to classroom assignments by scholars and pedagogues and *conservateurs?*

RICH SINCERELY BELIEVES that poetic tradition is a kind of theft: she herself, according to the fable is a new maker of a mosaic of traditions, her *trouvailles* pulled uniquely from the wreckage. But the good girl who no longer sits at anyone's feet—this presentation, too, is traditional, and it can grow tiresome: "I'd rather / taste blood, yours or mine, flowing / from a sudden slash, than cut all day / with blunt scissors on dotted lines / like the teacher told." She writes as if all her teachers were cereal boxes.

Her actual teachers were the second generation of modernists, in poetry and criticism. But in relation to modernist poetry generally, which she picks at with an air of baffled annoyance, Rich's critical role has now become as specialized as that of a clearance-signing petty bureaucrat of the Ming dynasty. She is the professional scold—the famous living rebuke to all those famous dead delinquents. "Look at their politics," she says and says again. Her refrain practically becomes a parody of itself, as if she were saying "How bad they were!—Eliot, Pound, Stevens, Tate, the lot. (Sometimes I think Whitman was better, then again sometimes not.) How little they paid for their errors! And yet, something sticks in my mind about those poems. Or maybe it doesn't really, or shouldn't, I can't remember, I'm not really sure. Don't bad politics make the poems worse? Aren't they *shot through* with sin? Maybe that's too harsh; no, maybe it's the justice of History. But here, here is the poem, see for yourself." And then she quotes and scolds and pats and scolds some more.

The revelations in *What Is Found There* all happen at furious speed—a sign, perhaps, of boredom in the compiler—and the shorthand leaves you blinking to make sure what point has been made. Was that a new mug shot just now, or an old one held up for re-exposure? In Rich's undergraduate lecture notes,

> penciled on the endpapers of the copy of *Four Quartets* that I still have, I find: "This = problem of a Christian poem in a secular age—you can't accept it unless you accept Christian religion." The lecturer was F. O. Matthiessen, one of Eliot's earliest interpreters, who one year later, in a suicide note, described himself as a Christian and a socialist. He was also a homosexual.

Well, and? Should he have said "a Christian and a socialist and a homosexual," his suicide note rewritten to your canons of discretion and honesty? Or do you mean that there was something weird about such a man admiring Eliot? The notebook-keeper cannot be bothered, she has gone on to something else.

The most unexpected entry is on Stevens. Of the established poets of the older generation, he was the one from whom Rich learned most, the one to whom she returned for surprise and self-renewal. She has some interesting short observations on "The Idea of Order at Key West" and *The Man with the Blue Guitar.* But she singles out as startling achievements two lyrics much less widely known, "Dry Loaf" and "The Dwarf." One must have read a good many commentaries on Stevens, including appreciations by other poets, to see how uncommon these choices are, and how much they tell about Rich. Both poems explore a vein of sharp realism wrung out almost to drabness. Slightly incantatory, they do not try to sing. The notes are merely placed, just so, a remembered deposit, a trace. Rich admires "Dry Loaf" and "The Dwarf" for the way they show the poet "capable of shedding any predictable music"; and this was the moment in *What Is Found There* that reminded me that Rich is a poet. By the end of the chapter, she is back at the mill of denials and permissions. Stevens's was, after all, a poetry of "the riven self, the emotionally unhappy white man with a 'fairly substantial income,' the fugitive in the imagination who is repeatedly turned back by a wall of mirrors." Then comes a dutiful mention of "the collective poetry" of every culture, and with a last reassuring bump-down the chapter is over.

Regarding the most original American poets, Whitman and Dickinson, Rich over the years has moralized herself into an ambivalence so perfect that she is now equally uncertain of her past and present opinions. On the one hand, "Didn't they," in spite of appearances, "seem to fit their age, these 'beginners'? Didn't they act out precisely the chartered roles, the constructions of white, middle-class masculinity and femininity that suited the times?" Let us try to recall. Middle-class masculinity: "Steep'd amid honeyed morphine, my windpipe throttled in fakes of death, / At length let up again to feel the puzzle of puzzles, / And that we call Being." Middle-class femininity: "Dare you see a Soul *at the White Heat?* / Then crouch within the door." Those quotations are not in these notebooks, and indeed how could they be?

Sensing something faintly wrong, on the next page Rich takes back every word: "They were a wild woman and a wild man, writing their wild carnal and ecstatic thoughts." That feels closer to the truth, but the conclusion is utterly forbidden by an aphorism that greets us twelve chapters later, under the heading "What does a poet need to know?"

That to track your own desire, in your own language, is not an isolated task. You yourself are marked by family, gender, caste, landscape, the struggle to make a living, or the absence of such a struggle. The rich and the poor are equally marked. Poetry is never free of these markings even when it appears to be. Look into the images.

Of course, this "tracking" is a job that can be done, and in a modern society someone will be found to do it. Whether a poet needs to regard it as a sacred task, whether to treat it so is consistent with the writing of poetry: these are separate questions, of no necessary interest to the tracker.

Recall that the challenge was that we simply "Look into the images." I looked into these:

> Beyond siroccos harvesting
> The solstice thunders, crept away,
> Like a cliff swinging or a sail
> Flung into April's inmost day—
>
> Creation's blithe and petalled word
> To the lounged goddess when she rose
> Conceding dialogue with eyes
> That smile unsearchable repose—

Maybe, there, you can read the whole story just as Rich says you should be able to: Hart Crane, white, middle-class, homosexual, downwardly mobile, child of a grasping loveless marriage, tied forever to a place called Chagrin Falls, Ohio, spoiled, a drunk, a born evader, but keenly faithful to two destructive parents, incidental compensatory idealizer of black men (see "Black Tambourine" and "The River," passim) and later of one white woman (see "The Broken Tower"). For just a moment, it may all come into focus, until a second voice says: "You, fast-track critic, are a liar and a cheat." And suddenly it seems again that these are not images at all, let alone extractable social markings, but words, amazing words.

WHAT IS FOUND THERE contains some evocative passages that deserve a better setting: a rare glimpse of a Great Blue Heron on the roof of a house next door; a description of the making of maple syrup, with a page on how the custom and its product are threatened now by the prevalence of acid rain. The politics of these notebooks, as of Rich's recent poems if they could settle for less than everything, would have to be called broadly "environmental." In the notebooks she conveys her feeling for this cause as a passion bigger than resentment, and it is a pity that she should have chosen so diffuse a medium. One feels that a chance has been squandered by an advocate who can speak firmly and not pompously of the things she loves, many of which she sees dying out. Yet Rich has been misled from the start by an analogy between poetic activity and political activism.

"You cannot," she remarks, "tell how [the feelings in politics and poetry] will connect, spreading underground from rootlet to rootlet till every grass blade is afire from every other." But it makes a difference whether the connections occur across a society or in the mind of one person. It matters for what we can suppose the metaphor of fire to mean, and it matters for the sorts of links that will be felt between one root and another. Too credulous a regard for this analogy has taken Rich in her career from poetry to daily poetry to daily prose. She wrote good poems, fairly early, of an inventive delicacy and humor that she has come to disdain; and, later and less often, poems with the tenacity and the earnestness that she has come to prefer. She has written vivid prose, and useful agitational prose, but somewhere on the way a poet who aspired to journalism turned into a journalist troubled by her love of poetry. It is an adaptable blend, likely some time to send up greener shoots than the present notebooks—but not to be confused with the pursuit of either activity in its happiest state.

1993

FOURTEEN

John Ashbery:
The Self against Its Images

Ashbery writes about life with the guarded pleasure of one who cannot possess it. "Only love stays on the brain," he says, in a consolatory gesture that typically stops halfway—love, "and something these people, / These other ones, call life." When he speaks of love, he means something different from what the others would mean. The choice of the word *brain* may suggest the strangeness of his conception. It is the sort of word favored by poets who do not exalt imagination into "mind," but refer it back to an impulse from the senses: Shelley and Whitman, for example, as against Wordsworth and Stevens. In the context then, love is a material trace of spent passion, which exists in memory only. But it would be credulous to judge from the choice of a word. If the occasion seemed right, Ashbery would be prepared to say that love persists in the mind. He knows the rhetorical possibilities of English as well as any living author, and, apart from the standard poets, has kept a record of his debt to miscellaneous others. He writes in one place of "using what Wyatt and Surrey left around," but he might have added Landor, Clare, Beddoes, F. T. Prince, Caroline Lamb, and A. Conan Doyle. His poetry needs a various support system. It seeks after all to chart the look and feel of modernity in America, a place where people live in constant relation with each other though their lives only touch at points. The good of memory is the evidence it gives that they did touch once.

What has love to do with the writing of poetry? Ashbery comes close to an answer in the concluding lines of "Street Musicians," which compare the memory of any action or passion to an inscription on the landscape, a deposit with a signature that happens to be ours.

> Our question of a place of origin hangs
> Like smoke: how we picnicked in pine forests,
> In coves with the water always seeping up, and left
> Our trash, sperm and excrement everywhere, smeared
> On the landscape, to make of us what we could.

So to the question, What did our love make of us? the poet has to reply: not what we wished; only a deformation which we cherish anyway. Yet writing has an advantage over unassisted memory. It slows down the processes of annihilation by placing a small monument in their path—indeed, this is the motive of "Street Musicians," which begins with the report of a death. Also, unlike experience, writing has a pathos that changes slightly at times, as its feelings move from person to person. These features help it to survive, and to commemorate a way of life that may have lacked a name.

The poet's tone of complicity implies that his elegies belong to all of us. But who are we? People who start to call a thing "life" once we know that we care for it. By contrast, the poet is someone who keeps thinking about the commonness and even the sordidness of the thing we chose. His attachment to this unnatural work makes him an exile; and he elects as a companion someone named *you*. Placed beside the latter personage, we look no different from "the others." Such have been the premises of Ashbery's poems, from *The Double Dream of Spring* on—conventions so familiar by now that it feels pedantic to rehearse them. It remains a puzzle why the game of pretended solidarity and genuine concealment should occur as steadily as it does in his writing, which allows few things to happen twice. But Ashbery has gone far to explain it in "Syringa," one of his unshakable triumphs, with patient eloquence and an uncharacteristic depth of allegorical detail.

> Orpheus liked the glad personal quality
> Of the things beneath the sky. Of course, Eurydice was a part
> Of this. Then one day, everything changed. He rends
> Rocks into fissures with lament. Gullies, hummocks
> Can't withstand it. The sky shudders from one horizon
> To the other, almost ready to give up wholeness.
> Then Apollo quietly told him: "Leave it all on earth.
> Your lute, what point? Why pick at a dull pavan few care to
> Follow, except a few birds of dusty feather,
> Not vivid performances of the past." But why not?

All other things must change too.
The seasons are no longer what they once were,
But it is the nature of things to be seen only once,
As they happen along, bumping into other things, getting along
Somehow. That's where Orpheus made his mistake.
Of course Eurydice vanished into the shade;
She would have even if he hadn't turned around.
No use standing there like a gray stone toga as the whole wheel
Of recorded history flashes past, struck dumb, unable to utter an intelligent
Comment on the most thought-provoking element in its train.
Only love stays on the brain, and something these people,
These other ones, call life. Singing accurately
So that the notes mount straight up out of the well of
Dim noon and rival the tiny, sparkling yellow flowers
Growing around the brink of the quarry, encapsulizes
The different weights of things.
                                        But it isn't enough
To just go on singing. Orpheus realized this
And didn't mind so much about his reward being in heaven
After the Bacchantes had torn him apart, driven
Half out of their minds by his music, what it was doing to them.
Some say it was for his treatment of Eurydice.
But probably the music had more to do with it, and
The way music passes, emblematic
Of life and how you cannot isolate a note of it
And say it is good or bad.

Orpheus, first of poets, likes the "glad personal quality / of the things beneath the sky," and he naturally assumes his poetry will bring them closer.
If it did so, it would cooperate with his need for ordinary companionship
and love: "Of course, Eurydice was a part / Of this." But the poem means
to disappoint any hope that poetry can redeem these things.

As the plot advances, one comes to see that Eurydice's loss was a necessary condition of the power of Orpheus's music. The comic feeling with
which Ashbery invests this catastrophe is partly owing to the good-natured
pessimism of Apollo's challenge. A healer and prosodist whose laws of balance Orpheus has broken, he speaks for the monuments of the past
against the genius of the present, and the drama of the poem follows from
Orpheus's silence here. It is Ashbery who speaks for him: "But why not? /
All other things must change too." Harold Rosenberg wrote of "art's aim
of changing the landscape," and for Ashbery this ideal must never be allowed to relax into a figure of speech. The effects of Orpheus's song are ac-

cordingly described in a present tense that would suit an epic hero: "He rends / Rocks into fissures with lament." Heroic as it may be, such language offers a view of art's influence on life that is not ameliorative. If, to pursue Rosenberg's aphorisms a step further, "the Rocky Mountains have resembled fake art for a century," the solution is to change it all on earth. Alter the position of the trees, the mountains, the creatures, by enchanting them with music, so that they come nearer just for the sake of listening. This renewal of the present, however, is accomplished not only by the loss of Eurydice, but by the expulsion from the poet of any sense of his effect or reward. Moralists have their own explanation of his fate—"Some say it was for his treatment of Eurydice"—but readers and listeners feel otherwise: "probably the music had more to do with it, and / The way music passes." In proportion therefore as Orpheus sang accurately, his notes will have been scattered with a reach and pattern that looks altogether aimless.

So far, we have a picture of the artist as a person so receptive to the stimulus of present things as to be unconscious of his role in creating them; so that, even before being torn apart, he is a character who exists in fragments. A regret of the moralist of art is that the reward for the artist's unique sacrifice can never be timely enough. But this comes from mistaking admiration of Orpheus's music for direct sympathy with Orpheus. The truth is that his music, like a poet's word, is curiously indifferent to him, as it is to any wisdom it may seem to manifest:

> But how late to be regretting all this, even
> Bearing in mind that regrets are always late, too late!
> To which Orpheus, a bluish cloud with white contours,
> Replies that these are of course not regrets at all,
> Merely a careful, scholarly setting down of
> Unquestioned facts, a record of pebbles along the way.
> And no matter how all this disappeared,
> Or got where it was going, it is no longer
> Material for a poem. Its subject
> Matters too much, and not enough, standing there helplessly
> While the poem streaked by, its tail afire, a bad
> Comet screaming hate and disaster, but so turned inward
> That the meaning, good or other, can never
> Become known. The singer thinks
> Constructively, builds up his chant in progressive stages
> Like a skyscraper, but at the last minute turns away.
> The song is engulfed in an instant in blackness

Which must in turn flood the whole continent
With blackness, for it cannot see. The singer
Must then pass out of sight, not even relieved
Of the evil burthen of the words. Stellification
Is for the few, and comes about much later
When all record of these people and their lives
Has disappeared into libraries, onto microfilm.
A few are still interested in them. "But what about
So-and-so?" is still asked on occasion. But they lie
Frozen and out of touch until an arbitrary chorus
Speaks of a totally different incident with a similar name
In whose tale are hidden syllables
Of what happened so long before that
In some small town, one indifferent summer.

In showing how the poet's words recede into a name, then a tale, and at last hidden syllables that tell of an unknown place, "Syringa" concludes with an observation on art in general. Wherever the center of attention appears to be, it will turn out that the action was somewhere else.

The long line and the calmly elaborating syntax of this poem are, in fact, borrowed from Auden's "Musée des Beaux Arts," which makes a similar point more explicitly. The result feels unexceptional in a poet whose sense of the decorum of style is always keen. Yet the very presence of the echo suggests a revision of Auden's teaching. His poem told us that we *could* isolate a note in the song or a figure in the painting, though the old masters would never help us by displaying it prominently. This was in keeping with Auden's belief that wisdom, even if only the wisdom of human limitation, could be derived from art for the sake of life. But Ashbery supposes that the observations of art enter our life as knowledge when it is already too late. About suffering, his old masters are never wrong because they are never right, and how could they be, when the suffering includes their own? As for the scholarly setting down of "unquestioned facts" about their careers, it is concerned with just the things they themselves do not regard. Meanwhile, their words have been withdrawn, leaving a blank that engulfs "the whole continent" in blackness. If the words return at all, it will be as "a totally different incident with a similar name." Ashbery's trope for the place of such recurrences is "some small town, one indifferent summer"; in "Self-Portrait in a Convex Mirror," he called it "pockets out of time." What he points to in either case is the inscrutability of change in art as in history. To put it another way, revision is a later reader's word for invention, and originality is a name for success that may be repeated under a new aspect. But for the poet, "not even relieved / Of the evil burthen of the words," both of these ideas are unintelligible.

The poet's ambition has been to become a totally different incident with a similar name, that is, to achieve ignorance of himself through his singing. To others eager for self-knowledge, this makes him "a bad / Comet screaming hate and disaster, but so turned inward / That the meaning, good or other, can never / Become known." It will not do to translate his ignorance as a side effect of conscious boldness. He is a disaster even to himself. And in these circumstances, the burden of the survival of his words is such that he would prefer to be relieved of it. "Stellification / Is for the few"—the we'll-make-you-a-star syndrome being the invention of later readers and not of poets—but how many would want it? At the end of "Syringa," one realizes how far perfection of the work, as Ashbery reads it, must always be from any conflict with perfection of the life. But that is because the two have no relation to each other at all. The poet's individual disasters or windfalls, if he has either in a notable degree, will be taken as they are dealt out, free of any connection with the energy that his words carry past him. Ashbery's understanding of these matters has enabled him to appear at once the most confident and the least arrogant of poets.

Nevertheless, the others, whose personal quality the poet has attested, seem to have passed out of sight. Probably this had to happen. Ashbery cared for them less than he thought, and only as one might care for the sympathizers of the poet in "Alastor," baffled lookers-on who minister to his wants but are dead to a fate they cannot touch. This is plain in an earlier poem, "Parergon," which looks like a sketch for "Syringa." The others there declare they are "happy in our way of life," but the poet denounces them, "O woebegone people," and concludes "It is always time for a change." The change, of course, comes to him alone, though they marvel at his passing:

> He took his pleasure, savage
> And mild with the contemplating.
> Yet each knew he saw only aspects,
> That the continuity was fierce beyond all dream of enduring,
> And turned his head away, and so
> The lesson eddied far into the night:
> Joyful its beams, and in the blackness blacker still,
> Though undying joyousness, caught in that trap.

The poet had promised that his listeners would enter "each other's lives, eyes wide apart, crying"; and it may be noted that Ashbery commonly associates this image with the hope of natural sympathy. Indeed, the promise here as in "Syringa" is identical with the shared gesture of Whitman's poetry, the breaking of the lilac sprig.

Syringa denotes the genus of lilacs, and its name implies the animation of nature by a divinity. But the poet Ashbery has described is hardly fit to perform the act of binding and healing that his words prophesy. He says, "Share it with the others," even as he thinks, "Hide it." There are poets who honor a friend by addressing him in public as a second self. Ashbery sounds like one of them, yet his feeling is different. When he ceases to write on behalf of us, and addresses "you" instead, he means only himself, farther in. Once again the contrast with Whitman is revealing. His usual self was a stand-in for all possible others in the democracy he imagined. Ashbery on the contrary summons his "you" as part of an attempt to keep America outside himself. This isolation he clearly regards as a necessary ruse in the project of continuing as a poet at all. He speaks of America in a variety of metaphors: network, shadow, crosshatching, and sometimes "the juice," as a maniac driver talks of *giving the thing more juice*. But all of these converge on a single fear. America had better be treated as an abstract postulate, an uncharted terrain on which poetry somehow emerges. Were it incorporated into a poet's ambitions, it would leave nothing personal to be said.

THE GAME OF still talking to the others—not despising but amusing them, in the knowledge that their lives "matter too much and not enough, standing there helplessly"—seems to me the leading motive of Ashbery's work. His remains the original idiom of our time, and yet it is really a composite of styles, which owes its distinctness to the speaker's need of shifting tones. Ashbery began ventriloquizing in earnest with the voice of the pedantic lecturer, in openings like these from "Decoy," "Definition of Blue," and "Soonest Mended": "We hold these truths to be self-evident"; "The rise of capitalism parallels the advance of romanticism / And the individual is dominant until the close of the nineteenth century"; "Barely tolerated, living on the margin / In our technological society." Another voice, that of the genial big-city topographer or tourist of daily habits, had already been heard in episodes of "The Skaters," before it took over the whole narration of *Three Poems* and of "Grand Galop." This may be the version of Ashbery that most readers cherish. But from the start it alternated, and only flourished in balance with, the half-visible landscapes and personalia of a native abstractionist. These can be glimpsed in the montages that open "Sunrise in Suburbia," "Fragment," and "Fantasia on 'The Nut-Brown Maid,'" and that return at intervals to give many poems a tacit command of detail that is haunting. It seems pertinent that the ground note of the latter idiom comes from Auden's early verse, from poems like "To throw away the key and walk away," "From the very first coming down," "Will you turn a deaf ear," and "It was Easter as I walked in the public gardens." The subject of those poems was a conspiracy that was destined to fail, a you whom chance would easily part from me.

Ashbery sometimes imagines a happier ending for one of us. In showing what it is, and at what cost it is imagined, I will be saying very little about style. Yet the motif that will emerge, with its self-contained plot, may be inseparable from the deflections of a style like Ashbery's. It has to do with the exposure of a self that is diminished by experience, pictured side by side with the concealment of a self that is untouchable by experience. The first is associated with figures of commercial reproduction and, above all, photographs. The second is associated with figures of reflection. *Picture,* therefore, must be taken in an almost literal sense. As for the interest of these things, it belongs in the first case to the worldly fortunes of the author, and in the second to the hidden fate of his words. The moral weight of this contrast for Ashbery will be apparent from the quotations alone, without a great deal of comment. The only circumstances he asks his reader to take for granted are self-evident: that, for example, the rise of capitalism parallels the advance of romanticism; and that the poet is among those who are barely tolerated on the margin of society. What he brings back from the margin to the center he will no longer recognize as his.

The poem called "Summer" is among the most available of Ashbery's shorter pieces; and yet, through several readings its plot may remain obscure.

> There is that sound like the wind
> Forgetting in the branches that means something
> Nobody can translate. And there is the sobering "later on,"
> When you consider what a thing meant, and put it down.
>
> For the time being the shadow is ample
> And hardly seen, divided among the twigs of a tree,
> The trees of a forest, just as life is divided up
> Between you and me, and among all the others out there.
>
> And the thinning-out phase follows
> The period of reflection. And suddenly, to be dying

Is not a little or mean or cheap thing,
Only wearying, the heat unbearable,

And also the little mindless constructions put upon
Our fantasies of what we did: summer, the ball of pine needles,
The loose fates serving our acts, with token smiles,
Carrying out their instructions too accurately—

Too late to cancel them now—and winter, the twitter
Of cold stars at the pane, that describes with broad gestures
This state of being that is not so big after all.
Summer involves going down as a steep flight of steps

To a narrow ledge over the water. Is this it, then,
This iron comfort, these reasonable taboos,
Or did you mean it when you stopped? And the face
Resembles yours, the one reflected in the water.

The initial sound which means something nobody can translate is the sensory trace that may lead to a strangely valued memory, or to the writing of a poem. It is something one keeps hold of unawares and may return to by accident without knowing why. But "the sobering 'later on,' / When you consider what a thing meant, and put it down," exists for the poet alone. The shadow, which enters the poem soon after, evidently belongs to the world outside, with its mindless and unconsidering energies. It depletes, and itself causes the thinning-out phase that is another name for dying. We are told its effect is to blot out every lingering impression from the "period of reflection" that has come before. This, then, is the power that the poet sets himself against. The aim of his poem is to induce a second period of reflection.

At the moment of writing, however, "the loose fates serving our acts" have control of us; and they retain it all the more fiercely for their apparent graciousness: "This iron comfort, these reasonable taboos." So the poem as it nears its close is poised before a contentment it sees as killing. The last five lines take place in this ominous pause, and every element of the figure they make is equivocal—possibly menacing, possibly consoling, like the attitude of a human figure bent over a reflecting pool, whose next action we cannot predict. The narrow ledge over the water seems to afford a transition to some different state of being; but what would that be? And the stopping that is spoken of—is it a moment of death, or of being transfixed by an image? The deceptive syntax of the last line-and-a-half brings all these riddles into coherence. What the picture has led us to expect is a face looking at its own reflection. But on inspecting the grammar, one observes that "the one reflected in water" can refer equally to "yours" and "the face," which are in any case the same thing: they are the reflection itself. Where the logical structure of the poem makes us look for a relation between object and copy, the closing lines yield an object that exists only in reflection. One may conclude that this moment itself is the "later on" which the poem meant to realize, from its impulse in "that sound like the wind / Forgetting." Yet the reflective permanence we are shown, in which a self-recognition is sealed tight from experience, has something of the finality of a death.

I interpret the poem allegorically, as a shadow play about poetry, and how it relates to the life it borrows from. Words that we return to always have the sort of deadness that this reflection has. To borrow Ashbery's phrase in "Tapestry," they are written *dead on the line*. Their character derives from the wearying and unbearable experience of the one who wrote them, but none of this appears on their face. It presents rather a surface which we cannot pry beneath. So experience, which made its way into reflection because it mattered too much, passes wholly into reflection, until it does not matter. The conversion, if that is the word, of pleasure and pain into expression, also suggests an advantage that poems have over poets. They can show at any moment a fixity which the poet lacks. But they command our interest by two other traits as well: ignorance, and the power to grow without dying. The first of these traits may be hard to see as the virtue Ashbery requires it to be. I would explain it in the following way. The narrow ledge from which the poet imagines himself crossing over into another "phase" is the means by which he imagines connecting himself with other persons. But this aim has to be disappointed. What he will succeed in joining is his reflection with their gaze, or his words with their reading. In the latter event particularly, it will be impossible to say what has been gained. And yet his surmise that the action may be transitive moves the poem from a first to a second reflection, and from "dying" to "you."

Some explicit proverbs on the uses of ignorance take up a section of "Grand Galop." The premise of this marvelous poem is a walk around New York City, where unforeseen halts are above suspicion:

Someone is coming to get you:
The mailman, or a butler enters with a letter on a tray
Whose message is to change everything, but in the meantime
One is to worry about one's smell or dandruff or lost glasses—
If only the curtain-raiser would end, but it is interminable.

But there is this consolation:
If it turns out to be not worth doing, I haven't done it;
If the sight appalls me, I have seen nothing;
If the victory is pyrrhic, I haven't won it.
And so from a day replete with rumors
Of things being done on the other side of the mountains
A nucleus remains, a still-perfect possibility
That can be kept indefinitely. And yet
The groans of labor pains are deafening; one must
Get up, get out, and be on with it. Morning is for sissies like you
But the real trials, the ones that separate the men from the boys, come later.

Quite frequently in Ashbery's poetry, one comes across the figure of some-one bringing a letter on a tray—usually as a screen figure for the nameless person who is coming to get you, to break up your conspiracy with your-self. When the image is central—as in the bland epigram "At North Farm," to which Ashbery gave a mistaken prominence by printing it at the front of *A Wave*—he cannot use it. But here, as the bearer of a charge of duties from the other side of the mountains, the figure has a purpose. It stands for all the servants who are masters in disguise, the loose fates serv-ing our acts, whose claim the poet must resist. He does so here by doing nothing: "If it turns out to be not worth doing, I haven't done it; / If the sight appalls me, I have seen nothing; / If the victory is pyrrhic, I haven't won it." He saves himself an unembarrassable role in the play that is his future, by assuring that the curtain-raiser will be interminable.

Yet the curious power of these lines is that they persuade, and one ends by feeling he was right to guard himself. It is carried off largely by the sug-gestion about sight: experience, these words seem to say, is so monstrous a spectacle that once seen we would wish it to have been unseen. Lurking somewhere beneath the phrase may be an echo of *King Lear*, at Cornwall's reply to the prophecy of revenge by Gloucester—"I shall see . . . " "See't shalt thou never"—and the pathetic recurrence to the same thought at the end, in Gloucester's "I see it feelingly." A similar context in "Soonest Mended" incidentally discloses an echo of "Nothing will come of noth-ing." In the earlier poem too, doubts about the worth of knowledge have led to a self-humoring wish for total inertia:

Better, you said, to stay cowering
Like this in the early lessons, since the promise of learning
Is a delusion, and I agreed, adding that
Tomorrow would alter the sense of what had already been learned,
That the learning process is extended in this way, so that from this standpoint

None of us ever graduates from college,
For time is an emulsion, and probably thinking not to grow up
Is the brightest kind of maturity for us, right now at any rate.
And you see, both of us were right, though nothing
Has somehow come to nothing.

In moments like these, which undo in advance anything that it would be possible to do, the self-protective instinct seems to express a stronger will than mere action could. And in the lines that follow in "Soonest Mended," Ashbery will identify action with deferral as such—"For this is action, this not being sure, this careless / Preparing, sowing the seeds crooked in the furrow, / Making ready to forget." What is at stake is a truth not of experience, but of our thinking about experience, which Ashbery wants to build on.

Many people think of action or suffering as something that just happens. You may choose whether or how much to learn from it, whether or how early to get up in the morning so as to expose yourself to a lot of it, but experience is what you read in the letter brought on the tray. The only way out of the predicament is to have written the letter. Yet the person who decides not to read it may show an authority like that of the writer himself (as an ideally steady correspondent would be too busy to open his mail). In this light it looks as if the reasonable exhortation, "Get up, get out, and be on with it," is another bridge like the "narrow ledge" in "Summer," placed there to stop us from crossing. To confirm the suggestion, Ashbery gives his next lines—"Morning is for sissies like you," and so on—in one of the hugely inauthentic Other People's Voices that interrupt many of his poems for a line or two. Here it strikes the note of a rotarian call to order. The effect is spurious, yet no other voice is heard in favor of testing the rumors "of things being done on the other side of the mountains," which may well be the other side of the street. The passage moves a long way toward framing the desirability of ignorance as a virtue for experience. Yet we know that this will not do. It can be supposed a virtue only in art, and even there for the work alone and not its maker. "Grand Galop," however, points to a risk Ashbery takes throughout his writing. He appears to speak from the wisdom of ordinary action and suffering; but he does so by describing the pathology of art as the pathology of daily life.

OUTSIDE ART, what would it mean for a moment of experience to attain the fixity of words written dead on the line? This is a question that Ashbery has looked at again and again. The moment, of course, simply passes into oblivion; but it can achieve a sort of counterfeit immortality; and his poems often discuss the process by which that happens. Photography may be seen as just such a process, and as a metaphor for others, because it is the medium in which most people recognize themselves as the heroes of their own lives. Ashbery finds the result disturbing, most likely on two counts. It imitates the durability of language while feigning the easy survival of personality which words deny. At the same time it presents an image that can never vary—unlike words, which expose "a totally different incident with a similar name." One of Ashbery's finest short poems, "City Afternoon," regards the capture of memory in a photograph as another name for death, against which poetic reflection may appear as an act of recovery.

> A veil of haze protects this
> Long-ago afternoon forgotten by everybody
> In this photograph, most of them now
> Sucked screaming through old age and death.
>
> If one could seize America
> Or at least a fine forgetfulness
> That seeps into our outline
> Defining our volumes with a stain
> That is fleeting too
>
> But commemorates
> Because it does define, after all:
> Gray garlands, that threesome
> Waiting for the light to change.
> Air lifting the hair of one
> Upside down in the reflecting pool.

The veil of haze is said to "protect" the old photograph, but only in the paradoxical sense in which weakening faculties may protect the body from consciousness of its decay. For the end that is hidden to the subjects of the picture is to be "sucked screaming through old age and death"—a fearful image which plays on our belief that time-lapse photography opens up a reality hidden to the eye. The death mentioned in "City Afternoon" is startling, in that it includes an idea of fate. The single aspect under which both may be known Ashbery calls "America."

To resume the comparison with Whitman: though Ashbery has a deep emotional affinity with his poetry—as he does with Eliot's in "Preludes," "La Figlia che Piange," *The Waste Land,* and "Marina"—the local or national community he reflects upon either exists without relation to the individual, or frustrates his wish "To step free at last, minuscule on the gigantic plateau— / This was our ambition: to be small and clear and free." That may seem to leave American poetry with the task of defining itself as "a kind of fence-sitting, / Raised to the level of an aesthetic ideal"; but when Ashbery does invoke America, it appears as a contingent presence that cannot be seized by art. Another poem, which he published close to "City Afternoon," in *Self-Portrait in a Convex Mirror*, bears the evangelical title "The One Thing That Can Save America." Starting with a recital of place-names for their own sake, it seems ready to yield a warmer view of the subject than one has seen elsewhere in his work. Yet it warns that while "places of known civic pride, of civil obscurity" still have a personal value for the poet, their claim may be hostile to his.

> These are connected to my version of America
> But the juice is elsewhere.
> This morning as I walked out of your room
> After breakfast crosshatched with
> Backward and forward glances, backward into light,
> Forward into unfamiliar light,
> Was it our doing, and was it
> The material, the lumber of life, or of lives
> We were measuring, counting?
> A mood soon to be forgotten
> In crossed girders of light, cool downtown shadow
> In this morning that has seized us again?
>
> I know that I braid too much my own
> Snapped-off perceptions of things as they come to me.
> They are private and always will be.

Notice the suggestion that it is America's shadow that seeps into our outline, America itself that has taken hold of us and made our consciousness of ourselves incommunicably private. And the moment this is recognized, "we" is displaced by "I." The speaker of the last three lines can no longer possess a version of America but only his snapped-off perceptions.

There is always a coolness like this when Ashbery speaks of his part in the general life. The last lines of "City Afternoon" have their chill, yet they try to make an affirming memory from the very sense of conditioned life, which America induces and the photograph depicts: the progression of verbs in these lines is "seeps," "defines," "commemorates." We risk having our outline determined by the fine forgetfulness that seeps into it from our conformity to a stereotype. But maybe, if the stereotype matters too much, it really does matter; it "commemorates, / Because it does define, after all." A nostalgia for standard commemorations is one of the unsorted elements in Ashbery's work, and it can easily join the mood of a poignant and personal nostalgia; as when, near the end of "Grand Galop," he remembers faces and emblems from a high school graduation: "Impossible not to be moved by the tiny number / Those people wore, indicating that they should be raised to this or that power." A more recent poem, "Cups and Broken Handles," winds down in a similar way, with Ashbery thinking "Isn't it too bad about old things, old schools, / Old dishes," but then turning back on the elegiac rhythm he had begun: "Our strength lies / In the potential for motion, not in accomplishments, and it gets / Used up too, which is, in a way, more effective." The potential is used up by being frozen in memory like a snapshot: it preserves an idea of a self that time destroys. This is, as the title admits, a method by which we are broken down, though something survives of us in a shape we did not choose. The likelihood that the idea we end with is for the best (because there is no alternative) haunts Ashbery as it haunted Proust.

Thus a personal irony may be felt to qualify the geniality with which his writing accepts the claim of public images. It grants itself as many slogans, endorsements, familiar appeals, and healthy attitudes as the audience will bear: seen from a distance, it has a wised-up look. But the performance alludes to, it does not trust, what "these people, / These other ones, call life." As naturally as possible, Ashbery bends to the impulse to talk with them about the pageant of every day, of which a photograph may capture a choice moment. His own vision of the city is almost a photographic negative of this one. It appears with great power at the close of "Self-Portrait in a Convex Mirror," and is meant for a single speaker and a single listener:

> We have seen the city; it is the gibbous
> Mirrored eye of an insect. All things happen
> On its balcony and are resumed within,
> But the action is the cold, syrupy flow
> Of a pageant. One feels too confined,
> Sifting the April sunlight for clues,
> In the mere stillness of the ease of its
> Parameter.

The city, like the photograph but unlike the self-portrait of this poem, represents a force of anonymity, the enormous confinement in which a name and a face are trapped and lost. When, in a poem written many years later, "Whatever It Is, Wherever You Are," Ashbery writes of a person captured in the same flow, he still presents his memory as "an old photograph of you, out in the yard, looking almost afraid in the crisp, raking light that afternoons in the city held in those days." In view of these other images, the invention of the last lines of "City Afternoon" is the poise with which they hold in solution two distinct perspectives, that of nostalgia and that of a fateful retrospect. The achievement owes something to the complexity of the subject, which is at once America, the city, and our memorials of both.

But the "threesome" in the photograph are not waiting for the light to change as a painter waits. Rather, they are waiting for the shutter to click and the trap to close. Why then does their posture so curiously recall the pause of the hidden self in "Summer," as it withdraws into a reflection— as indeed the poem's final image, "Upside down in the reflecting pool," seems to repeat the final image of "Summer"? What I believe interests Ashbery is how the mass productions of culture make an uncanny double of the reflections sacred to art. As Proust's narrator saw in thinking about the last photograph of his grandmother, the flaw of the reproduced image suggests a truth about knowledge. "What is restored / Becomes stronger than the loss as it is remembered": that is the way Ashbery puts it in "A Wave." But one can frame the truth in words that afford less comfort. A vivid memory is a lie whose value we secure for ourselves in exchange for a death. This means that an image which merely stimulates memory can be a subject for art only to the extent that the artist defends against it. The city is composed of just such images, as Ashbery remarks in "Self-Portrait"; it wants "To siphon off the life of the studio, deflate / Its mapped space to enactments, island it." A response that the poem considers is to refine one's tactics of evasion, and take satisfaction from the self's "swerving easily away, as though to protect / What it advertises." But this is usually followed by a stronger defense.

The following lines of "Self-Portrait" seem to me written in earnest, and they concern the image-maker's touch that converts all art into play.

> "Play" is something else;
> It exists, in a society specifically
> Organized as a demonstration of itself.
> There is no other way, and those assholes
> Who would confuse everything with their mirror games
> Which seem to multiply stakes and possibilities, or
> At least confuse issues by means of an investing
> Aura that would corrode the architecture
> Of the whole in a haze of suppressed mockery,
> Are beside the point. They are out of the game,
> Which doesn't exist until they are out of it.

The anger of the lines is directed against the can't-miss formats of cultural appropriation which now go by the name of postmodernism. Ashbery thinks of art on the contrary as the writing of a text—an act indistinguishable from the concealment of a self—which disperses the "haze of suppressed mockery" and withdraws the "investing aura" from images. A work of art, therefore, for as long as it feels original, is a work against commerce.

A lot of nonsense has been written about Ashbery's relationship to the painters whose work he admires or partly admires. He made a good joke about it once, by entitling a poem "And *Ut Pictura Poesis* Is Her Name." Still, he has described, with a personal sympathy, his sense of the heroism of modernist painting; and his allusions appear to concentrate most on the first generation of abstract expressionists: on Pollock, in his essay "The Invisible Avant-Garde," and, from the look of it, on de Kooning in the central passage of "Syringa."

> "The end crowns all,"
> Meaning also that the "tableau"
> Is wrong. For although memories, of a season, for example,
> Melt into a single snapshot, one cannot guard, treasure
> That stalled moment. It too is flowing, fleeting;
> It is a picture of flowing, scenery, though living, mortal,
> Over which an abstract action is laid out in blunt,
> Harsh strokes. And to ask more than this
> Is to become the tossing reeds of that slow,
> Powerful stream, the trailing grasses
> Playfully tugged at, but to participate in the action
> No more than this.

Those grasses belong unresistingly to nature, as the "playful" copyists belong to the acceptance world of culture: they are beside the point. Being part of nature in this sense means guarding the moment with a passive receptiveness. Being part of culture means losing oneself in its protective haze. The parallel helps to indicate a last feature of the allegory in "Syringa," according to which every break in culture is a disruption of nature, and is felt by the usual spectators simply as a catastrophe.

IF THESE COMMENTS on image and reflection, on the anonymous photograph and the expressive self-portrait, have suggested a consistency in Ashbery's thinking about art in general, the impression ought to be deepened by a reading of "Wet Casements." I am not sure whether to call it a poem. Yet it has Ashbery's characteristic virtues of "wide authority and tact" and expounds what eighteenth-century critics used to call an original sentiment; so that, if one read it knowing nothing else of the author, one would want to call him a great writer of some sort. It is worth stopping at the epigraph to the poem, which comes from Kafka's "Wedding Preparations in the Country": "When Eduard Raban, coming along the passage, walked into the open doorway, he saw that it was raining. It was not raining much." The quotation ends there but, a page further on in the story, one finds a more revealing passage. Raban imagines recounting to some passerby the dull feverish unpleasantness of his existence, and says of himself: "So long as you say 'one' instead of 'I,' there's nothing in it and one can easily tell the story; but as soon as you admit to yourself that it is you yourself, you feel as though transfixed and are horrified." Kafka's is preeminently a story about the self-image of the hero and the way it is constituted by the fancied approval and disapproval he sees reflected in the faces of others. They may have seemed to Ashbery the same sort of others whom the poet just glimpsed as he fled in "Parergon," the people whom he deserted in order to meet them some day "under a better sky." Evidently, the poet's valor came from his indifference to their claim, whereas Raban's pathos comes from his submission to it.

Allowing for the distinction between Kafka's self in the story and Ashbery's in the poem, the distance that has to be passed in going from "one" to "I" remains a common subject of both narratives. Yet the perplexity that Raban felt from being unknown and unremarked, the author of "Wet Casements" feels as much from being known and remarked:

> The concept is interesting: to see, as though reflected
> In streaming windowpanes, the look of others through
> Their own eyes. A digest of their correct impressions of
> Their self-analytical attitudes overlaid by your
> Ghostly transparent face. You in falbalas
> Of some distant but not too distant era, the cosmetics,
> The shoes perfectly pointed, drifting (how long you
> Have been drifting; how long I have too for that matter)
> Like a bottle-imp toward a surface which can never be approached,
> Never pierced through into the timeless energy of a present
> Which would have its own opinions on these matters,
> Are an epistemological snapshot of the processes
> That first mentioned your name at some crowded cocktail
> Party long ago, and someone (not the person addressed)
> Overheard it and carried that name around in his wallet
> For years as the wallet crumbled and bills slid in
> And out of it. I want that information very much today,

Can't have it, and this makes me angry.
I shall use my anger to build a bridge like that
Of Avignon, on which people may dance for the feeling
Of dancing on a bridge. I shall at last see my complete face
Reflected not in the water but in the worn stone floor of my bridge.

I shall keep to myself.
I shall not repeat others' comments about me.

The poet shows no interest in the looks, impressions, and attitudes that he sketches, until he begins talking to himself, or to the aspect of himself represented by "your / Ghostly transparent face." By the time one comes to the phrase "how long you / Have been drifting; how long I have too for that matter," one feels that his intimacy with "you" is all-important.

Ashbery said once that he thought of himself as John and the person who wrote his poems as Ashbery, and this made it interesting to hear at times what others were saying about Ashbery. John, I think, wrote this poem in defense of the fortunes of Ashbery's name. He had been a listener often at parties where correct impressions of himself were overlaid by the self-analytical attitudes of others; had, like Whitman, heard himself "called by his highest name" by those who were out of the game, which did not exist until they were out of it—a game that emerges from the mysterious enchantment of self with self. In response, he starts this new conversation with "you." But the motive that prompts the utterance is his anger at learning that his name has been circulated—overheard, and picked up by someone it was not meant for—with the result that it took on the currency of rumor and not of fame. Two metaphors come so close together, in accounting for the reaction, that one cannot well distinguish between them, or between them and the name they are figures of. The metaphors evoke a piece of paper in a wallet and an old photograph. To retrieve the name by recovering these would mean to belong truly to one's experience, and at the same time to remain inseparably oneself. One cannot, however, do both. The name is irretrievable, and the poet builds his bridge from the recognition that things are so. People may dance there just for the feeling of dancing on a bridge; yet the place is his; it bears the reflection of his face for him alone. I do not know whether Ashbery was conscious of revising the last lines of "Summer" in these last lines of "Wet Casements." But one cannot help placing the two endings side by side; and the revision shows a larger change of perspective. The reflection at last has become still more figurative than it was at first, and the poem has become as strange to the poet as it is to the others. His reward, such as it is, has to be surmised from the unhurried power of the final couplet, which with its two assertions joins in a single vow.

Inward allusions like these betray a strength of self-concern that is nearly obsessive, and that produces the uneasy proportion of excitement and delay in Ashbery's great poems and stray experiments. It is in the nature of his work even now to continue hoarding such properties. *I want it back,* he says again near the end of "A Wave," of his memorials of an earlier loss; and in the shorter poems of *A Wave,* he is still reflecting on the images I have traced in *The Double Dream of Spring, Self-Portrait in a Convex Mirror,* and *Houseboat Days:* even in a poem called "Try Me. I'm Different," with its chagrin at the possibility of being lost to the future, among "those streaming with a present so heavy / And intense we are subdued by it." He appears to share in the present without being subdued, passing from line to line as on a stairway with new spars of planking, linoleum stumps, painted railings, or different-sized steps down, to complicate the way at every turning. And yet his house, as he says to himself, "is built in tomorrow," while his possessions dwell in the past. There is a character in one of Eliot's poems who asks, "Are these ideas right or wrong?" and Ashbery provokes his readers to ask the same question, though it cannot be answered in poetry. Gradually, a style of thinking and feeling make a home for themselves, and we call it our home. But to the extent that American speech and mores have always directed themselves to a present they do not inhabit, his poems touch us with the sense of a more general fate.

> Your realness is real to me though I would never take any of it
> Just to see how it grows. A knowledge that people live close by is,
> I think, enough. And even if only first names are ever exchanged
> The people who own them seem rock-true and marvelously self-sufficient.

They will go on seeming so and he will go on taking none of it, while "a reflected image of oneself / Manages to stay alive through the darkest times, a period / Of unprecedented frost, during which we get up each morning / And go about our business as usual." These last lines, from "A Wave," form a natural commentary on the lines above, from "The Ongoing Story"—a title Ashbery invites us to take or leave, with the modest implication that the story may be ours.

1986

FIFTEEN

Hemingway's Valor

It is the sentences that first draw a reader in to Hemingway's writing:

> They were old eyes now but they were in a young man's face gone old as
> driftwood and nearly as gray.

Then, further in, the longer sentences:

> All of the operations of bull raising to one who loves bullfighting are of
> great fascination and in the testings one has much eating, drinking, com-
> panionship, practical joking, bad amateur cape-work by the aristocracy, of-
> ten excellent amateur cape-work by the visiting bootblacks who aspire to be
> matadors, and long days with the smell of cold, fall air, of dust and leather
> and lathered horses, and the big bulls not so far away looking very big in the
> fields, calm and heavy, and dominating the landscape with their confi-
> dence.

And as the paragraphs are built up, each to its separate climax, a varied
pace and steady rhythm mark a path as intricate as the emotional turnings
with which both cooperate:

> The room was long with windows on the right-hand side and a door at
> the far end that went into the dressing room. The row of beds that mine
> was in faced the windows and another row, under the windows, faced the
> wall. If you lay on your left side you could see the dressing-room door.
> There was another door at the far end that people sometimes came in by. If
> any one were going to die they put a screen around the bed so you could not
> see them die, but only the shoes and puttees of doctors and men nurses
> showed under the bottom of the screen and sometimes at the end there
> would be whispering. Then the priest would come out from behind the
> screen and afterward the men nurses would go back behind the screen to

come out again carrying the one who was dead with a blanket over him down the corridor between the beds and some one folded the screen and took it away.

Narrative has to give information, of course. But if that is all one believes it can give, then Hemingway's manner will seem just a manner.

The passages I have quoted are from *Islands in the Stream, Death in the Afternoon,* and *A Farewell to Arms.* The scenes that they capture—the glimpse of the eyes of a dying sailor; the casual festivity of a bullfight practice; the routines of a hospital room, seen with the huddled watchfulness of a soldier who will not die—have all been measured distinctly and consideringly, and the prose registers a fine keeping with the progress of separate recognitions. Yet Hemingway is often said to have been a *monotonous* writer. Doubtless, to those who make this charge, it implies that there was a small, self-enclosed, set of "experiments" which were always notably his. Meanwhile, a larger set was waiting to be tried, and he affected to ignore it. The sort of experiment in question, however, merely exemplifies an ideal of virtuosity. It pays off in the excitement of certain works, and in conceptions more than in works. But none of these is expected to link up with the larger pattern of a career; the worth of such a pattern, indeed, is what is being challenged. That would have been one problem with virtuosity, from Hemingway's point of view. Another was the hope it seemed to suggest that originality might go hand in hand with technical progress over a single artist's life. Crediting no such ideal for himself and no such hope, he aimed to write a prose as variously informed as his chosen idiom would allow.

Among the personal graces of the sentence about the bullfight practice, one notices first how the comma in "cold, fall air" (often, as Hemingway knew, the color effect of inferior writers) is earned by the modifications of feeling involved, and then made good by the full breath that the pause opens up. There is an almost languid pleasure in the extra *and* that follows; and in the play of *lathered* against the noun before it. The sense of alert complicity in an enfolding habit of life has been sharpened already by the jostling rhymes of *long-smell-fall.* One is thus prepared to feel that the big bulls are "not so far away" for them to look "very big" after all, as the eye dwells on them; and as it dwells on the ordinary fields, they take on the dignity of a landscape, with a dominant mood that belongs alike to the author and his subject. In the very different workmanship of the soldier's report from his bed, the cramped neatness of the room emerges plainly from the syntax that divides the whole ward into clauses evenly spaced: "and another row, under the windows, faced the wall." One has been shown in just in time to learn what awaits one here—"If you lay on your left side . . . If any one were going to die." And the mingled hope and fear are drawn from the felt force of the unsaid: every euphemism that this patient must have heard seems to be contained in the one he could not possibly have heard, "the one who was dead." Through the latter part of the description, the "men nurses" return like an uncertain omen; and when the death comes it is in the careful file of doctors and priest, in the right-angle turn "down the corridor between the beds," until all euphemism is reduced to a gesture: "and someone folded the screen and took it away."

As all of these passages testify, sensations matter to Hemingway before people do. This seems to me a necessary and not an incidental feature of his writing, for it relates to two aspects of his identity as an author: the unconfiding self-trust of his heroes; and the interest he shares with them in death as a climax of life's moments. But that is to frame his concern melodramatically, as he himself rarely does. It would be fairer to say that death interests him not as the end of sensations but as a limit drawn close around them. It gives them a meaning, as an outline gives definition to a picture. As for what this has to do with a career of writing, an answer may be pieced together from certain comments in *Death in the Afternoon* and *Green Hills of Africa*. In the latter book Hemingway remarks somewhat cryptically: "I have a good life but I must write because if I do not write a certain amount I do not enjoy the rest of my life." This may appear to admit his need, as a commercial writer, to produce a consistent style with a signature. His work, he would then be saying, is done to supply a craving for fresh stimulants in life itself—a life which his writing simply reflects, and to which it is subordinate. But that is not what Hemingway meant. Rather, his work, for him, has the quality of a *made thing*, which he of all others has added to life. The result is seemingly pointless. Nevertheless, it endures because it is alive with purpose, as life itself is not. So he must write in order to be released back into his experience and then go on, without knowing why he does, until enough traces collect for him to deposit again in the form of writing. Experience, as such, gives the pleasure that he lives for; writing, as such, does not; but the two are mutually dependent in this way.

People who find a purpose in their very lives Hemingway seems to regard with intense but distant admiration. His portrait of Robert Jordan, the hero of *For Whom the Bell Tolls*, is an attempt to show the forming of such a person by events. It does not quite succeed because Hemingway could never credibly realize the weight of external circumstances on an individual. Still, his respect for this kind of character rested on a belief that there were other disciplines as complete as that of writing. A version of that belief (partly hidden, then dramatized, with an effect of unmotivated sentiment) may be traced again in his identification with Colonel Cantwell, the hero of *Across the River and into the Trees.* Cantwell's virtuousness is understood as an almost public fact; a thing it would be tedious to rehearse in detail. With him, the shaping circumstances pass from view entirely. But here as elsewhere in Hemingway's writing, the error of tact betrays, not a lapse of taste, but the keenness of a too implicit artistic intelligence.

One of his later stories, "The Denunciation," renders with unexampled adequacy the discipline of life that he cares for outside art. Patrons of the Madrid restaurant Chicote's always keep coming back, to renew a sense of companionability which they can find nowhere else. This feeling has much to do with the antifascist struggle, but, as the narrator sketches the place, it comes to represent a wider trust in human solidarity. Sitting at a table one evening talking to a friend, he spots at a table across the room an old patron, Luis Delgado, who has not turned up at Chicote's since he went over to the Fascists. It is a puzzle why he should risk this exposure now. Maybe he was feeling reckless or high-spirited, or nostalgic for the intimacy at Chicote's. Or, maybe, he has come to spy. A waiter, looking on, grows nervous and asks the narrator, who as a journalist is nearly one of the authorities, whether it is not now his duty to report Delgado to the security police. That would lead to his arrest and probably to his being put to death. But the waiter is a good republican and a businessman. The narrator, however, answers with less decision than he is expected to show. He can see the rightness of betraying Delgado, the traitor. But he has a scruple. An action like that goes against the feel of the place, and perhaps even of the cause: the very things that have brought him and, for all he knows, Delgado back to Chicote's on this evening. The waiter does make the call anyway, and Delgado is arrested.

It is, till now, hardly more than an anecdote. But, as an afterthought, the narrator phones the security police from his hotel, to check up, he says, on Delgado, adding that it was he that made the first call. The final paragraph reads:

> All we old clients of Chicote's had a sort of feeling about the place. I knew that was why Luis Delgado had been such a fool as to go back there. He could have done his business some place else. But if he was in Madrid he had to go there. He had been a good client as the waiter had said and we had been friends. Certainly any small acts of kindness you can do in life are worth doing. So I was glad I had called my friend Pepé at Seguridad headquarters because Luis Delgado was an old client of Chicote's and I did not

wish him to be disillusioned or bitter about the waiters there before he died.

The suggestion is that the teller of this story has a finer sense of duty—the sort of duty that leads back to a common good—than the waiter and all others who obey the rules of citizenship or the logic of social virtue. His conduct in telling the lie is, in fact, like the artist's in its concern with a non-utilitarian design. Yet it remains unlike the artist's in that it has no self-regarding origin or end. For him, "the rest of my life" is all there is.

SO FAR, what I have said about Hemingway would hold true of some other writers, starting perhaps with Stendhal. But in no other writer does one find the same curious fit between a sense of a calling and a choice of both style and subject. Hemingway's books are about light, air, wind, "the folklore of the senses"; and they mean to instruct. One can learn from reading them how to clean a fish; where a bad hunter is satisfied to have placed a shot; the parts of the stadium a matador will most avoid on a gusty day; what wines to savor and what to imbibe in quantities; and why a man is sometimes excited by a woman who cuts her hair short. Outside their proper story, all of these data may look stark, pretentious, or absurd. Once placed, they are beyond ridicule. But the depth of Hemingway's interest in such things would seem to be archaic rather than modern. That is to say, he makes them all appear strangely substantial, as they can be only in a phase of culture where poetry and knowledge are one. The modernity comes in with his personal motive for finding them important. For they are his by choice and not by inheritance. They alone establish that he, he especially, was here and had a place in the general life. In the absence of these things, he would be lost.

The significance of the mere record of things done or felt, both to Hemingway and the characters who echo his tacit motive, was clear as far back in his work as "Big Two-Hearted River." A Nick Adams or a Jake Barnes is alive while he feels the change of his pulse, or the warmth of the day on his skin. And Hemingway's usual practice is simply to assume that his readers know the anxiety that prompts such testings from moment to moment. Until the publication of *The Garden of Eden,* one would have said that he refused, in principle, ever to reflect aloud on what his writing aimed to achieve. But the force of his repetitions brought out two irreducible beliefs: that experience is a loss, a deformation of oneself; and that one can guard against it by perfecting a craft, or a code of practical wisdom, or by writing a masterpiece. These were secrets of the laboratory, not to be published in the parlor, though, when faced by the literal-minded-ness of his researches, Hemingway was capable of showing a delicate self-mockery. Among the barroom scenes of *Islands in the Stream* is an exchange in which the hero, Thomas Hudson, a painter, is asked to tell about "the happiest time you remember"; the prostitute who makes the re-quest (and who somehow knows that Hudson is Hemingway's stand-in) adds the interesting warning, "And not with smells." He replies: "It has to have smells." But certain prejudices about style—about the devices that can help or hinder the weaving of life into something stronger than life—have for Hemingway an authority fully as great as that of the things he de-scribes. There has never been a writer whose love scenes were as apt as his to divagate, between endearments, into pedantic corrections by the lovers themselves of each other's grammar and usage.

About the nature of writing and the characters of writers, Hemingway has a lot to say in *Death in the Afternoon,* most of it solid sense and some of it extraordinary. The argument he used to persuade himself that bullfight-ing was an art turned upon its purposeful ordering of a tragic spectacle— "the education of the bull," up to the moment of recognition that comes with its death. It is an understood artifice that a bull who starts by know-ing too much cannot be fought in any case. Grant this, says Hemingway, and all that concerns you is the pure line that is traced by the moving fig-ures of the matador and the bull. The analogy seems to be with ballet. In both, because the work goes on in a live medium, real mastery can occur only a few times in one lifetime. But as Hemingway points out, there is a further disadvantage in bullfighting. Even when the art is perfect, it makes an impression only while it is happening. In this it is the opposite of writ-ing, which is dead once committed to the page, but exists to be renewed in the experience of the reader. In a remarkably sustained passage of *Death in the Afternoon,* Hemingway reflects on the shadowy immortality that comes to the matador, whose fame, compared to the painter's or poet's, is as sure as it is evanescent.

> If it were permanent it could be one of the major arts, but it is not and so it finishes with whoever makes it, while a major art cannot even be judged until the unimportant physical rottenness of whoever made it is well buried. It is an art that deals with death and death wipes it out. But it is never truly lost, you say, because in all arts all improvements that are logical are carried on by some one else; so nothing is lost, really, except the man himself. Yes, and it would be very comforting to know that if at his death all the painter's canvases disappeared with him, that Cezanne's discoveries, for example, were not lost but would be used by all his imitators. Like hell it would.

Suppose a painter's canvases disappeared with him and a writer's books were automatically destroyed at his death and only existed in the memory of those that had read them. That is what happens in bullfighting. The art, the method, the improvements of doing, the discoveries remain; but the individual, whose doing of them made them, who was the touchstone, the original, disappears and until another individual, as great, comes, the things, by being imitated, with the original gone, soon distort, lengthen, shorten, weaken and lose all reference to the original. All art is only done by the individual. The individual is all you ever have and all schools only serve to classify their members as failures. The individual, the great artist when he comes, uses everything that has been discovered or known about his art up to that point, being able to accept or reject in a time so short it seems that the knowledge was born with him, rather than that he takes instantly what it takes the ordinary man a lifetime to know, and then the great artist goes beyond what has been done or known and makes something of his own.

The artist, then, who makes a permanent object and the artist who executes a single performance have in common a peculiarly intense individuality. The only thing that favors the creation of a text over the surpassing of the spectator's expectations of every previous contest is that it allows a falling away of the creator's own "unimportant physical rottenness." But according to Hemingway, that makes a tremendous difference; for, as he observes, "Memory, of course, is never true."

Yet both kinds of art produce examples of personal energy; and a single idea of tradition will cover both. Hemingway's conception here is not less subtle than T. S. Eliot's in "Tradition and the Individual Talent." But he does rely on a less congenial figure of thought. The works in a tradition, says Eliot, form an ever-enlarging "constellation" which shifts slightly with the addition of the "really new" work. By contrast, Hemingway admits only an individual idea of tradition itself and is inclined to look at the whole aggregate of original works as an unfinished sequence of *choices*. Each marks a separate path and a separate sacrifice; and the character of each is defined by what it omits. A great writer is differentiated from others, he remarks in another place, by selecting more readily than they the knowledge that can become uniquely his. "There are some things which cannot be learned quickly and time, which is all we have, must be paid heavily for their acquiring." So the great writer who "must pay," like the others, "a certain nominal percentage in experience," seems to have "a quicker ratio to the passage of time." The meaning on which all these dicta converge, that art gains from a forfeit of experience, is not what one would expect to find in Hemingway. It seems better suited on the face of it to a writer like Henry James. That Hemingway should so insist on it in a book that deals with bullfighting suggests that his pursuit of this minor art had just the personal motive he sought to disclaim.

When he first saw a bullfight, Hemingway recalls, he disliked the *banderillas,* which "seemed to make such a great and cruel change in the bull" by enforcing "the loss of the free, wild quality he brought with him into the ring." Only later did he learn to appreciate that their effect was to sober the bull and make him aim more surely; until, at last,

> when I learned the things that can be done with him as an artistic property when he is properly slowed and still has kept his bravery and his strength I kept my admiration for him always, but felt no more sympathy for him than for a canvas or the marble a sculptor cuts or the dry powder snow your skis cut through.

These last analogies are incongruous; the climactic image is shocking. But, evidently, in any spectacle like this, Hemingway is bound to feel the same detachment and fascination in the presence of the unimportant physical rottenness which drops away when something from life is turned into something in art. In a bullfight, that happens before one's eyes; with the restriction that it can happen only before one's eyes. Hemingway returns to the bullfights again and again, notwithstanding his awareness of the restriction. His affinity for the spectacle, as he makes us understand, is based on temperament after all, and not on his definition of a major art. He writes in the same vein, in *Green Hills of Africa,* of "freezing myself deliberately inside, stopping the excitement as you close a valve, going into that impersonal state you shoot from." For what compels his attention, not as the scene of all great writing but of his, is the instant organization of life that can happen with death.

Other artists have other subjects and greater ones. Hemingway wanted, he says, to study bullfighting for the discipline it would give his writing, but he adds that it is a narrow sort of discipline. To learn how to describe a death accurately seemed within his grasp in his late twenties. To approach a great subject, such as the change of heart that may alter a whole life, was beyond his powers then. His touchstone here was Tolstoy, who, at the end of his career, he knew he had still not begun to rival. If one asks why in all the years between he never properly aimed at that kind of mastery, the answer will be unenlightening. It takes us back to the sheer force of his affinity for something narrower. But Hemingway's regret at having allowed a temporary focus of his craft to become the subject matter of his art may be deduced from another episode of *Green Hills of Africa.* After a particularly clumsy and brutal day's hunt, he thinks for a while about the different pleasure he might feel if, "instead of trailing that sable bull, gut shot to hell, all day, I'd lie behind a rock and watch them on the hillside and see them long enough so that they belonged to me forever." But this is a choice he is never able to make in any of his books. Even the artist-hero of *Islands in the Stream,* when asked, in the middle of the Second World War, to paint an apocalyptic satire of Cuba, prefers instead to hunt Nazi submarines; the sailor in the very first sentence I quoted will at last be photographed like any other big kill, to prove that the right materials were used to create the finished work. So for a moment the human body too becomes only "the dry powder snow your skis cut through."

Indeed, given his absorbing interest in this way of seeing, the question about Hemingway might just as well be turned around. How did he manage to hold himself back from it as much as he did? One explanation for his restraint, I think, is that the very specialization of his subject gives him a counter-charm against its inhumanity. Thus his belief that the matador is himself a work of sculpture issues in something more than aesthetic concern with the sort of people who are matadors. Both in *Death in the Afternoon,* and its sequel, *The Dangerous Summer,* all the more interesting fighters are subjected to a continuous moral inquest by their chronicler. It is sometimes assumed that Hemingway's usual hero is a man of supreme courage, beyond challenge by his rivals or by the multitude who observe his doings from the security of their noisy perch. But his books contain no such character: the stereotype is in fact a composite creature, with traits drawn from a few of his characters, from an unrewarding side of the author himself and from his shallower comments outside of his books. As it happens, one of the heroes of *Death in the Afternoon* turns out to be the matador Gallo, whom Hemingway appreciated at once for his method of attack and the frankness with which he tempered bravado with prudence.

> He was a great bullfighter and the first one to admit fear. Until Gallo's time it was thought utterly shameful to admit being afraid, but when Gallo was afraid he dropped muleta and sword and jumped over the fence head first. A matador is never supposed to run, but Gallo was liable to run if the bull looked at him in a peculiarly knowing way. He was the inventor of refusing to kill the bull if the bull looked at him in a certain way, and when they locked him up in jail he said that it was better that way, "all of us artists have bad days. They will forgive me my first good day."

Hemingway's feeling for the valor there may be in a completed work, or in the artist who is condemned to be the work himself, does not finally depend on either facing a defeat or carrying off a victory.

But a man like Gallo belongs to the comic side of things; a tragedy has to have a tragic end; and Hemingway tells us whenever he can that this is where his interest lies. Still, among the most memorable scenes of his fiction are several in which he seems to confess the unassimilability of his view of life and death. Thus in *Islands in the Stream,* Thomas Hudson is made to say an oddly charitable thing about the dying sailor:

> "Don't bother him," Thomas Hudson said. "He's a good Kraut."
> "Sure," Willie said. "They're all good Krauts when they fold up."
> "He hasn't folded up," Thomas Hudson said. "He's just dying."

It is Hudson's crony, Willie, who plays up to the old painter by invoking the ethic of the great death; and he is firmly rebuked. The worst moral fault with which one can charge Hemingway as a writer is that he sometimes does show people like Willie in a favorable light.

Why did that have to happen? Writing as personal as Hemingway's, and as closely bound to the writer's hopes for himself, is liable to all the influences of resentment, apathy or defensive fear which can create "a transition of the soul." It is as if at times Hemingway's sympathies were forced into a thin channel. He is then capable of equating imaginative survival with survival, and survival itself with life. It is plain such a mood could end in sadism, but my feeling is that in Hemingway it seldom does. Rather, it confirms a tendency already noticeable in his work, by which, in order to be sure of a hidden power in himself, he has to serve as the witness of a privation. Whenever this pattern asserts control of his imaginings, he is close to nihilism—that is, to a liberty of action founded on a want of belief. There remains the anomaly that, for him, the action, once taken, must be justified by a principle of morality.

Hemingway is probably the most striking instance in modern art of a man for whom the motives and the justification of action have suffered this kind of permanent division from each other. But he is clear about why so often the action that appeals to him is violent action. This follows, as he says in *Death in the Afternoon,* from "the feeling of rebellion against death" which can only be had by killing: "Once you accept the rule of death thou shalt not kill is an easily and a naturally obeyed commandment. But when a man is still in rebellion against death he has pleasure in taking to himself one of the Godlike attributes; that of giving it." When, therefore, an artist chooses to give death, it confirms his sense that all life, apart from his work, is a drawn-out siege against the *nada* that it will not conquer anyway. On the other hand, the man of action will choose to *give death* more often, because his life embodies a less acceptable fate. The phrase itself is a weirdly aggressive euphemism—as if composed to suit a killer's muffled solemnity. Only by excluding things from life can he prove the solidity of the choice he represents; those exclusions lie about him in the dead forms of the beasts he has killed. They might just as plausibly be the corpses of the men he has killed or otherwise forced to submit to his design. Hemingway's objection to war, so far as one can tell from his writings, was only that it took such acts of power off their proper individual basis.

I have been taking a concentrated but I hope a truthful view of Hemingway's subject. The result may be to make him more strange than he had seemed, without making him appreciably more sympathetic. There are, however, precedents for the withdrawal from ordinary living, the sense of experience as foreign rather than given, which he required in order to accomplish his work. One, as I have suggested, is James; and the comparison is worth pursuing a little. The dramatic situations that both writers care for are apt to center on a moment of sudden reduction or literalization; though for both a story is dramatic enough if the reader is kept uneasily thinking about the mere possibility that such a moment will occur. The surprise may come either through a reversal or an intensification of the habits of daily existence. But it has a moral: that the exalted pleasures and sensations of life (what James likes to allude to in a word like *impression*) arise from, and are answerable to, some particularly coarse fact. Hemingway's pride in the fact and James's embarrassment at it mark a trivial difference beside the agreement they share about its significance. In Hemingway, it is true, one is always on the brink of a small discovery, and it usually has to do with the body; whereas James constructs whole works to delay such a discovery, and when it does come it is in a discussion of money. To borrow the slang of these literalists, Hemingway's writing is about what the body can take; James's is about what the money will bear; but in both cases this is something they show all the time and can never quite say. The sum of the books that got written, it must be added, is less satisfying in Hemingway's case than in James's, but not because his gifts were slighter. The reason is rather that, given so choice an asceticism, he still sometimes wanted to have his life both ways. He wanted, himself, to serve as a sure witness to the very experience he had to break with, a witness whose report would have the irreducible clarity of a fact. It is this that gives his fiction (in episodes where a slow revenge is extorted from a worthless soul) and his first-person journalism (in passages that weigh the author's sacrifice of raw materials for a sublime effect) their occasional overtones of greed. The greed is always calculated and always intelligent, but in the defeated manner of a guardian of already cherished monuments.

MINE IS THE first generation in which it has been fashionable to revile Hemingway. Like Byron, he is held strictly to account for the conceit that bound his writing to his celebrity. Unlike Byron, he lacks the protection of self-irony. Some part of this reaction he certainly earned: there are whole tracts of his life in which nothing edifying can ever be sought. But the recent and familiar picture of him is so oddly limited that it now seems necessary to recall the distinct fame he enjoyed in the twenties and thirties. At that time he was known, above all, as "a writer's writer"—a character differing markedly from the creator of a signature. He was not the preceptor for a school of masculine pleasures, and not the property of the American Literature that since has claimed him. He came to prominence with the European avant-garde of the twenties, for whom *Ulysses* was the great work of a new age of literature. Hemingway thought that Leopold Bloom was the highest invention of that book (the judgment neither of a sportsman nor a prig), and he was one of the few contemporaries about whose writing Joyce in turn spoke with consistent respect. The idea that he looked on writing as something to be done between rounds of social éclat—that, in short, he pretended not to be a writer—is the most falsifying report about him and the easiest to expose. In this respect indeed, the type he fits is Johnson and not Byron. He thought of the dull business of composition as a trial requiring all one's nervous faculties.

There used to be people who dismissed Hemingway because they had loved his books in their youth. Now my impression is they do it because they have read a little, and heard some unpleasant things, and that is that. But somebody is reading him. The past two years alone have seen the publication of a long biography by Jeffrey Meyers and an expanded version of *The Dangerous Summer,* the bullfight articles that Hemingway wrote for *Life* in 1959. Before that, there had been a comprehensive biography by Carlos Baker, and *Islands in the Stream,* a posthumous abridgment of the trilogy on the sea which Hemingway drafted in the late 1940s. Then last year Scribners published *The Garden of Eden,* a section, heavily edited, of the autobiographical novel which formed his other big project of the years after the Second World War. And now comes a third full-length biography, *Hemingway: The Life and the Work,* by Kenneth S. Lynn. Compared to Baker's *Life,* this one has rather uneven proportions: about half of it deals with Hemingway in the twenties. This shows anyway that Lynn's interest began with the work and not the life; that it ends there too is fortunate, and uncommon in a modern biographer. Meyers's *Hemingway,* well informed as it was, seemed to have been written from a quasi-moral disapproval of Hemingway, and it punished him with strenuous quotations from his enemies. Lynn plainly likes his hero, without being credulous about him. His book is not going to displace Baker's; yet it has its own distinction as a thoroughly qualified revision of a legend. Here is an example of the sort of thing I mean. In the First World War, Hemingway served as an ambulance driver and was wounded in exactly the manner described in *A Farewell to Arms*. He received a medal for heroic conduct because, as an Italian friend is made to tell Lieutenant Henry, this was a time when medals went out freely to the men fresh from America. Hemingway never seriously pretended (except once, in a speech to students at his old high school) that he had gone back to the front, as his hero does, or that he had enlisted early to fight with the Italian shock troops and stayed through the Caporetto retreat. Nevertheless, some of these things do happen in *A Farewell to Arms,* and the story about Hemingway himself made the rounds; it was repeated by critics, and not fully challenged by Baker; and it appears now as part of the "note on the author" in the paperback edition of the novel. Lynn is exceptional among Hemingway's biographers in not trusting his books as a fair index to his life. He does, I think, tend to read Hemingway's life back into his books, but that is another matter.

It is hard not to see his life in any case as a great subject for a biography. After hearing its facts rehearsed often enough, one starts to think they are "representative"; and then the idea of some one being representative seems more mysterious than it ever did. It has nothing to do with being all mankind's epitome, or even the special case favored by a few. What his life most suggests is the power of the exception to make us forget the rule—a power that lasts for a generation or more, until different readers come in search of a different hero. Lynn also brings us back to two aspects of Hemingway's development that have not before received the emphasis they deserve. First, the degree to which the passion of his life was involved to the very end with the father he loved who killed himself and the mother he hated who lived on: the father, a good doctor and anxious husband, who took him hunting and fishing, on house calls and emergency visits, and made him a grown-up early; the mother, a devout believer in culture, who taught him that acting respectably and writing cleanly would be "money in the bank." Equally, in this account as in no other, we are made aware how stunning, recurrent, and finally disastrous were the series of physical injuries that Hemingway sustained throughout his life, from the wounds to his leg and head in the war to the two plane crashes he suffered in 1954, on a last trip to Africa. These accidents, though they do not explain his long spells of depression, must have lengthened the shadow in which his recoveries were always expected to begin. Also, they made him brave with his fortune: at any moment it could seem already to have done its worst. The bare recital of his chronic pains helps to make sense, for example, of his behavior in 1944, in a bivouac of the American army on the allied march to Paris, where he calmly ate his dinner, helmet off, while German bombs poured down and every soldier took cover in the basement. At work in incidents like this was something much less happy than a formal display of stamina. Nevertheless, I agree with Lynn that none of the evidence suggests a process of deterioration which impaired his ability to write; on the contrary he produced, in the last two decades of his life, thousands of pages besides those of the posthumous works we have seen. What may in part have failed in him was a capacity for self-criticism. Yet he spent many months in the late fifties revising the sketches he had made years earlier for *A Moveable Feast*. And to judge even by the present, much foreshortened, version of *The Garden of Eden* (which Lynn rightly praises for its "brilliant, drastic editing" by Tom Jenks), his last effort as a novelist was also his most ambitious.

Lynn's theme, and he needs it less than he supposes, is what he calls the "cross-sexual experimentalism" that runs through Hemingway's work. He keeps a sort of running tally on the incidence of women cutting their hair short, or challenging men to approve their intention of cutting it short, and he observes that the outward change commonly goes with a reversal of sexual positions. There is a level at which all this is simply true. Catherine Barkley's "I want us to be all mixed up," in *A Farewell to Arms,* is only the clearest signal of a motif that touches many of Hemingway's stories, and that becomes the focus of the action in *The Garden of Eden*—a novel, from one point of view, about nothing but haircuts, breakfasts, and spirited talk concerning their finer points. This is at any rate a potent fantasy, but Lynn wants to honor it as something more: he is not quite sure what. In consequence, the reader is heaped with strange and unamalgamating materials, which suggest everything from a quirk to a compulsion, while the biographer stands to the side and implies that much will be made of it some day. Yet, for Lynn, the good of this hobbyhorse is that it keeps him from riding another as hard as he might have done. He belongs to the current crop of suspicious critics. They come in orthodox and heterodox varieties, and he is of the orthodox: those, namely, who know for sure that every impulse of social idealism is a form of political naïveté or worse. So, around the time of the Spanish War, he starts to hector his subject with caption-sentences like the following: "At no point during [Hemingway's] visits to Spain did he consider reporting the conflict from the Nationalist as well as the Loyalist side." But Hemingway never pretended to be a reporter in this debased, unreal, and quite recent sense of the word—the sense according to which a reporter's duty is not only to be truthful but to fake a "responsible" tone of impartiality which, as a thinking being, he cannot possibly credit.

Hemingway had a keen sense of politics almost from the first. His masterly report in the early twenties of an interview with Mussolini is still worth looking up: it gets to the bottom of him fast (with the help of a wolf pup Mussolini had the poor judgment to try and use as a prop). One may also recall such things as the discerning remarks, made in passing in *Death in the Afternoon,* on the importance of cobblestones to revolutionaries, and how solid paving has done more for tyrannies than any weapon known to their police. In short, he used his eyes and ears, in politics as in everything. Nor was he ever a crier up of "two moralities"—one for the war whoop and one for the sermon. *For Whom the Bell Tolls* is proof of his steadiness here, with its dry portrait of the Stalinists, whom he had expected to admire, and the cold epigram about La Pasionaria. Hemingway, in these matters, had nothing to learn from his biographer, or from anyone living then or now. He was a man of fierce democratic instincts, like Whitman, who happened, unlike Whitman, not to care for most of the people he encountered in daily life. But their cause was real to him. Of the Spanish War itself, even before his first journey to the front, he observed that "the Reds may be as bad as they say," but "they are the people of the country" and the war is between them and "the absentee landlords, the moors, the Italians, and the Germans." Even Orwell's summing up in "Looking Back on the Spanish War" was a little more rhetorical than that. By contrast *The Fifth Column,* the one work he wrote *hors de combat,* is just a bad play with some good boasting. It accords to Spain all the reality of *X,* where *X* is any field of action offered by the times; and it was denied a more than moderate success on Broadway only because Humphrey Bogart was not on hand to utter its one great line: "We're in for fifty years of undeclared wars and I've signed up for the duration. I don't exactly remember when it was, but I signed up all right." This statement had its chief importance even then as a promise by the writer himself. Hemingway kept it and was still keeping it twenty-two years later, when Castro's revolution touched him closer to home, and he did not affect to greet it with dismay.

Johnson argued in the *Rambler* that there are times when a biographer is obliged to be a moralist. Famous men like Addison, or for that matter Hemingway, who are able to fashion a public character for themselves, have to be held answerable by posterity: that is part of taking them seriously. The principle still seems to me a good one, but as hard as ever to set fair limits to. Literary critics and sensational journalists tend to write biographies from opposite motives (misplaced custodial reverence or the hope of an opportune unmasking) but either way they get the lives of artists wrong and their moralism is noxious. Lynn, however, fits neither of these categories; his work is the slightly chastened homage of an old fan; so that his moral judgments, when they enter at all, are often very valuable. He has his fullest occasion in the account of Hemingway's break with Sherwood Anderson. From their first meetings in Chicago, Anderson had been cordial and generous to Hemingway, without any air of patronizing. He wrote a statement of praise to appear on the jacket of *In Our Time* and brought Hemingway together with his own publisher, Horace Liveright. Yet in these first months of his public reception, Hemingway was growing heartily sick of hearing himself classed in the school of Anderson and Gertrude Stein, and seeing his reviewers pick out some of his early stories as imitation Anderson. This grievance joined his wish for a bigger publisher and provoked his writing of *The Torrents of Spring*, an out-and-out parody of Anderson's *Dark Laughter*. Hemingway's strategy was to force Liveright either to insult his most celebrated author (by publishing the book) or to give the disappointed parodist an opening to terminate his own contract (by refusing to publish it). The upshot was just as he planned: Scribner picked up *The Torrents of Spring* and stayed with Hemingway ever after. This sort of maneuver is common enough. What makes Hemingway's conduct peculiarly unpleasant to review is his wish, even as he was betraying Anderson, to keep up his friendship with him by working out an honorable explanation. In a letter written at the time he appealed to his friend's good nature, with the help of some sophistry: (1) he was just being the good critic that Anderson needed then; (2) he could think of doing it only because he was the lesser writer of the two; (3) anyway, he was right to want to withdraw from Anderson's patronage, even if an unsympathetic reader might see his gesture as somehow ungrateful. Lynn comments: "Quite possibly, this utterly grotesque argument was the work of a man who was drunk." What I think Lynn misses elsewhere is the drama of Hemingway's retractions. Other original writers whose egotism served them pragmatically—Wordsworth and Frost both come to mind— have also burned a path for themselves with methods just like these. But Hemingway, though he is often disingenuous when first confronted, is almost never so in the long run. His *Letters* contain a retrospective view, in another letter to Anderson, of the whole business of Liveright and *The Torrents of Spring*, in which he concludes of himself: "What a horse's ass."

He could say this without a fuss because he knew it was not the whole truth. But how did he look to others? Two observations have stayed with me through two thousand pages of Hemingway facts. One is from Gregory Clark, a war veteran who knew Hemingway at the *Toronto Star:* "a more weird combination of quivering sensitiveness and preoccupation with violence never walked this earth." The other is from Damon Runyon: "Few men can stand the strain of relaxing with him over an extended period." But what comes through in every report is the impression of a captivating energy. This worked its charm most tellingly on friends who never became quite intimate and who remained uncertain of his affection. Dorothy Parker wrote well, often, and always admiringly of Hemingway's work; but she made the mistake of talking to him once about an abortion she had had. By having done it at all she disturbed a part of him that was always less bohemian than his surroundings; but she doubtless offended a much deeper piety by alluding to it in the course of ordinary gossip. Some time later Hemingway composed a rancorous, painfully ugly, free-verse satire on her life (complete with anti-Semitic slurs), which he had the prudence not to publish and the ill grace to insist on reading aloud to several of their mutual friends. Parker heard of this and forgave it; her last words about him are said to have been: "Tell me the truth. Did Ernest really like me?" A similar attachment kept his first two wives, Hadley Richardson and Pauline Pfeiffer, close to him long after he had ruined the marriages with insult and infidelity. From the sheer force of his energy, their own self-love came to be linked with his. The psychoanalytic word for that kind of power is narcissism; it is said that in any battle of wills the narcissist always wins, for he has an unbeatable advantage: to him the other person's claims are never real. But there is another way of putting this. The narcissist loses the world for the sake of winning all the people in it (those, at least, who have the luck to meet him). From the preceding notes on Hemingway's writing, it ought to be clear why such a pattern of conduct suited his art. When, close to the age of fifty, he started to reflect on his life as a whole, he wrote two novels that resemble each other as allegories of narcissism: *Across the River and into the Trees* and *The Garden of Eden.* It is curious to realize that both of these books, one with a military hero in his fifties, the other with an artist-hero in his twenties, belong to nearly the same period of composition; and that Hemingway chose to publish the less impressive of the two, in which the problem is exemplified, rather than the more impressive in which it is fully understood and judged.

Given the dangerous consistency of Hemingway's self-trust, the most unexpected fact to emerge from this biography is the resourcefulness with which he accepted intelligent criticism. His best reader beyond any doubt was Fitzgerald. Of the long opening chapter of *The Sun Also Rises,* which gave the backgrounds of the characters, only a short sketch of Robert Cohn survived Fitzgerald's objection to the "elephantine facetiousness" of the tone. A less definite problem with the novel, he thought, was that Jake Barnes's pathos was still missing a last, low note; for, in his scenes with Brett, he did not really seem like an impotent man; more like a man in "a sort of moral chastity belt." Again, in the manuscript of *A Farewell to Arms,* he noticed that Hemingway was able to regard his hero with a degree of retrospective irony, while for the heroine he retained every solemn feeling he must once have cherished for the woman on whom she was based. "In consequence unless you make her a bit fatuous occasionally the contrast jars—either the writer is a simple fellow or she's Eleonora Duse disguised as a Red Cross nurse." It remained an unequal friendship, however, partly owing to a streak of hero worship in Fitzgerald, and partly to Hemingway's unconcealed disgust at any hint of slack self-discipline. He read *The Crack-Up* as the confession of a man who was finished. By these reflections written close to suicide, Fitzgerald also violated an unspoken canon of Hemingway's writing and action alike—one, however, that might have been deduced by any careful reader of "A Clean, Well-Lighted Place." It was about this time that Hemingway worked into "The Snows of Kilimanjaro" the now-famous anecdote concerning "poor Scott Fitzgerald" and his illusions about the rich. Fitzgerald commented with propriety on the scandalous ease of that *poor:* "If I choose to write *de profundis* sometimes, it doesn't mean I want friends praying aloud over my corpse." Beside, as he knew, the truth about the exchange was very different from the anecdote. Fitzgerald was not present when it took place, at a lunch in New York that brought together Hemingway, Maxwell Perkins, and Mary Colum. And, in fact, it was Hemingway who said he had been getting to know the rich and they were "different"; and Mary Colum who made the reply he later took as his own, that the only difference was they had more money. Of course, Hemingway's report improved both sides of the conversation. But as a specimen of his practice, it is enough to make critics permanently wary of interpreting his writing much in the light of facts drawn from his life.

Yet that is what Lynn has tried to do; his subtitle should have been "the life in the work." There is a general difficulty with this method of analysis, which is not quite summed up by saying that writers sometimes do imagine. Even if we could find a traceable source for every detail, the fact would remain that life is less rigorously organized than art. This does not mean that a thorough immersion in archives may not yield a blunt and otherwise inaccessible wisdom about a writer's provocations. For example, faced by the three dozen variants Hemingway produced for the end of *A Farewell to Arms,* one might say (though Lynn does not) that anyway Catherine Barkley had to die, because Agnes von Kurowsky jilted the author and he never got over it. But the status of such remarks will never be critical; for they give no help at all in thinking about a book. Lynn's speculations on "the work" belong to the same limbo of possibly trivial secret knowledge. He says in a gloss of "The Battler": "At last, [Hemingway] had reason to hope that he was on his way to the literary championship of the world. But was his excitement unalloyed, or was it edged with an inexplicable dread?" The question is graceless, as well as rhetorical, in just the way the story is not. Similarly "Fifty Grand" is here interpreted as an apology for Hemingway's escape from his contract with Liveright: Benny Leonard (said to be the prototype of the dirty fighter in the story) is actually Horace Liveright, and "Behind the facade of a cynical and brutal boxing story lay Hemingway's ugly wish to believe that a Jewish publisher had hit him in the groin, so to speak, and that therefore it was all right for him to reply in kind." Notice how easily the first substitution (Leonard for the fictional boxer) shades into the second (Liveright for Leonard). If fictions were problems in algebra, these quadratic equations would solve them. *The Sun Also Rises* affords the widest such opportunity in all of Hemingway's work; and Lynn has a very full day there. He comes close to suggesting that Jake Barnes is a male lesbian, on the grounds that Natalie Barney and Djuna Barnes lived, respectively, at 20 Rue Jacob and the Hotel Jacob, in Paris.

Still, this way of reading is in fact revelatory in two important instances. *The Torrents of Spring* contains a sexual triangle, with an old waitress and a younger one competing for possession of the hero, Scripps O'Neill. Lynn reads it as a straightforward diagram of Hemingway's transition, during the writing of the book, from his wife Hadley to Pauline, whom he was on the verge of marrying. As Meyers showed in his biography, the decision to publish the book at all was associated in Hemingway's mind with the decision to make public his split with Hadley. And even at the time, both elements of the crisis were unmistakable—the more so because Hadley recommended against publishing the book and Pauline was staunchly in favor of it. What is odd is that none of them, including Hemingway, seems to have read the story as a roman à clef: the mask of parody was in this case authoritative and complete. A more patent instance in which a work served as a map of a still going relationship was *The Fifth Column.* There, as Lynn points out, Hemingway not only declared his new attachment to Martha Gellhorn, but gave a full portrayal of the temperamental discord that would end their marriage almost a decade later. *The Fifth Column,* however, remains his least rewarding work of any length, *The Old Man and the Sea* alone excepted. To decode, it may be agreed, is sometimes also to interpret, but only with writing in which the carpet is all figure.

"A master miniaturist, a poet essentially": such appears to be Lynn's final verdict on Hemingway as a writer. It is not false, but it sounds a little satisfied, and without more details one cannot know what to make of it. How the life and work accord with each other, rather than corroborate each other's data, is the subject that opens up when life and work have been rehearsed on separate stages. To take just one resistant piece of evidence: John Dos Passos, who by the end of his life had no reason to spare Hemingway any just reproach, made the unpredictable comment that he had been a "builder up" and not a "breaker down" of the women he married. One can explain this by supposing that, from the force of example, his constant and heedless activity gave an involuntary encouragement to some others, who did not always care if self-absorption was at the bottom of it. A point of rereading his work after reading about his life is to see how some such quality gets into writing. It seems to be there under enormous repression. The effect is "miniature" if you like; but nothing could be more wrong than the idea that it comes from *paring down.* His work, in the short stories above all, is an act of displacement and concentration, but it neither simplifies nor clarifies. It is worth repeating in this context what early readers like D. H. Lawrence and Virginia Woolf noticed immediately: that Hemingway's insistent concern with personal power derives from a fear of its opposite. His men of action are never far from inertia.

THE MOST WOUNDING truth ever published about Hemingway was in a chapter of Wyndham Lewis's *Men Without Art.* The heroes of Hemingway's books, said Lewis, are "*those to whom things are done,* in contrast to those who have executive will and intelligence." This charge of passivity is so apparently counter-intuitive and yet, as one reflects on it, so plain a fact about his work, that one is not sure with what degree of paradox it was uttered. By subtitling the same chapter "The Dumb Ox," Lewis did, however, imply that the impression left by such characters was scarcely foreseen by the author himself. Hemingway, and not just the type he wrote about, was here being denied intelligence. Now Hemingway seems to me so much more intelligent a writer than Lewis that the description of him as a primitive hardly calls for refutation; and by "executive will" Lewis is very likely to have meant that Hemingway would have been a wiser citizen of the twentieth century had he been more of a Fascist. So to see the worth of what Lewis was saying, one has to turn from the political design of his criticism and go back to the comment itself. I will do that presently but I have first to deal with another obfuscation.

For Lewis, in the same place, attempted a broad characterization of Hemingway's prose. He called it *steining*. In that one-word cartoon, he was hoping to nail down forever an opinion that had already become commonplace. Versions of it have continued to appear in posthumous assessments of Hemingway, and the judgment will bear some looking into. There is a trick of Hemingway's early prose, from repetitions of rhythm, of emphasis or of single words, that was there for him in Gertrude Stein if he needed it. But Stein's repetitions are logical: they thicken the medium without adding to the representation. Whereas Hemingway's repetitions always mean to confirm or darken the texture of the scene he is describing. That is why hers seem a kind of rhyming in prose while his carry an undersong of contest or excitement. Stein, also, wrote according to a principle: "Prose is the balance the emotional balance that makes the reality of paragraphs and the unemotional balance that makes the reality of sentences and having completely realized that sentences are not emotional while paragraphs are, prose can be the emotional balance that is made inside something that combines the sentence and the paragraph." Hemingway wrote to no such principle. In every sentence, he retained a tact for the weight of individual words; for him, their history was an almost audible measure of their weight. These generalizations may be tested against, for example, the opening and closing paragraphs of *A Farewell to Arms,* and any pair of comparable passages in a novel by Stein. The truth is that she, Hemingway, and Sherwood Anderson all at this time shared a certain bias of anti-affectation, and occasionally it tended to produce in all their work sentences of a certain size and shape, roughly corresponding to the idiom of unhackneyed journalism. But they invented the style before the journalists got to it. And they were up to different things.

As a writer of prose, therefore, Stein is only instructive as Hemingway's antithesis. But in her lecture "What Is English Literature," she gave an accurate and original view of the situation they shared, as American writers coming after the last Victorians. Stein remarked there how the unit of vivid utterance in English had gone from the word in the Renaissance to the sentence in the eighteenth century (Swift and Goldsmith are her examples) all the way to the paragraph at the end of the nineteenth (in Swinburne, Browning, and Meredith). In this last period, English literature has been so busy with its possessions, both linguistic and political, that its medium little by little has been refined to assure the registration of that fact alone. The result is that, in the twentieth century, it can describe a new thing only in passages that take on a certain vagueness from their very bulk. It is as if English writers needed ever-widening views to show how vision could be deployed as an instrument of possession. Original work, even when it gets done in this way, will be confined to "daily island life," understood as a habitual property. You can see the difference, says Stein, between this and American literature, if you compare all the English writers of the age with their contemporary Henry James. He, too, writes in paragraphs rather than sentences, and needs that much space to achieve a single observation; but, above each of his paragraphs, there floats something impalpable, a certain heft in the atmosphere; and that diffusive ideal and reward come from the author's effort to construct a reality out of nothing given. American writing on this view is the reverse of imperial: rather it is unpropertied, and chiefly original in that it shows the difficulty even of owning itself. The analysis throws a new light on Stein's famous remark about Oakland, "There is no there there." She may have meant it to be an American compliment after all.

But let us return to the creations of this atmosphere—*those to whom things are done*. Hemingway's characters are men and women without a place. It is pertinent that he wrote no novel with an American setting, and very few stories after his earliest, unless one counts the border operations of *To Have and Have Not*. Placelessness is a condition of the nihilism I mentioned earlier, but it is also, for the reasons that Stein gave, a kind of deliverance for the writer. These characters, as much as their author, because they are always on the move, can build their lives in keeping with a theory that belongs uniquely to them. Nothing else will ever anchor them. A last comparison with James may help to remove any trace of parochialism from such a quest. James's men and women create a life for themselves purposively, through the acquisitions of art and artifice. Indeed, they are often preoccupied with works of art as the final determinant of what their lives can mean: the hero of "The Middle Years" and the heroine of *The Spoils of Poynton* are in this sense remote examples of an identical predicament. But Hemingway's characters have to make their lives for themselves by impulse alone, and with the means available to every man and woman. His, therefore, is a leveling aesthetic, as Lewis sensed in the twenties and as Communist reviewers would notice rather late, with the appearance of *To*

Have and Have Not. Anyone, Hemingway seemed to be saying, with normal human equipment could live the richest kind of life that he as an artist had imagined. Only, if they were not artists, they had to do it by acts of inward and not outward creation. Here we come back again to the distinction proposed in *Death in the Afternoon,* between two sorts of art and two sorts of discipline. That distinction now looks weaker, for it covers not just major and minor arts but the work of individuals in general, in all the uses they make of their lives. Yet at this point Hemingway's interests contract, almost convulsively, and he reckons that his story about the artist can only be the story of a sacrifice. Once, he says, those who are not makers of art begin to think about their lives, they are not far from thinking about the death that unsettles every human design. They are then, under whatever name, interested in art. If, further, they come to resent the artist's privilege in "using" his life, they will want to take revenge however they can.

Hemingway wrote the story of such a revenge in "The Short Happy Life of Francis Macomber." The artist there is a hunter, a coward at first and aimless in his work, who recovers his courage and attains the mastery of a perfect kill, but at the cost of being murdered by his wife, who could endure his impotence until made jealous of his art. *The Garden of Eden,* in all but its surface properties, is another version of the same story. The hero is a novelist, David Bourne, whose early career has been paid for by his wife, Catherine; and the action covers their honeymoon, and their discovery together of a second woman, Marita. As we are shown from the start, David lives in his writing, and not in his life itself. Yet for the honeymoon, he joins Catherine in a regimen of bicycle trips along the Riviera, swimming, and picnics on the road or in the hills above. Apart from these outings, David and Catherine share a life of narcissistic fantasy. She is always cutting her hair shorter and bleaching it whiter, and having his cut and bleached to look like hers. They are pictured again and again, and speak of each other, as twins, or as the same person, and with that comes the exchange of sexual roles that is almost customary in Hemingway. But in this novel, at last, he gives the theme to the story it wanted all along.

There is a strong suggestion here that the novelist has taught his wife everything and made her part of his materials; and again, that his power followed naturally both from his isolation and from the command he enjoys in his work. The look-alike games play out the meaning of such a conquest, and give the first faint premonition of a battle. As soon as Marita enters the scene, she seems to attract both David and Catherine more than they do each other; she is, after all, the first addition of something different in a life that has become pure echo; and it is with this recognition that one sees how far David has overstepped the necessary boundary between an artist and his experience. Catherine's revenge has two phases: the seduction of Marita, and the burning of all of David's manuscripts. The last incident seems to have been drawn from Hemingway's experience as well as his reading. In 1922, when his marriage with Hadley was already in trouble, she lost a valise in which she had placed the originals, typescripts, and carbon copies of all the writing he had done in Europe. The novel frames the catastrophe as an act of conscious aggression. But, formally, the plot of *The Garden of Eden* repeats that of *The Light That Failed,* with a notable exception. The two women of Kipling's novel—the aspiring painter whose envy of the hero's gift stops her from loving him; and the vicious serving girl who scrapes his masterpiece to an illegible smear—are here collapsed into the single figure of Catherine. Close as Hemingway was to the actual and literary patterns for his story, his conclusion touches a surprisingly selfless vein of dramatic truth. We are left with the suspicion that this act of revenge was somehow, humanly, justifiable: it is a terrible way, but the only way, for Catherine to assert the claim of her life against David's art. And when their marriage ends abruptly and David takes up with Marita, the same story is poised to begin again. Marita may be dark and Catherine fair, but nothing can disturb the "inner core" David writes from, which "could not be split or marked or scratched."

One detail I think shows better than any other Hemingway's own understanding of what is at stake between Catherine and David. When she burns his manuscripts, she still manages to rescue from among them the *cahier* that is merely a diary of the time he has spent with her. Could this, she asks, now serve as material for stories to write in place of the lost ones? She has the pride and selfishness of an artist, without art. Thus, Hemingway's imagination of her fate is involved with his recognition of his own; and it is this that makes him able to write the catastrophe as well as he does. *The Garden of Eden,* it seems to me, provided a way for its author to admit something to himself which he had kept well hidden after *The Sun Also Rises.* His notion of a perfect pairing was really a treacherous game, after all, even though it helped to distract the people he kept near him. For it expressed his need to reduce all life to a kind of frictionless sheen. This may be consoling for an artist like David Bourne, whose imitative practice of love helps to conceal or protect an inner core. It is nothing like that for Frederic Henry when he becomes "the same" as Catherine Barkley. The relevant episode is near the end of *A Farewell to Arms,* when he has to spend parts of days alone; and the Catherine of that book tells him:

"All you have is me and I go away."

"That's true."

"I'm sorry, darling. I know it must be a dreadful feeling to have nothing at all suddenly."

"My life used to be full of everything," I said. "Now if you aren't with me I haven't a thing in the world."

All that can occupy such a vacancy is the work of art, and it commonly does so in the most unpromising settings. One recalls that in *Across the River and into the Trees,* Cantwell's ecstasy is reserved not for his lovemaking with Renata in a gondola shrouded by the Venetian mist, but for the portrait of her which he keeps in his hotel and which has become more vivid to him than she is herself. It is the same with David and his manuscripts.

What is new in *The Garden of Eden* is the stinging clarity with which it portrays the condition of knowing such an abstract love while being unable to trust its permanence. Catherine, talking of the countryside they have been seeing, confides to David, "I don't want to die and it be gone." He replies, "You know what you saw and what you felt and it's yours." Yet it will not be hers when she dies; and that is the thought she cannot stand. "Then," he concludes, "don't let it happen till it happens. Look at the things and feel." It is a therapy offered by the author and his hero alike. But she is comfortless because she knows the terms of both sides of the sacrifice; and, after burning the manuscripts, she gives an explanation of her own:

> "I want to talk about them," Catherine said. "I want to make you realize why it was necessary to burn them."
>
> "Write it out," said David. "I'd rather not hear it now."
>
> "But I can't write things, David."
>
> "You will," David said.

The last reply is shaking, and it can only mean: she will write (if she will) because, having given useless pain, she has come part of the way to being a writer already. It is thus in keeping with every tension of the story, when, in its very last moments, David moves from love and hate to something like sympathy with Catherine, but only after reading a letter that she has written.

> He had never read any other letters from Catherine because from the time they had met at the Crillon bar in Paris until they were married at the American church at Avenue Hoche they had seen each other every day and, reading this first one now for the third time, he found that he still could be, and was, moved by her.

Memory, of course, is never true, not even the memory of so many interlocked, indistinguishable days. But reading does for this hero just what living never can; and his returns to the letter hold more truth for him than any memory.

THE GARDEN OF EDEN is the only novel Hemingway wrote in which he brought into the open something like the view of writing that he first declared in *Death in the Afternoon*. But the novel is emotionally daring for another reason: it goes some way to connect this attitude with the pathos of a single author's life. It may therefore supply the sort of master clue Hemingway's biographers have wrongly sought in Paris or Havana. For the novel has a story within the main story, a narrative of the hunt for a powerful elephant in which David, as a child, accompanied his father, and first came to know his father well. The story is told by paraphrase or indirect discourse, but the result anyway is finely suggestive. In narrating the hunt, by contrast with the outward chronicle of David's marriage, Hemingway all along stresses its differentness from common experience: a quality he tries to catch by returning to a time before sense impressions have closed into memories. Here, it is the father who is associated with the giving of death and with the recovery of something from life by words. The quest he leads is altogether as relentless as those Hemingway would later describe himself leading in Africa, when, at the age of thirty-five, he was already asking to be called Papa. So by writing this story, the son hoards all the weight of an old accusation against his father; the elephant they were chasing had seemed, when shot, "to sway like a felled tree and came smashing down toward them. But he was not dead. He had been anchored and now he was down with his shoulder broken. He did not move but his eye was alive and looked at David. He had very long eyelashes and his eye was the most alive thing David had ever seen." Compare, now, with these sentences given from a boy's perspective, the description of the dying bull in which Hemingway likens him to "the dry powder snow your skis cut through." The latter way of feeling belongs to the father. But it seems to be part of the moral of *The Garden of Eden* that the writer Hemingway was destined to be was always a compound of this father and this son.

> He had intended to ask his father about two things. His father, who ran his life more disastrously than any man that he had ever known, gave marvelous advice. He distilled it out of the bitter mash of all his previous mistakes with the freshening addition of the new mistakes he was about to make and he gave it with an accuracy and precision that carried the author-

ity of a man who had heard all the more grisly provisions of his sentence and gave it no more importance than he had to the fine print on a transatlantic steamship ticket.

Yet within *The Garden of Eden,* the motive of the African story remains buried quite deep. It is a "given"—wholly a matter between David and his father, and therefore between Hemingway and himself.

If a puzzle remains somewhere in the design of all of Hemingway's writing, it lies in the process by which this second story recedes into a stark background of daily phenomena, and we are left only with the one face of the hero and the actions that define him. But that, mostly hidden, work of reduction does seem related to a larger movement of Hemingway's writing, by which every reader comes to feel his distinction. Much of the drama of his work goes on in a transitory pause of action, where a human figure slips away from the scene that has held it provisionally, but the narrator's eye rests for an extra beat on the chance surroundings. Stories like "A Clean, Well-Lighted Place" and "Hills Like White Elephants" even figure the effect in their titles. But, of course, it is more than an effect; it is almost the statement of a purpose for writing. In his Nobel Prize speech, which was not about man but about prose, Hemingway said: "Things may not be immediately discernible in what a man writes, and in this he is sometimes fortunate; but eventually they are quite clear and by these and the degree of alchemy that he possesses he will endure or be forgotten." This will serve as a defense of all that his work does salvage, now that the author himself has passed from the scene. His shadow has merged with the landscape, far outside the range of English, where one can feel it in Waugh, in Orwell, and in Beckett. It is there in the closing montage of Antonioni's *The Passenger,* with the scene of death in a quiet room and the long look out to the drive, where a woman tramps slowly back and forth in the white dust. The composure of such moments was a temperamental necessity for Hemingway. That it should have become inseparable from the very idea of modernity is one of those accidents that are not less fateful than the choices of a life. A future that knows Hemingway from a distance will sort out better than we can now the proper fame of his words. By the focus of a body of work, no one has ever done more, or more swiftly or admirably, to change the way that writing was practiced and thought about. He belongs to the company—more select, in fact, than the masters themselves—of those who have made a whole period imaginable for art.

1988

SIXTEEN

How Moral Is Taste?

Why do we want to be spectators? The dignity of being seen to stand aloof may be dismissed as a reason. In most settings, nobody sees us; it is we who watch, unseen. Yet everyone has felt the guarded satisfaction of looking on while something happens. Bullfights and auto wrecks offer arenas of spectatorship in which our interest will not bear too close a scrutiny. Art seems to be a different matter: it has been said that art calms the emotions of the spectators; so that we seldom pause to ask how art itself supplies the emotions that make a person sufficiently agitated to become a spectator. Within the ancient genres of epic and tragedy, to create or behold a work presumed an interest in scenes of suffering. The same hardly appears to be true of comedy—or of modern genres of painting like portrait, landscape, and still life—and yet displacements of motive are possible everywhere. Hobbes's definition of laughter as *sudden glory* (glory in the defeat of an ambition whose slip and fall we had the luck to observe) reminds us that even the more tranquil walks of art may lean on interests difficult to disclose. Fortunately, on this delicate subject I can enlist the impartial testimony of a fable.

"The Bonfire" is a poem by Robert Frost that starts with an unnamed voice suggesting a prank to some unnamed listeners:

> "Oh, let's go up the hill and scare ourselves,
> As reckless as the best of them tonight,
> By setting fire to all the brush we piled
> With pitchy hands to wait for rain or snow.
> Oh, let's not wait for rain to make it safe.
> The pile is ours: we dragged it bough on bough
> Down dark converging paths between the pines.

Let's not care what we do with it tonight.
Divide it? No! But burn it as one pile
The way we piled it. And let's be the talk
Of people brought to windows by a light
Thrown from somewhere against their wallpaper.
Rouse them all, both the free and not so free
With saying what they'd like to do to us
For what they'd better wait till we have done.
Let's all but bring to life this old volcano,
If that is what the mountain ever was—
And scare ourselves. Let wild fire loose we will—"

He wants to talk them into starting the biggest fire they can make within their power to end it. The blaze will rouse the neighbors—will command a kind of distinction, however deplorable. To accomplish this from the fuel that dry brush or that living trees supply will be to create a thing of beauty and terror—something to scare the neighbors, but also to scare ourselves. Who are "we," in this poem? After the opening lines, a second voice comes in: "'And scare you too?' the children said together." The speaker's audience evidently is a group of children. He must be a grown man or anyway a much older boy. And in the remaining hundred lines, he tells of having once before started a fire.

He was scared that other time (there may have been more than one other time). "Why wouldn't it scare me to have a fire / Begin in smudge with ropy smoke, and know / That still, if I repent, I may recall it, / But in a moment not," A fire like this may start with "a little spurt of burning fatness" but soon nothing but "fire itself can put it out"; and before that happens "It will have roared first and mixed sparks with stars," become like a flaming sword, "Made the dim trees stand back in wider circle." The sport of this, the "fun" (to use Frost's own word in other places) comes mainly from the capriciousness of the wind—so willful an element of the scene that you can think "Something or someone watching made that gust." The wind can make the flame go "tip-down," make it "dabble the grass" and show "the merest curl of cigarette smoke." But once it really takes hold, the only way to stop the fire is to smother it: "A board is the best weapon if you have it," but at the time that he speaks of, the man says "I had my coat." Still talking of that earlier scare, he says he risked being terribly burned because "the thought of all / The woods and town on fire by me, and all / The town turned out to fight for me—that held me." He was lucky that time, though, and still cherishes a secret pride. "I'm sure no one ever spread / Another color over a tenth the space / That I spread coal-black over in the time / It took me." He speaks here of making a fire as one would speak of making a painting. He "won" against the blaze, stopped it and framed it, and the neighbors came to admire without knowing why, while he stood aside in triumph with "a sort of scorched Fourth-of-July feeling."

The children listening are more scared now, but the speaker tells them that is what they wanted, it is what people always want; and he adds: "What would you say to war if it should come?" "Oh," they say, "but war's not for children." The poem ends with the man's response:

> "Haven't you heard, though,
> About the ships where war has found them out
> At sea, about the towns where war has come
> Through opening clouds at night with droning speed
> Further o'erhead than all but stars and angels,—
> And children in the ships and in the towns?
> Haven't you heard what we have lived to learn?
> Nothing so new—something we had forgotten:
> *War is for everyone, for children too.*
> I wasn't going to tell you and I mustn't.
> The best way is to come uphill with me
> And have our fire and laugh and be afraid."

My summary and quotations have softened the impression this extraordinary poem makes when you read it straight through.

The bonfire (I take Frost to be saying), looked at in a certain way, for its brilliance and exhilaration and the surprise of its power, may be an apt analogy for a work of art. Or rather, it brings to mind certain moments in works of art and the associated sensations they provoke, the sort of moments and sensations that make us laugh and be afraid. To experiment with the analogy in this way, Frost must have meant it in earnest. He offers it as a reminder how far in the presence of any intense and rousing spectacle, the kind that occurs in nature and in art and is sometimes called sublime—how far, in such conditions, we grown-ups turn into children much like those in the poem. The work of art, like the fire, matters because it brings its audience close to a scene of risk.

I WILL BE discussing here the non-moral theory of art which Frost's analogy implies. The theory has this interest, that it is credible and commonly held, and it seems to explain at times a large, at times a small but significant part of our experience of art. Its limitations are obvious. The psychology of the sublime—the state of emotions which the speaker of "The Bonfire" exemplifies and presumes in his listeners—is concerned only with the response to works of art. It gives no help at all in analysis. We cannot say what it would mean to suppose the relation of one poem to another to be like the relation between one fire and another. A world of tacit conventions, of historical inheritances, conscious or unconscious elaborations and revisions, everything implying the willing use of the mind gets stinted in this account. But the theory has the advantage over more refined conceptions that its intent is not apologetic. It offers one of the few explanations that are plainly not nonsense, of the motives of our interest in poetry, painting, film, and other man-made excitements of uncertain effect. It is, indeed, a sense-theory to the point of being sensational. The usual reaction to it, in the branch of criticism which from now on I will call aesthetic, has been to accept and then to moralize the theory: what begins as sheer sensation, it is said, comes to be transformed by personal or social mediation into something more exalted, "Of quality and fabric more divine." But there is a difficulty hard to overlook in passing like this from description to justification. The enthralled spectator who then becomes an aesthetic theorist is in the position of Frost's speaker saying about his experience, "I wasn't going to tell you and I mustn't."

There are obstacles at the scene of art itself to any judgment that tries to stand outside the sense of being held and watching. By the end of "The Bonfire," the poem knows how much we may disapprove of this sort of play, and it sides a little with our disapproval; but there is a question whether the effort to hold back and judge the scene can be more than half-hearted. The action is arranged to help us condemn the speaker, with his perverse need of a life so strangely fuelled: he is (we see) a bully, and will lead the children into mischief; the poem being mostly spoken by him helps us to see that vividly. The children have no real chance against a man like him, so much more experienced at building fires and at telling stories. They may laugh but they are certainly scared. And the danger touches not only themselves but society: the fire, which may be an incident of a longer manic spree, has the energetic impact and the arbitrariness of any transgression. In this sense, we who read are rather like the baffled neighbors the man remembers from his last fire: if we caught him we would know what to do; but looking at his effects without thinking, we are lost in unwilling admiration. While the poem thus offers all the proper machinery of disapproval, it leaves us too inquisitive to disapprove. The children for their part have been interested and not only scared. They are interested in the thought of war.

I have used the words *sublime* and *beautiful* so far only in passing but in the Burkean way that makes them emotional opposites with a similarity deriving from their power to capture attention. The beautiful draws us fondly in, as to some irresistible attachment; the sublime makes us stand back, and stand still in an attitude of awe. As Burke says, marking the difference: "We submit to what we admire, but we love what submits to us." The beautiful for Burke is the more definite and customary idea, a binding motive of sexual and, for that matter, of all social relationships. But the sublime interests him more because it is associated with the heights and depths of tragedy and with the sufferings of actual life. Any thinker indeed who supposes as Burke did, that an intimate relation exists between art and life, will be drawn to speculate on the sublime by the character of the disasters which this descriptive category brings into focus— the sudden dissolution of a psychological habit, and the sudden dissolution of a social order. Why do we want to look at catastrophes?—look so long at them, and so far into them? Is the motive in some sense moral, moral anyway, though at some remove? Or is it less than, or other than, moral? In *A Philosophical Enquiry into the Origin of Our Ideas of the Sublime and Beautiful,* Burke's answers are quite clear but they are given in a section of the book which, though no more elusive than the rest, has drawn little commentary. The reason is not so much a lack of skill in the commentators as a resistance to the simple sense of what Burke is saying. He makes smaller claims for the autonomy of art and different claims than we expect from an eighteenth-century authority on taste. He has everywhere a matter-of-fact acceptance of the human taste for catastrophes. This interest of life he identifies completely with our interest in art.

It might be said even now, as it was at the time, that with so crude a reduction he places his argument beyond the reach of taste. But taste—the word, and the general idea that connects it to the senses—has had an ambiguous history from the start in English. The French *goût* and the Italian *gusto* suggest an unmistakable identity between the physical and the mental: they point to the sort of fact we can prove on our pulses. *Taste,* by contrast, was a word that from the first seemed to take in and gloss over the distinctness of active and passive senses: fastidiously, dutifully passive— and active with a libertine authority. Aesthetic theory from Burke's time to ours has split this difference, and one can see why the profession of criticism should have wanted it to do so. If taste is a testing, a sifting, a conscious incorporation of bodily data, then a promise seems to be held out that works of art will be good for the person who knows them. After all, we have a human mechanism for validating the experience. Taste of the

unaccommodated sort that interests Burke, taste eager and possibly reckless and certainly susceptible, delivers no such promise. To consider its effects in this light may put a thinker on the path to iconoclasm—a reform
of art that clears away art as we know it—and that was in fact the path followed by Rousseau in his *Letter to D'Alembert*. His practical observations
there resemble Burke's but he arrives at dogmatic conclusions from a belief
in the reform of human nature. People, says Rousseau, want to put into
practice what they see on the stage; they look at works of art to get ideas of
things to do; or maybe, once exposed to certain conventions or anomalies
in art, they are in the position of irresistibly entertaining those conventions or anomalies in practice. Burke, too, in his discussion of tragedy
thinks that the force of example is strong, but he trusts that in the normal
case people will stop at a vicarious contentment: "We do not sufficiently
distinguish what we would by no means choose to do, from what we
should be eager enough to see if it was once done. We delight in seeing
things, which so far from doing, our heartiest wishes would be to see re-
dressed." This observation rests on his analysis of the motives of art, from
the previous section, entitled "Sympathy," to which I now turn.

Sympathy is a strange word to choose. For Burke's sense does not fit
what we would now call sympathy, or what anyone in his time would have
called sympathy. In the modern sense, which has not changed much over
two centuries except that for intense sympathy we now reserve the word
empathy—in this sense, sympathy means feeling for or feeling with someone else, drawing as one does so upon one's personal resources of experience and one's knowledge of the other person. Sympathy in Burke's sense,
though it includes this element of fellow feeling, shares nothing of the accompanying premise of beneficent mutual sensitivity and vulnerability.
All he means by sympathy is, the state of being held to attention by helpless feelings *about* someone else, who at the moment is visibly suffering. To
have the sense of the pain of another person, while one watches that person suffer: that, I think, stating it as neutrally as possible, is the Burkean
idea of sympathy.

Let us try now to follow him in his own words:

> Sympathy must be considered as a sort of substitution, by which we are put
> into the place of another man, and affected in many respects as he is af-
> fected; so that this passion may either partake of the nature of those which
> regard self-preservation, and turning upon pain may be a source of the sub-
> lime; or it may turn upon ideas of pleasure; and then, whatever has been
> said of the social affections, whether they regard society in general, or only
> some particular modes of it, may be applicable here.

Notice that formally the impression may be either of pain or of pleasure—the person we watch may be doing or suffering; in a state of prosperity or adversity. I have emphasized pain in keeping with Burke's remark elsewhere that "the idea of pain, in its highest degree, is much stronger than the highest degree of pleasure; and that it preserves the same superiority through all its subordinate gradations." Pain, like pleasure, as he understands it is a brute sensation; and neither can be blended with the other; though for the feeling of conscious cessation of pain or a lifting away of its weight, Burke reserves the counter-intuitive word *delight*. Such pleasure as we take in sublimity, then, is of this oddly negative sort. And the sympathy we feel is not personal, not positive. To argue as he does that sympathy with someone else's pain is an instance of "substitution" is to place it on a par with other logical or clinical leaps of the mind; but as Burke goes on to say, borrowing a conclusion from Hume's *Treatise*, "the influence of reason in producing our passions is nothing near so extensive as it is commonly believed"; and without a sense of the utility of such unreasoning substitutions, without a knowledge of the conversion by this means of pain into delight, one will have no way to account for the fact that "objects which in the reality would shock, are in tragical, and such like representations, the source of a very high species of pleasure."

In the next section, on the effects of sympathy, Burke comes to the paradox that concerns him most: that delight is more interesting and possibly more intense when we are watching "our fellow creatures in circumstances of real distress." He says, conspicuously now with the sublime and not the beautiful in mind, "I am convinced we have a degree of delight, and that no small one, in the real misfortunes and pains of others; for let the affection be what it will in appearance, if it does not make us shun such objects, if it makes us dwell upon them, in this case I conceive we must have a delight or pleasure of some species or other in contemplating objects of this kind." This goes against what has become the prevailing opinion of qualified judges of the arts, that the delight in question is *not* sensational, that it is in fact detached or contemplative and somehow vindicated in advance, because it comes to us shaped by an intervening mood of judgment. Burke is emphatic throughout the *Sublime and Beautiful* in dismissing such a hypothetical mood as false. He thinks we can know it is false by introspection. One of the few critics who ever caught the exact drift of his thinking here was Hazlitt, in an essay on the character of Iago:

> Some persons more nice than wise, have thought the whole of the character of Iago unnatural. Shakespeare, who was quite as good a philosopher as he was a poet, thought otherwise. He knew that the love of power, which is

another name for the love of mischief, was natural to man. He would know this as well or better than if it had been demonstrated to him by a logical diagram, merely from seeing children paddle in the dirt, or kill flies for sport. We might ask those who think the character of Iago not natural, why they go to see it performed—but from the interest it excites, the sharper edge which it sets on their curiosity and imagination. Why do we go to see tragedies in general? Why do we always read the accounts in the newspapers, of dreadful fires and shocking murders, but for the same reason?

Curiosity, says Burke (and Hazlitt confirms the intuition), is enough to account for our continued presence at any scene of suffering, at a sufficient distance. This curiosity is another name for the love of power, or the love of mischief which is a kind of power and a kind of play.

IF WE NOW ask, "Is this way of feeling right or wrong, is it good or bad to indulge?" we are likely to feel pulled in two directions. Sympathy in the ordinary sense is good because it reminds us of our necessary relations to other people, through similarity. This, in turn, suggests compassion, pity, charity, and the possibility of help. But the idea of sympathy for Burke does not necessarily suggest any of these things. To sympathize is to watch someone suffer, with the feeling of mere fascination that comes from knowing that the person, like oneself, is human. The feeling may partake of *morbid* fascination, even to a degree of voyeurism—that, and a refined detachment in which the coarse actualities of suffering are lost. This uncomfortable connection of feelings about art with feelings about life is what made the *Sublime and Beautiful* seem implausible to many of its early readers. I think that Burke took satisfaction, in the way Freud did, at bringing to light the suppressed probabilities of the human mind and doing so under a flatly prosaic and apparently scientific cover. His picture of sensational morbid interest as the motive that holds our attention at a scene of suffering, is probable in exactly the manner of Freud's analysis of substitute gratification as a leading motive for the creation of art. That analysis made it possible for Freud to apply an idea of sublimation to the transfigurative work by the artist upon his human materials. Yet Burke's account is the less moralized of the two. Freud, characteristically, made out a fertile source of regret in the inquisitiveness of the young Leonardo da Vinci: "He neither loved nor hated, but questioned himself whence does that arise which he was to love and hate. . . . Not to love before one gains full knowledge of the thing loved presupposes a delay which is harmful. . . . One has investigated instead of having loved." Burke would have seen nothing to regret in this development. At the scene of the sublime, for him, nothing like sublimation occurs. It is a scene of excited attention, and if the excitement produces thought of any kind that thought remains inscrutable. At most, it may lead to the reflection that we live in a world where things like this can happen.

From a longer perspective, Burke does offer one possible more-than-sensational reason for the presence of spectators at a scene of suffering. The justification is teleological, though its end is not, as in other eighteenth-century theories, the knowledge of propriety in art or an expansive ideal of benevolence. Burke speculates instead that the instinct for witnessing such scenes may aid the survival of the human species.

> Whenever we are formed by nature to any active purpose, the passion which animates us to it, is attended with delight, or a pleasure of some kind, let the subject matter be what it will; and as our Creator has designed we should be united by the bond of sympathy, he has strengthened that bond by a proportionable delight; and there most where our sympathy is most wanted, in the distresses of others. If this passion was simply painful, we would shun with the greatest care all persons and places that could excite such a passion; as, some who are so far gone in indolence as not to endure any strong impression, actually do.

We are formed by natural design, then, to take an active and in some degree a delighted interest in scenes of suffering. The design may look perverse but it serves the derivative interest of compassion: "the delight we have in such things," Burke concludes, "hinders us from shunning scenes of misery; and the pain we feel, prompts us to relieve ourselves in relieving those who suffer; and all this antecedent to any reasoning, by an instinct that works us to its own purposes, without our concurrence." We would, that is to say, in the most impartial of moral worlds shun altogether such scenes of misery, and decide whom to help and why to help them as a matter of principle or expedience. Or, supposing ourselves to be unconcerned, we would pass by such scenes altogether, for what is simply repellent simply repels. But in the moral world we inhabit, mixed with the feelings of disgust are also feelings of delight. The same instinct that keeps us looking may stimulate us to offer help. Burke thus concedes that passive beholding may eventually lead to compassionate action. On his theory, it would seem that it might for the same reason lead to wanton or brutal action, but he does not address this other possibility.

Now let me anticipate an objection. Burke had very different things to say about taste in the *Reflections on the Revolution in France*. He says there that the moral judgments we learn at the theater, and especially when watching the progress of a tragedy, prepare us for the judgments we shall have to make in actual life. The theater, therefore, and the arts generally are a "school of moral sentiments." Taste in this later Burkean view, as part of the system of manners, shows us just where morality comes in to edify the craving for uninstructed excitement. More particularly, taste educates us in a suitable appreciation of dramatic justice, an eager interest in seeing that virtue should prosper and vice be punished. But taste of the sort Burke speaks of in the *Reflections*—a habit of feeling that is moral through and through—by the time we inherit it has been thoroughly socialized. That version of taste does not appear in the *Sublime and Beautiful*, except in the introduction he wrote for later editions: in this cautious after-thought, taste is defined as a habit that reconciles our palate to "alien plea-sures." Whereas the inference from the original text had been that the pleasures remain alien, and, further, that taste, whose evolution is strongly marked by its origin, begins not as a habit of feeling but rather as a hunger for extraordinary stimulus. We venture to taste the alien pleasure because we do not know how not to.

Faced with these two aspects of taste, a regulative habit on the one hand, and on the other an adventurous motive, we may naturally try to harmonize them but it will always involve the sacrifice of taste in the latter and less eulogistic sense. We then stand liable to miss the recognition Burke made, which was, I believe, that the cause of our interest in art is psychological before and after it is moral. This is a recognition, of course, that one can find shared by a few later writers. Of the scattered sources I have discovered to confirm the theory, I want to quote just one passage from William James—partly because James's style in these matters, being far from either the clinical or the theatrical extreme, makes the view feel unexceptional but not less strange than it really is. In the chapter on habit in his *Psychology*, James had followed the ameliorative logic of Burke in the *Reflections*. He doubtless therefore surprised his audience at the banquet of the Universal Peace Congress of 1904 when he asserted that "Man lives *by* habits indeed, but what he lives *for* is thrills." Imagining a world without war, James continues:

> In such a stagnant summer afternoon of a world, where would be the zest or interest? The plain truth is that people *want* war. They want it anyhow; for itself, and apart from each and every possible consequence. It is the final bouquet of life's fireworks. The born soldiers want it hot and actual. The non-combatants want it in the background, and always as an open possi-bility, to feed imagination on and keep excitement going. . . . War is hu-man nature at its uttermost. We are here to do our uttermost.

James's purpose was not to defend war but rather to inform his audience of the strength of their antagonist, to remind them of the difficulty of finding something else as interesting to satisfy the same instinct. My suggestion, following Burke, is that we extend the application of these remarks to the taste for art which may likewise be irreducible to habit. Suppose then we say that in the aesthetic as in the practical realm, man lives by habits but what he lives for is thrills. How true is this? What part of the experience of art may it decisively account for? And what elements that have perhaps been filtered out of other accounts may it turn our attention back to?

The answer to these questions ought to be by a practical test. My first example is trivial and personal but useful just because being so commonplace some version of it has occurred to everyone. On television a few months ago I was watching the shelling of Sarajevo with my six-year-old son beside me. The family policy is to exclude the violent images when they can possibly be avoided, but not to avoid an explanation when they come unexpectedly. I had time to turn it off, but shirked the policy on this occasion, and let the footage run on. A bit late for any improving pretense I finally did switch the channel: things on the screen were becoming too stark. My son at that point said indignantly, "Don't turn it off! I want to see it." Maybe the only allure came from its having been forbidden. But I suspect he wanted to see it in spite of the policy for the same reason that I wanted to see it in spite of myself. We talked afterward a little; but I am drawing on what I think I remember of my childhood thoughts when I try to explain his. "They are people doing those things," he was thinking. "Those are some of the things people do." Elizabeth Bishop in her poem "In the Waiting Room" suggests the last part of this thought: the child saying to herself, as she looks at photographs of a hunt or a war, "You are one of *them*." But childhood moments like this do not yet enter the domain of art. My next example comes from an intense experience of art with a narrow emotional range.

Just before Christmas 1985, two teenagers in Reno, Nevada, Ray Belknap and James Vance, shot themselves with a 12-gauge shotgun. Vance survived the blast disfigured; and five years later the case of *James Vance et al. versus Judas Priest* was heard in a Reno courtroom. Vance and his family and Belknap's family had become convinced that the suicide pact was an irresistible result of the attachment the boys then felt to the music of the heavy-metal band Judas Priest. The music, the plaintiffs argued, had drawn Vance and Belknap to the brink of a scene of danger they could not distinguish from their own lives; the fascination of this music with violent risk, and with violence against the self, so fiercely claimed their attention that they became its casualties. The spectator's sense of impassioned delight in the bare survival of a danger from experience, had here passed into an act of self-destruction, an act that may have been partly involuntary. All my details of the case are taken from a remarkable documentary film by David Van Taylor, *Dream Deceivers,* which was shown last year in the *P.O.V.* series on public television.

James Vance and Ray Belknap came to be addicted to violent music, but long before that their lives had stumbled. Belknap shot a cat with a dart, stole money from home, ran away to Oklahoma, stole a pair of sunglasses. "Everything he ever did he got caught." Vance told a social worker once that he "couldn't think of anything good" in his own life. His mother, who brought him up on the Bible before the music took hold, thought for a long time that he was getting to be "obnoxious," "a punk." Vance particularly relished one line from Judas Priest, "Everything he touches fries into a crisp," and both boys had experiences of their own to match the line. Yet no one who knew them really doubts that when they listened to the music in James Vance's room, a powerful force did enter their lives. They would come out of these sessions with fantasies—with talk of getting hold of automatic weapons and killing lots of people.

To my ear the sound of Judas Priest is insistent, intense, monotonous, and at times as seductive as the hard-rock music of the sixties from which it descends. Characteristic titles like "Island of Domination," "Genocide," "Ripper" give some impression of the sadistic treatment here of apocalyptic themes. But the music is pitched to the interests of quite young adolescents: sex, it says, is forbidden and good; and so is music like ours. Leaving home and leaving life are easily turned into metaphors for each other. Often, too, the lyrics have the dramatic form of lamentation, the object of pity being someone young and misunderstood, and the deliverer of pity the chorus of singers who express bitter resentment on the victim's behalf. "He had enough, he couldn't take any more, / He found a place in his mind, and slammed the door, / No matter how hard they tried, they couldn't understand"—and the song goes on to speak of the world as a place "not fit for living in." The followers of the band, if this film's selection is not misleading, are many of them teenage drifters close to suicide. And yet, what is absorbing in this side of the documentary record is how very distantly the lives of the singers are related to the lives of the audience their music has found.

Most days until the age of sixteen, Rob Halford, the lead singer of Judas Priest, walked from his council flat past an ironwork factory and heard the concussion of steam hammers that would become the beat of his music. As he recounts this fact, the anecdote seems well rehearsed, something plainly that he has made an impression with before. Anyway, his story points to a major fact about the group that seems unknown to the fans outside the Reno courthouse. The style of Judas Priest, as they present themselves, is a British and a working-class style of rebellion. Yet with this music James Vance and Ray Belknap of Reno identified themselves completely, while their own almost unconscious rebellion took no coloring from it. They wanted the music for its vibrations. And if we agree that sympathy is a kind of substitution, where in this case can we draw the line between art and life, intention and effect, legitimate sympathy and a mistaken empathy? In taking their listeners to the brink of a thrill, Judas Priest were trying an extreme experiment with the usual dangers of art. Practical effects are always a live possibility in this realm, and the idea of sympathy we have looked at offers no guidance either in blaming artists, or in exempting them from blame. It is not clear how, apart from the narrowness of the appeal, the offense of the heavy-metal band differs from that of the author of an epic or a tragedy.

I want to add that James Vance's experience of the music, to judge by the things he says about it on film, was deeper than what most of us can feel at most times about the greatest poetry, shockingly deeper than the experience of the musicians themselves. They talk of "getting on with our career" and see the trial as a tedious interruption: "Perpetual movers that we have been, ever since we were born, life is sort of standing still at the moment." Vance quotes his mother's remark that "I would say the lyrics like scripture," and adds: "There was a song for every mood, and a mood for every song." He speaks with difficulty, his face collapsed from the wreck of the blast and half repaired with a fissure down the middle of his forehead. Thinking back on his sessions with Ray Belknap, he observes: "Judas Priest sang a lot about the cosmos—songs like 'Epitaph' and 'Dreamer' and 'Dream Deceiver' [recorded as 'Dreamer Deceiver']. The music was just beautiful. We would get power from it, and our emotions would just soar with the music, and they would go up and down and up and down, and it was like a drug, like a narcotic. It wasn't just this one night, it was always like that." Vance's judgment even after the death of his friend is closer to reverence than to reproach.

At the trial in Reno where Judas Priest were finally acquitted, the legal issues were whether the music contained subliminal messages, and, if so, whether the messages had an effect on listeners. What no human tribunal could dislodge was James Vance's conviction that the music "led us, or even mesmerized us, into believing that the answer to life is death." The idea of suicide came into the minds of both Ray Belknap and James Vance in the presence of the music. But the strategy of the defense lawyer, which succeeded, was to establish that Vance's was a "highly dysfunctional family." He had fallen out with his mother earlier, without any help from Judas Priest. His stepfather was sometimes rough with him, and had a history of alcohol abuse. A line of exculpation for the singers was open here; and David Van Taylor's film goes with it some of the way. Most likely when he started on the subject, Van Taylor felt the propriety, as well as the advantages in irony, of a principled aesthetic defense of Judas Priest. Possibly he felt much the same when he had finished. But some way beyond the canons of evidence of the courtroom, we are brought back to the sense in which Vance loved a chosen feeling from art, and so far entered into the feeling that he trusted it with his death.

He says near the end that though he talks to his friend Ray now "like a dead person—I don't expect an answer," he did get an answer once from the song he calls "Dream Deceiver," which he paraphrases: "The figure under the willow tree asked them if they were happy / And they said they didn't know, / He took them by the hand / And up and away they go." On the night of the shooting, "We were following the dream deceiver." James Vance later died in a hospital where he was in treatment for depression, under circumstances medically anomalous and possibly indicating suicide. Why did you call the film *Dream Deceivers?* asks the singer Rob Halford over the closing credits, and the director mentions that Vance, close to his death, had given the song this peculiar importance. "Did he? Well, that's the first I heard about that. Actually," says the singer, "it's about being took off by some kind of space being, like an astral planing kind of thing. I didn't really perceive that as a really meaningful, deep lyric." The blank response suggests what may be a usual failure of connection between artist and audience on the ground of the work of art. There is no reason ever to suppose that the thrills of the listener will correspond to the thrills of the singer. They have in common only a stimulus and an excitement.

I SYMPATHIZE with the person who having followed the analysis so far now complains, "Why do you torture us with this repulsive story? What can it possibly show except that some people have bad judgment in their choice of artists as in their conduct of life? That is regrettable, but we knew it before, and it points no moral for art." The case, I think, matters for this reason, that it differs from the normal case only in degree. If we admit that "poetry which excites artificial feelings makes us callous to real ones" and that "what men delight to read in books, they will put in practice in reality," then there is no impervious zone between these facts and the conclusion that the strong sensations people cultivate in the arts answer to a desire which they may choose to satisfy in other ways. What inhibits any of us from putting the desire into practice is fear of the law, or the force of custom, or certain inherent limits of human energy and invention. Yet most aesthetic defenses of artistic freedom have been founded on a pretense that the desire and its attendant possibilities do not even exist. The fear seems to be that if Burke's account of sympathy or something like it were accepted, the consequence would be censorship. That still leaves open the question whether we have any persuasive argument, drawn from the experience of art itself, against the utility of censorship. One had better first concede the almost compelling strength of the case on the other side. For every good use of art, there is a bad use, a repulsive putting into practice, that can be made to emerge as a deduction from the same work. There is no fictional character so terrible, provided he be singular enough, that someone will not say after reading or watching, "I want to be like him."

Our modern arguments for the protection of art have all converged on a few propositions both broad and false: that art, like no other human activity, fosters an immunity in the spectators from the contagion of example; that the artist must have led an exemplary life or a high-minded life, at least in relation to art; that the dangerous elements of a given work will always be rejected by the sane; that whatever most deeply offends in the work may turn out to be justified retroactively by a self-caricaturing intent. These explanations do not deserve to be believed. We hold on to them as a convenient consequence of the moralized idea of taste. But it may be true that without this pretense a society like ours would seek to impose a discipline on art. We live at a time when the well-educated want more than ever before to believe in the efficacy of cultural helps, and sooner or later this must make itself felt in a corresponding belief in the efficacy of cultural hindrances. A frank defense of art against regulation ought not to appeal from the strong moralism of censorship to the weak moralism of art's supposed freedom from practical effects. It ought rather to begin with the question: "In separating ourselves from this (as it seems) instinctive resort of human ingenuity, what else would we be trying to separate ourselves from?" Here again I find Burke useful. He remarks in a curious and anti-aristocratic thought: "It is our ignorance of things that causes all our admiration, and chiefly excites our passions. Knowledge and acquaintance make the most striking causes affect but little. It is thus with the vulgar, and all men are as the vulgar in what they do not understand." Art, I take this to imply, when it touches us most nearly brings to mind the intractability of what we do not understand. It maintains contact with what Jean-François Lyotard (commenting on the *Sublime and Beautiful*) calls "the threat of nothing further happening."

Let us say that the movement of the mind that compels attention in the presence of sublimity is a not-to-be-satisfied wish for knowledge and for survival. The awkward phrase is mine not Burke's. One possibly deliberate inadequacy of his presentation is that it omits to give an example of the relation between the sublime and sympathy in his special sense. But he may have thought his quotation of Milton's lines about Death in *Paradise Lost* would serve that purpose:

> The other shape,
> If shape it might be called that shape had none
> Distinguishable in member, joint, or limb;
> Or substance might be called that shadow seemed,
> For each seemed either; black it stood as night;
> Fierce as ten furies; terrible as hell;
> And shook a dreadful dart; what seemed his head
> The likeness of a kingly crown had on.

Burke relates this description to his chosen categories of obscurity, terror, and privation. But his instinct in quoting the passage may have favored once more a psychological motive. Satan, in darkness, exploring Chaos, moving toward the world into which he himself will introduce death, is interested in knowing and is afraid to know the outward shape of an impulse he contains in himself. The language of the lines is of groping, stretching, or searching for resemblances where none appear, and that too fits a dramatic recognition in which Death will prove to be Satan's child. In these lines Satan feels, and the reader with him, something of the father's natural emotion in the face of a son he has reason to fear. But the progress of the description also strangely mimics the posture of any sympathetic spectator as Burke has described that spectator earlier in the *Sublime and Beautiful*: peering at a thing as yet unknown, questing further toward the danger it may pose, and at the same time shrinking from that danger.

This sort of encounter is at the heart of epics. If one omits the chases and retreats, and the rhetoric of challenge and counter-challenge, the fight in the *Iliad* between Hector and Patroclus comes down to a single moment in the presence of which every reader is both expectant and surprised.

> Coming behind you through the dust you felt
> —What was it?—felt creation part, and then
> APOLLO!
> > Who had been patient with you,
> Struck.
>
> His hand came from the east,
> And in His wrist lay all eternity.

At such moments a destiny is contracted to an instant, and fate itself is allegorized in a name. In the version here, which I take from Christopher Logue's *War Music,* the inaccessibility of the god to human purpose is stressed by the book's original typography, which blazons APOLLO! black-on-white across two pages of text in blinding capitals. The success of this utterly literal effect is hard to account for—except, perhaps, on the theory that we form an idea of a great shock only by analogy with a smaller shock we have felt close to home.

To show the persistence of this way of feeling let me close with two illustrations of the modern sublime. In Stanley Kubrick's film *The Shining,* a child haunted by premonitions of disaster, and other sorts of shadowy telepathic knowledge, goes out to play in the corridors of a gigantic hotel in the Rockies which his father and mother have moved into for a winter. They agreed to be caretakers and live in complete isolation, to allow the father to write his book, though he will not write it and there are early signs of the mania or distraction that will drive him later to commit acts of violence against his family. This scene shows the child's first freedom in the vast and unfamiliar building when he explores an upper floor on his tricycle: since there are no carpets, the wheels make a grinding roar as he plows between the rows of closed-up rooms. The camera is mounted low, about the level of the handlebars, making it hard at first even to trace the action. All we hear is the roar of motion, all we see is the view too close to the ground and, more disturbing, the abrupt ninety-degree turns that expose the long vista of one more hallway to be explored. One's fear is that the sound will suddenly stop, or that it will be overwhelmed by another sound, or that the hallway will not be empty. When at last in the middle of a corridor the boy sees looming the ghosts of twin sisters murdered in the hotel a long time before, his emotion is a compound of fear and curiosity. Was he trying to frighten himself? Do we think we ought to be frightened on his behalf? His inquisitive response and our terrified response are two sides of the same human phenomenon.

In the same director's *2001: A Space Odyssey*, the charge of dramatic interest is tied to the battle of wits between two astronauts and the computer HAL. The story hangs on whether this will prove to have been a battle of wills—whether, that is, the computer is in fact a conscious agent—and here the story touches a potent fantasy of the general culture. HAL is a compliant friend to the astronauts up to a point, but shows alarming signs of disagreement and of trusting its own authority, and so they isolate themselves behind the window of a soundproof chamber to discuss what to do with HAL, and they decide to incapacitate it. The scene is a few seconds of the two men speaking in profile, seen through the pane of glass; but we realize it is shot from HAL's point of view and that HAL is reading their lips. One of the astronauts then goes out in an exploring craft to trace an apparent failure in the system; as he walks into space, attached to the vehicle only by a cord, we see like a solitary eye the red light of the vehicle in a three-part rapid montage: close, closer, closest. The next moment, HAL will cut the cord and send the astronaut slowly hurtling through space, but this is the moment that counts. In an instant the computer HAL with his mechanical outworks is personified. He was reading the astronauts, and now we see the eye that reads, and have the beginning of an answer to the question, Does it have a will?

The kind of fear, or the delight nearly related to pain, which all of these moments carry is more familiar in movies than in the other arts today. The sensation that such moments produce certainly fits Burke's definition of astonishment—"that state of the soul, in which all its motions are suspended, with some degree of horror." What seems, however, from his own use of Milton, to be partly distinct from horror is a mood of absorbed uneasy anticipation. I have stressed the point of view of the cinematic shots to make them vivid if possible, yet the odd feature of the passages from Kubrick, as of the lines from *Paradise Lost* and Christopher Logue's *Iliad*, is how they make point-of-view no longer matter. The apprehension from which we look at the scene does not belong to any participant in the drama, nor is it exactly the standpoint of our consciousness as spectators. It puts us in the place of an intelligence that would come as close as possible to the thing it fears without passing into actual danger. That is why in looking at such moments, person and place vanish and one is left with an inscrutable impression which may be translated imperfectly as "I am implicated." In response comes the half-voluntary movement of grabbing or touching the person beside one just when the near horror comes so much nearer as to be almost intelligible. The explanation which everyone has thought of and no one has found satisfactory is that we do it to be sure of company. Maybe we do it because we want the feeling of keeping the thing at bay and having it near and we want both feelings at once. The gesture by which we do bring something near is an instinctive irrational adjustment toward that end.

WITH MY ARGUMENT now almost sunk in sensations, I need to recall the commanding alternative theory that has received no attention here. The successor to Burke's account of pain in the *Sublime and Beautiful* is Kant's system of aesthetic judgment in the *Critique of Judgment*. The argument there will claim to include an empirical interest in the spectator but at the same time will associate taste with something larger: an act of self-reflection that must be understood against the background of nature and humanity as a whole. On this view, the response to a work of art, far from being non-moral, carries the full resonance of, may even be another form of, the assertion of moral freedom. In the purposiveness without purpose, the finality without final cause of the work of art, one recognizes the general human striving to grasp an object that exceeds comprehension, and one is exalted by the very consciousness of that fact. With the same recognition, one starts to see how human representation may participate symbolically in the kingdom of ends that human action requires. This argument does more than add to Burke's speculations on sympathy; it disposes of them, if true. But for that reason it would be tactless even to pretend to consider the two accounts together. Kant's is founded on a hope about art, Burke's is founded on a suspicion.

Yet it is impossible to keep in its pure state the opacity of Burke's sublime moment—a problem which suggests that the experience is bound to become reflective in spite of itself. According to his analysis, the sense of sublimity must always be unthinking; it is a sudden stopping short at an obstacle or privation. But the feeling of sympathy which draws us to the occasions of the sublime will unavoidably be influenced by reasons as well as motives. Once we start to explain the primitive interest of a scene, to say why it held *us* watching so long, we have commenced to interpret and passed from astonishment to reflection. Nor is anything to be gained by an ascetic refusal of explanations. The omitted gloss will have crept into the neutral description if only as an undertone. Any practicing critic can recall plenty of examples that show how hard it is for a report of supernatural excitement to evade the various rational subtexts that lie in wait. It follows that there is this much truth in the ideal of reflective distance which criticism derives from Kant: when one distinguishes an "art emotion" from the reductive responses that hold no interest at all—"Me, too"; "It makes you realize how lucky you are"; "The book offended us"—simply by making the distinction one has already gone some way into a curriculum of analysis. One has begun to evoke the ways in which art may survive as an image that is exemplary and not just affecting; a bearer of thought that feels like enthusiasm, and not of an enthusiasm that is the counterfeit of thought. That is a subject for another story. If, meanwhile, the idea of sympathy resting on fear makes sense to people with a knowledge of art—people for whom the study of art is not a profession, a solemn compulsion, or a conscious avocation—one may wonder why so many close to the arts have had an interest in rejecting this view. I can offer only a hint, from observation.

Licensed judges, collectors, and critics of art, including the soulless kind who describe themselves as cultural workers, are led to think affirmatively about the claims of sympathy by their need to suppose that their own speculations and judgments add up. For them, it must come to be seen that art itself, or the right way of knowing art, involves a therapy with appreciable results. Keats reported meeting a gentleman at the exhibition of the Elgin Marbles who said, "I believe, Mr. Keats, we may admire these works safely." The connoisseur and the cultural worker are interested in showing that we may admire these works safely, though their terms of appreciation may vary: one critic's fluent harmony of expressive tensions is another's tour de force of ironic subversion. In the lexicon of praise these judgments perform the same function. Both try to make art safe for personal consciousness, and happy for social consciousness. The skeptical conclusion I have worked toward is that we may not admire these works safely but we will probably go on using them until another occupation comes along as interesting as our elective and maybe instinctive practice of exposing ourselves to the risk. To ask more, with a hope of benefiting either oneself or society, is to expect at once too much and too little of art. It is to live the life of that fictional person who will always have real followers, who "consulted his taste in everything—his taste alone perhaps, as a sick man consciously incurable consults at last only his lawyer."

1994

imagism, 9, 11–12

James, Henry: compared with T. S. Eliot, 35; compared with Hemingway, 211, 215, 226; conciousness and writing, 16
James, William: 43, 67, 73–74, 82, 105, 241; *A Pluralistic Universe*, 73, 74, 81; "Pragmatism and Humanism," 73; *The Principles of Psychology*, 70, 241; *The Will to Believe*, 70
Jarrell, Randall, 111
Jaurès, Jean, 152–53
Johnson, Samuel, 219
Josephson, Matthew, 53
Joyce, James, 3, 54, 216
Judas Priest, 242–45

Kafka, Franz, 202
Kahn, Otto, 60
Kalstone, David, 102
Kant, Immanuel, 250, 251
Keats, John, 15–16, 56, 62, 121, 251
Kermode, Frank, 15
Kierkegaard, Søren, 17
Kipling, Rudyard, 228
Kubrick, Stanley, 248–49

La Fontaine, 96
Lawrence, D. H., 111, 123, 135–36, 168–69, 173
Lewis, Wyndham, 224–25
Logue, Christopher, 248, 249
Lowell, Robert, 151
Lukács, Georg, 40
Lynn, Kenneth, 216–17, 218–20, 222–24
Lyotard, Jean-François, 247

Mallarmé, Stéphane, 3
Marlowe, Christopher, 62
Marvell, Andrew, 9
Matthiessen, F. O., 181
Maurras, Charles, 152, 157
Melville, Herman: *Moby-Dick*, 63
Mendelson, Edward, 132
Merrill, James: *The Book of Ephraim*, 144; "The Broken Home," 144; "Lost in Translation," 144; "Voices from the Other World," 147
Meyers, Jeffrey, 216–17
Milton, John, 58, 95, 247, 249
Monroe, Harriet, 54

Moore, Marianne: "Armor's Undermining Modesty," 92, 112; "Critics and Connoisseurs," 115; "Elephants," 98, 100; "Four Quartz Crystal Clocks," 91–92, 113; "The Frigate Pelican," 98–99; "A Grave," 93–95; "The Hero," 92–93; "In the Days of Prismatic Color," 96–97; "In This Age of Hard Trying," 104–5; "The Jerboa," 92–93; "Marriage," 95–96, 113; "Melanchthon," 100; "The Pangolin," 100; "The Past is the Present," 97; "People's Surroundings," 98; "The Steeple-Jack," 92; "To a Prize Bird," 107–8; "To Be Liked by You Would Be a Calamity," 103–4; "To Military Progress," 110–11, 114
Munson, Gorham, 53
Murdoch, Iris: "Against Dryness," 15; "On 'God' and 'Good'," 21–22; "The Sublime and the Good," 22

Niebuhr, Reinhold, 108
Nietzsche, Friedrich: 67, 68, 69; *Beyond Good and Evil*, 70–71; *The Birth of Tragedy*, 84–85; *Daybreak*, 89; *The Gay Science*, 73, 74, 76; *The Genealogy of Morals*, 76; *The Will to Power*, 70, 76, 77

Opffer, Emil, 57, 59
Orwell, George, 219
Ovid, 26
Owen, Wilfred, 1

Parker, Dorothy, 221
Parkinson, Thomas, 54
personality: Eliot on, 14–15; Keats on, 15–16; tacit assertion of, 25
perspectivism, 70–74, 117–19
Peterson, Margaret, 67
Pfeiffer, Pauline, 221, 223
Picasso, Pablo, 1
Plath, Slyvia, 5
Pound, Ezra: "Hugh Sewyn Mauberley," 101; "In a Station of the Metro," 12; word and deed, 157–58
Powell, Michael, 4
pragmatism: Jamesian, 73–74, 82; Nietzschean, 71–73
Proust, Marcel, 20, 199, 200